19· 36

Dissent and Disruption

PROPOSALS FOR
CONSIDERATION BY THE CAMPUS

A Report and Recommendations by
The Carnegie Commission on Higher Education

JUNE 1971

MCGRAW-HILL BOOK COMPANY

New York   St. Louis   San Francisco   Düsseldorf
London   Sydney   Toronto   Mexico   Panama
Johannesburg   Kuala Lumpur   Montreal
New Delhi   Rio de Janeiro   Singapore

". . . Man is born unto trouble, as the sparks fly upward."

JOB 5:7

*This report is issued by the Carnegie Commission on
Higher Education, with headquarters at
1947 Center Street, Berkeley, California 94704.
The views and conclusions expressed in this report
are solely those of the members of the Carnegie Commission
on Higher Education and do not necessarily reflect the
views or opinions of the Carnegie Corporation of New York,
The Carnegie Foundation for the Advancement of Teaching,
or their trustees, officers, directors, or employees.*

Contents

Important Note

Many exhibits are inserted in this report to illustrate or to amplify textual material and to suggest the many different approaches to the complex problems discussed. The inclusion of statements by other persons or groups in these exhibits does not necessarily imply our concurrence with the ideas expressed. Rather, our intention is to provide the reader with a range of relevant information.

Exhibits are referred to in the text at the end of the paragraphs to which they are relevant. All exhibits are quotations except where it is indicated that the exhibit was prepared by the Carnegie Commission staff, or was prepared from Carnegie Commission survey data.

Foreword

The Carnegie Commission on Higher Education will issue its final report and recommendations in 1972, after all its research projects have been completed. But many problems in higher education are urgent and need early action. The Commission issues special reports on such matters as soon as it has had an opportunity to review the relevant issues and develop specific recommendations.

This report, *Dissent and Disruption: Proposals for Consideration by the Campus,* concentrates on how dissent on campus may be protected and how disruption may be prevented.

To the many persons who were consulted and gave us helpful suggestions we wish to express our appreciation. Two studies sponsored by the Commission were of particular value: the large-scale survey in 1969 on attitudes of students, faculty, and research personnel directed by Dr. Martin Trow of the University of California, Berkeley, in cooperation with Dr. Seymour Martin Lipset of Harvard University and with the assistance of the U.S. Office of Education and the American Council on Education; and the survey regarding developments at the time of the Cambodian incursion in May 1970 by Dr. Richard Peterson of the Educational Testing Service.

We wish to thank the members of our staff, and especially Dr. Lois S. Gold, for their assistance in preparing this report.

Eric Ashby
The Master
Clare College
Cambridge, England

Ralph M. Besse
Chairman of the Board
National Machinery Company

Joseph P. Cosand
President
The Junior College District
of St. Louis

William Friday
President
University of North Carolina

1. Major Themes

1   The Carnegie Commission generally endorses the report of the President's Commission on Campus Unrest (Scranton Commission).

2   Dissatisfaction and disaffection on our campuses reflect many problems in American society—achievement of equality of opportunity for all American citizens, ending of the war in Vietnam, elimination of poverty, preservation and restoration of our physical environment, assessment and control of the impacts of technology, and responsiveness of our institutions to the needs of the people. Attitudes of unrest also reflect many problems on campus—including disagreements over forms of governance and over the substance of academic programs.[1]

3   We expect some of these attitudes of dissatisfaction and disaffection to persist for the foreseeable future, rising and falling dramatically from time to time in the extent and intensity of their manifestations.

4   Our concern in this report is that dissatisfaction and disaffection be expressed on campus in a constructive way and in accord with the principles of a free society. A campus has a fundamental obligation to conduct itself in keeping with the laws of our society, and also with its own high aspirations for reasoned discussion and reliance on persuasion. The gravity of the problems in society and on campuses accentuates the importance of this obligation and in no way relieves a campus or any of its constituent groups or any

---

[1] In coming months, the Carnegie Commission will issue reports on campus governance and on academic reform which will relate closely to the subject matter of this current report.

1

of its members from the duty to uphold the principles of a free and ordered society and thus to rely on reason and persuasion.

5 Public expressions of dissatisfaction on campus by students and faculty members take two broad forms: dissent and disruption.

Dissent must be protected.

Disruption must be ended.

To achieve these goals, repression must be prevented, and unnecessary harshness by law enforcement officers must be avoided.

6 Higher education is marked by great diversity. The overwhelming majority of campuses are peaceful nearly all the time. Most students and most faculty members oppose disruption. Solutions to disruption, therefore, must be aimed at the disrupters in particular and not at higher education or its component parts in general.

7 We recommend as important steps that can be taken by each campus toward discouraging and coping with disruption:

· Adoption, campus by campus, of a "bill of rights and responsibilities" for members of the institution. We suggest a model bill.

· Development by each campus of effective measures for consultation and contingency planning in the event of disruptive emergencies. We make a number of suggestions. In particular, a campus is not and cannot be a sanctuary from the general law, and, thus, must relate more consciously and effectively with the police than it did in earlier periods.

· Creation by each campus of effective judicial procedures. We suggest special consideration of the use of external panels and persons, and of the general courts for certain types of cases.

8 The campuses, in recent times, have moved from a condition of quiet acceptance of their general system of governance by most of their students to one of more profound concern; from a consensus among their faculty members about purposes and mores of conduct to sometimes intense dispute about both; and from public approbation to greater scrutiny and questioning. In a period of student acceptance, faculty consensus, and public approbation, practices of the past and unwritten understandings largely sufficed to guide a campus in its conduct. Today we are faced, regretfully, by conflict and confrontation, and under the new circumstances, more formal

codes, more clear-cut decision-making processes, and more independent judicial procedures are becoming necessary on many campuses. In particular, the campuses have discovered how much disruption can be caused by small proportions of their members and by a few participants from the surrounding community. The campuses are more enmeshed in the greater society of which they are a part, and also are less informal communities of colleagues and more formal entities marked by partisanship. The campuses—some more than others and each in its own way—need to reflect these changes. The new condition is a difficult one, and the changes inherent in it are often distasteful and controversial—but they are also essential.

9   We recognize that a campus is many things—a physical place, a shifting scene of people, a set of functions, a series of traditions, a body of rules and much else—but it is also a spirit. This spirit has been in the past and needs to be in the future the spirit of tolerance, of respect for the contrary views of others, of goodwill toward others as individuals, of the supremacy of persuasion, of concern for hard facts and careful analysis, of devotion to the well-being of mankind around the world, of the means of thought directed toward the ends of wisdom. This spirit is particularly in the care of the faculties of the nation—as they nurture and guard it well, so will it endure. If they do not, it will decay.

A very heavy responsibility thus falls on faculty members, for they are at the heart of all academic endeavors. The viability of a campus community depends, in particular, on their performance. They need to be alert to grievances, to be ready to accept constructive change, to be willing to cope with the problems of both protecting dissent and preventing disruption, and to be devoted to the preservation of independent scholarship and teaching.

2. Dissent versus Disruption

"Campus unrest" is neither a single nor a simple phenomenon. A clear distinction must be made between dissent and disruption as public expressions of unrest. This distinction is of especial importance since the American public considers "campus unrest" to be one of the leading problems in the nation and, by implication, expects something to be done about it. *(Exhibit 1: Public Beliefs about Current National Problems (table); and Appendix D)*

Dissent. Individual or organized activity which expresses grievances held against, or changes desired in, society or a campus or both. The activity is carried on within the limits of the democratic processes of freedom of speech, assembly, and petition. Dissent may be generalized around more than a single grievance or remedy and may have an ideological base. It often includes proposed solutions as well as complaints. *(Exhibit 2: American Civil Liberties Union: Distinction between Dissent and Disruption)*

Disruption. Activity which is not protected by the First Amendment and which interferes with the rights of others. Whereas dissent relies on persuasion, disruption is based on coercion and sometimes violence. Disruption may take two broad forms which differ in their severity and in the actions and penalties appropriate to dealing with them *(Exhibit 3: The First Amendment):*

1. Coercion. Interference with the normal activities of other persons and groups on the campus, but stopping short of violence. Persons are prevented from doing what they normally are able to do, or are forced against their will to do what they do not want to do and should not do. Examples include interference with a person's right to speak, obstructive picketing, and obstructive sit-ins.

5

EXHIBIT 1

Public Beliefs about Current National Problems

Gallup Poll: "What do you think is the most important problem facing this country today?"

Late May, 1970		Early August, 1970	
1. Campus unrest	27%	1. Vietnam War	24%
2. Vietnam War (including Cambodia)	22	2. Youth protests (campus unrest)	17
3. Other international problems	14	3. High cost of living	14
4. Racial strife	13	4. Other international problems (not Vietnam)	11
5. High cost of living	10	5. Air/water pollution	10
6. Polarization of American people	5	6. Racial problems	9
7. Teen-age problems/ juvenile delinquency	4	7. Crime and lawlessness	6
8. Crime and lawlessness	4	8. Drug use, drug addiction	6
9. Drug addiction	3	9. Polarization of public attitudes	6
Others	16	10. Teen-age problems	2
No Opinion	2	Others	10
	120%*	Don't know	3
			118%*

* Table adds to more than 100 percent because of multiple responses.

2. Violence. Behavior which willfully inflicts or seriously threatens to inflict physical injury on individuals, or damage to property, or both. Examples include beatings, rock throwing, and destruction of buildings. A severe form of violence is terrorism—planned, deliberate acts of violence by clandestine groups. Examples include bombings and arson.

Dissent is properly protected in a democracy; disruption must be sternly condemned, suppressed, and punished. The border line between dissent and disruptive interference is thus a crucial one and is sometimes difficult to draw. The strike, conducted within the law, is defined as dissent, as is peaceful picketing. A perplexing but common problem of drawing lines is the sit-in. We define it as *dissent* if no one is injured, threatened, or abused; no property

EXHIBIT 2

American Civil Liberties Union: Distinction between Dissent and Disruption

Picketing, demonstrations, sit-ins, or student strikes, provided they are conducted in an orderly and non-obstructive manner, are a legitimate mode of expression, whether politically motivated or directed against the college administration, and should not be prohibited. Demonstrators, however, have no right to deprive others of the opportunity to speak or be heard; take hostages; physically obstruct the movement of others; or otherwise disrupt the educational or institutional processes in a way that interferes with the safety or freedom of others.

Students should be free, and no special permission be required, to distribute pamphlets or collect names for petitions concerned with campus or off-campus issues.

SOURCE: *Academic Freedom and Civil Liberties of Students in Colleges and Universities,* American Civil Liberties Union, April 1970.

is stolen or damaged; no important activities are impeded; no crimes are committed or campus rules broken; and ingress and egress are not hindered. Like the nonobstructive picket line, the nonobstructive sit-in deserves consideration as a democratic means of expression; it may be viewed as a sedentary picket line. Disruption occurs when actions become coercive and obstructive and go beyond the legally conducted strike, peaceful picketing, the peaceful nonobstructive sit-in, and other persuasive actions. *(Exhibit 4: American Association of University Professors: Statement on Faculty Participation in Strikes; Exhibit 5: Guidebook to Labor Relations: Peaceful Picketing)*

Dissent is essential to democratic life. It generates new ideas, propagates their acceptance or exposes them to rejection, and evaluates their effectiveness if put into practice. Dissent lies at the

EXHIBIT 3

The First Amendment, Constitution of the United States of America

Congress shall make no law respecting an establishment of religion, or prohibiting the free exercise thereof; or abridging the freedom of speech or of the press; or the right of the people peaceably to assemble and to petition the Government for a redress of grievances.

EXHIBIT 4

American Association of University Professors: Statement on Faculty Participation in Strikes

The American Association of University Professors is deeply committed to the proposition that faculty members in higher education are officers of their colleges and universities. They are not merely employees. They have direct professional obligations to their students, their colleagues, and their disciplines. Because of their professional competence, they have primary responsibility for central educational decisions; they share in the selection of presidents and deans; and their judgment should come first in the determination of membership in the faculty. Where these principles (which are more fully stated in the 1966 *Statement on Government of Colleges and Universities*) are not accepted in their entirety, the Association will continue to press for their realization. We believe that these principles of shared authority and responsibility render the strike inappropriate as a mechanism for the resolution of most conflicts within higher education.

But it does not follow from these considerations of self-restraint that professors should be under any legal disability to withhold their services, except when such restrictions are imposed equally on other citizens. Furthermore, situations may arise affecting a college or university which so flagrantly violate academic freedom (of students as well as of faculty) or the principles of academic government, and which are so resistant to rational methods of discussion, persuasion, and conciliation, that faculty members may feel impelled to express their condemnation by withholding their services, either individually or in concert with others. It should be assumed that faculty members will exercise their right to strike only if they believe that another component of the institution (or a controlling agency of government, such as a legislature or governor) is inflexibly bent on a course which undermines an essential element of the educational process.

Participation in a strike does not by itself constitute grounds for dismissal or for other sanctions against faculty members. Moreover, if dismissal of a faculty member is proposed on this, as on any other ground encompassed by the 1940 *Statement of Principles on Academic Freedom and Tenure,* the proceedings must satisfy the requirements of the 1958 *Statement on Procedural Standards in Faculty Dismissal Proceedings.* The Association will continue to protect the interests of members of the profession who are singled out for punishment on grounds which are inadequate or unacceptable, or who are not offered all the protection demanded by the requisites of due process.

SOURCE: *AAUP Bulletin,* vol. 54, pp. 155–159, summer 1968.

Guidebook to Labor Relations:
Peaceful Picketing

FREE SPEECH Section 8(c) of the [National Labor Relations] Act—the "free speech" provision—must be considered. That section is relevant to all unfair practices. It provides that "the expressing of any views, argument, or opinion, or the dissemination thereof, whether in written, printed, graphic, or visual form, shall not constitute or be evidence of an unfair labor practice under any of the provisions of this Act, if such expression contains no threat of reprisal or force or promise of benefit." Thus, for example, abusive language and name-calling directed by union members or agents toward non-strikers is not unlawful if unaccompanied by threats or intimidation. However, Section 8(c) does not privilege speech or other expressions for unlawful purposes. Thus, strike orders are unlawful if the strike is one prohibited by law, and picketing for an unlawful objective is a violation of the Act, as are union attempts, by speech or otherwise, to force an employer to discriminate against employees in violation of the Act. . . .

PICKETING AND COERCION The U.S. Supreme Court has held that peaceful picketing is not such economic pressure as to constitute coercion of employees under Section 8(b) (1) (A) [of the National Labor Relations Act].

However, picketing, even for a lawful objective, may unlawfully restrain or coerce employees if it is accompanied by violence or other illegal conduct. Thus, picketing is unlawful where it involves physical attacks on non-strikers, threats against non-strikers, boisterous picketing of non-strikers' homes, blocking of plant entrances or exits, trailing non-strikers, damaging property of non-strikers, or invading the employer's premises. Mass picketing, as such, is not unlawful, unless it is reasonably calculated to deter non-striking employees from working. Thus, the fact that a non-striker was forced to walk around a group of strikers in order to enter the plant did not constitute coercion, even though the non-striker was somewhat inconvenienced thereby, where no attempt was made to prevent the non-striker from entering the plant. Moreover, even where as many as twenty pickets stood before an entrance twenty-three feet wide, the picketing was held non-coercive in view of the facts that none of the pickets engaged in any violence or threats and that the pickets specifically informed employees of the picketed employer that they were free to pass through the picket line if they wished to do so. However, blocking of plant entrances or exits is always unlawful, whether accomplished by mass picketing or by other means. . . .

EXHIBIT 5—continued

RESTRAINT OR COERCION OF EMPLOYEES

The NLRA's prohibition, in Section 8(b) (1) (A), of union restraint or coercion of employees works out in practice, usually, as a device for keeping unions and their agents from threatening physical violence to, or actually committing acts of violence on the person of, employees who refuse to participate in strikes or who refuse to join a union. The Act prohibits more than violence or threats, however; it also outlaws more subtle forms of coercion. . . .

PHYSICAL RESTRAINT OR COERCION

Both actual violence and threats of violence are unlawful restraint or coercion under the NLRA. The Act is violated by intimidation of, and threats of violence to, non-striking employees as they seek to enter a struck plant. In the case of non-strikers who seek to *work* in the plant, violent conduct interferes with their right to work during a strike (their right to refuse to engage in concerted activities); as to non-strikers who seek to enter for some other purpose, such as to pick up their tools, violent conduct is likewise illegal.

The mere grouping of large numbers of strikers outside a plant, however, is not necessarily unlawful. Mere force of numbers is not, in and of itself, restraining and coercive. However, "mass picketing" which physically obstructs plant entrances and poses a clear threat is unlawful. Thus, the fact that a non-striker was forced to walk around a group of strikers on a sidewalk in order to enter a plant does not mean that there was unlawful coercion, even though the non-striker was somewhat inconvenienced thereby, where no attempt was made to prevent entrance. On the other hand, where a large number of pickets congregated in an alleged "Taft-Hartley Demonstration," the gathering was unlawful where it physically obstructed plant entrances.

Threats of harm to non-strikers are unlawful, as is the actual beating of them. Even the carrying of sticks and stones is unlawful where directed and controlled by a union or its agents. Pursuing non-strikers, pulling them out of their cars, and telling pickets "to get out there and fight" are all restraint and coercion of employees. Destruction of property at a struck plant is considered to be a threat of physical violence against any employee who enters the plant.

SOURCE: *1970 Guidebook to Labor Relations,* Commerce Clearing House, Inc., Chicago, 1970.

foundation of a university; to create the factual and analytical groundwork necessary for critical assessment of ideas and actions is a major goal of education. Organized dissent and protest activity, within the law, are basic rights which must be protected on the campus—as they should be for all citizens everywhere. *(Exhibit*

6: *National Commission on the Causes and Prevention of Violence: Protest vs. Violence: Exhibit 7: Eric Ashby: The Discipline of Constructive Dissent)*

Disruption, on the other hand, is utterly contradictory to the values and purposes of a campus, and to the processes of a democratic society. Disruption is contrary to an atmosphere conducive

National Commission on the Causes and Prevention of Violence: Protest vs. Violence

The right to protest is an indispensable element of a free society; the exercise of that right is essential to the health of the body politic and its ability to adapt itself to a changing environment. In this country, we have endowed the right of protest with constitutional status. The very first Amendment to the Constitution protects freedom of speech and press and "the right of the people peaceably to assemble and to petition the government for a redress of grievances." The Amendment protects much more than the individual right of dissent; it guarantees the right of groups to assemble and petition, or, in the modern phrase, to demonstrate.

Group violence, on the other hand, is dangerous to a free society. All too frequently, it is an effort not to persuade, but to compel. It has no protected legal status; indeed, one purpose of law is to prevent and control it. Nor is group violence a necessary consequence of group protest. The violence of the Ku Klux Klan—the lynching of Negroes at the rate of almost 100 per year from 1890 to 1910—had little to do with protest; if anything, it was more a cause of protest than a response. The same may be said of the harsh treatment of Orientals on the Pacific frontier and the common use of violence to settle property and political disputes among competing groups in the early days of the American West.

It is true, of course, that group protest sometimes results in group violence. Violence may be committed by groups opposed to the aims of the protesters (as in the Southern murders of civil rights workers by groups of white militants); excessive force may be used by the public authorities, as in Selma in 1965; violence may be committed by some within the protesting group itself (as in the case of the Weatherman faction of the SDS). But the widely held belief that protesting groups usually behave violently is not supported by fact. Of the multitude of occasions when protesting groups exercise their rights of assembly and petition, only a small number result in violence.

SOURCE: National Commission on the Causes and Prevention of Violence, *To Establish Justice, To Insure Domestic Tranquility*, 1969.

EXHIBIT 7

Eric Ashby: The Discipline of Constructive Dissent

It has to be a constructive dissent which fulfils one over-riding condition: it must shift the state of opinion about the subject in such a way that other experts in the subject are prepared to concur. This is done either by producing acceptable new data or by re-interpreting old data in a convincing way.

It is a very austere form of dissent and it is difficult to learn. But it is this discipline of dissent which has rescued knowledge, in fields as wide apart as theology and physics, from remaining authoritarian and static. . . .

But despite many and frequent failures there is, in my view, a distinctive role of universities in systems of higher education: to teach the discipline of constructive dissent which changes ideas and advances knowledge.

From an address by Sir Eric Ashby, Vice-chancellor, Cambridge University, at the 10th Commonwealth Universities Congress, held in Sydney, Australia, August 1968.

to the rational assessment of problems and the constructive consideration of alternative solutions. It must be ended, in part, so that the right to dissent can be protected. It must be morally condemned and met promptly by the efforts of the campus and, when necessary, by application of the general law. The Scranton Commission on Campus Unrest particularly notes that "Faculty members who engage in or lead disruptive conduct have no place in the university community." *(Exhibit 8: American Civil Liberties Union: Statement on Campus Demonstrations)*

Dissent and disruption are not simply different methods of expressing the same point of view. Dissent respects the rights of one's fellow citizens; it relies on persuasion. Disruption is based on disregard for the rights of others; it relies on coercion. Dissent is essential in a free society. Disruption is destructive of legitimate democratic processes.

A major function of institutions of higher education, in a divided and troubled society, is to pursue knowledge that will help to resolve society's problems, and to educate students to be intelligent, tolerant, effective, and humane. To accomplish these goals, an atmosphere of free inquiry and expression must pervade the campuses. No matter how just one may consider his cause to be, violence and terrorism cannot be justified. "Victories" that may be achieved through such methods—and they are highly unlikely—

EXHIBIT 8

American Civil Liberties Union: Statement on Campus Demonstrations

The manner in which demonstrations have been conducted, at least in some notorious cases, must be condemned as disproportionate to the grievances of the students and as categorically in violation of basic principles of academic freedom. The fact that significant reforms may be won by violent action does not justify the resort to violence, even if such action seems plausible to some in a society marked by violence both internally and in its external actions, and even if an apparent justification after the fact seems to be provided by a violent response, for example a police action. The so-called "politics of confrontation" invites, and is intended to invite, such a response, but in so far as it seeks its ends by means which infringe on the liberties of others it is out of keeping with the principles by which and the purposes for which the university exists.

SOURCE: American Civil Liberties Union press release, June 25, 1968.

leave such an aftermath of ill-will and mistrust that they are self-defeating.

Most campus protest has taken the form of dissent, not disruption. However, there has been some tendency in the public reaction to protest activity to reject dissent as well as disruption. The American public seems to show limited tolerance for mass protest activities, even when these are within the bounds of the law. In 1968, a national sample of public opinion indicated that 52 percent of those responding would disapprove of protest marches *that were permitted by the local authorities.* This substantial disapproval suggests that many Americans may not distinguish sufficiently between organized dissent and disruption. Fortunately, most public authorities, most of the time, have respected this important distinction, although at times excessive police or National Guard action has been taken. [*Exhibit 9: Public Attitudes toward Protest: National Sample, 1968 (table)*]

The Commission recommends that evaluation of and response to events on a campus be based upon the distinction between dissent and disruption.

The Commission also recommends that dissent be protected as a democratic right and a major means of renewal for society; that repression be rejected.

Public Attitudes Toward Protest: National Sample, 1968

Attitude toward taking part in protest meetings or marches that are permitted by the local authorities:

Age	Percent disapprove	N
21–25	40%	133
26–30	39	150
31–50	48	550
over 50	65	482
Total all ages	52%	1315
Education	Percent disapprove	N
Less than H.S. grad	61%	528
H.S. grad	56	410
Some college	47	199
College grad	26	181
Total all levels of education	52%	1318

SOURCE: Prepared by Carnegie Commission staff from data from Survey Research Center, University of Michigan, 1968 Election Study.

The Commission further recommends that disruption be met by the full efforts of the campus to end it and, where necessary, by the general law, while guarding against excessive force by law enforcement personnel.

3. Many Problems, Many Individuals, Many Campuses

Responses to dissent or disruption on a campus must take into consideration that (a) there are many problems underlying current dissatisfactions; (b) there are many individuals with varied attitudes and behavior on a campus; and (c) there are many different campuses in the nation.

MANY PROBLEMS An examination of the factors contributing to protest activities on the campuses suggests that dissent and disruption reflect many changes, controversies, and problems in American society and in colleges and universities. Concern over these issues and problems ebbs and flows, and so, also, do campus protest activities.

The Scranton Commission has pointed to some of the conditions underlying campus unrest as:

. . . the advance of American society into the post-industrial era, the increasing affluence of most Americans, and the expansion and intergenerational evolution of liberal idealism. Together, these have prompted the formation of a new youth culture that defines itself through a passionate attachment to principle and an opposition to the larger society. At the center of this culture is a romantic celebration of human life, of the unencumbered individual, of the senses, and of nature. It rejects what it sees to be the operational ideals of American society: materialism, competition, rationalism, technology, consumerism, and militarism. This emerging culture is the deeper cause of student protest against war, racial injustice, and the abuses of the multiversity.

During the past decade, this youth culture developed rapidly. It has become ever more distinct and has acquired an almost religious fervor through a process of advancing personal commitment. This process has been spurred by the emergence of opposition to the youth culture, and particularly to its demonstrations of political protest.

Many, but by no means all, students share, to varying extents and in varying intensity, this broad set of values and perceptions of the world. Concomitantly, this new youth culture appeals not only to many students; some older persons also share its ideals in whole or in part. The ideals of the youth culture, however, do not necessarily imply that the means chosen to advance them are above reproach; in fact, some adherents disregard any moral concern about their choice of means in the name of the morality of their ends. Some of the means, more than most of the ends, pose difficulties for the campuses.

The more proximate causes of dissatisfaction among young people are seen in the reasons protesters themselves give for their actions:

- The conditions of minority and impoverished groups in the United States which involve inequality, injustice, and poverty in a society of affluence.

- The problems of war and peace, especially the Vietnam War, the growth of military technology, the bomb, and the escalating arms race.

- The problems resulting from the rapid growth of technology: deterioration of the environment and a sensed lessening importance of the role of the individual in a complex, postindustrial society.

- The problems of higher education, both internally and in its relationship to the wider society. These include the effects of institutions rapidly expanding in size; of traditional curricula offered largely unchanged despite the changing problems of society and the changing interests of students; and of the extent to which the campuses contribute to or fail to help solve society's injustices, inequalities, and inadequacies.

We conclude that dissatisfactions on campuses and their public expression should be viewed as the reflection of many problems and conditions both in society and on the campuses. Both campus and society share responsibility. Dissenters are also responsible for their choice of tactics in advancing their goals—for some of their tactics are the source of the dissatisfactions and negative reactions of the public at large.

MANY INDIVIDUALS There is a sense of dissatisfaction among many students about many things, but it is also important to recognize the varied extent of that dissatisfaction, its various sources, and its varied public expressions.

EXHIBIT 10

Undergraduates' Participation, Since Entering College, in at Least One Demonstration at Their College or Elsewhere, Concerning United States Military Policy, Ethnic or Racial Policies, or Administrative Policies of a College, by Carnegie Commission Typology of Institutions*

	All institutions†	*Doctoral-granting institutions*				*Nondoctoral: liberal arts and occupational programs*		*Liberal arts colleges*		*Two-year colleges*
		Heavy emphasis on research	*Moderate emphasis on research*	*Moderate emphasis on doctoral*	*Limited emphasis on doctoral*	*Comprehensive programs*	*Limited programs*	*I*	*II*	
Percent who participated	31	46	33	39	25	29	28	49	38	21
Percent who did not participate	69	54	67	61	75	71	72	51	62	79
TOTAL	100	100	100	100	100	100	100	100	100	100

* For a description of the Carnegie Commission typology of institutions, see Appendix C.

† For the undergraduate data, the population represented by the sample in the Carnegie Commission survey is persons who *entered* institutions of higher education as undergraduates for the first time during the fall terms of 1966, 1967, 1968, and 1969. These data were collected during December 1969 and January 1970 from all *entrants*, whether or not they were attending college at that time. All data reported from the Carnegie Commission survey have been weighted to compensate for differential rates of sampling among institutions of different types and differential rates of response among institutions. The weights for the undergraduate data will be revised to make use of additional information before further analysis of the data is undertaken, but the findings here will not be substantially affected by these revisions.

SOURCE: Carnegie Commission survey of undergraduates in 1969–70.

Most students engage in neither organized dissent nor disruption. As a broad conclusion, students may be divided as follows:[1]

Never engaged in organized protest activity	70%
Engaged occasionally or regularly in nondisruptive protest activity about aspects of a campus or society or both	30%

(Exhibit 10: Undergraduates' Participation in a Demonstration (table); and Appendix B)

While about half of all students feel that basic changes will be necessary to improve the quality of life in America, a substantial majority do not accept disruption and violence as appropriate means of change. Thus the issue is not that the campuses support disruption while society opposes it. The issue, rather, is how the substantial campus majorities against disruption can be effective against the minorities which occasionally or regularly engage in disruption. This is a common problem shared with society, because society also faces disruption and violence, including terrorism. The problem is not the campus versus society, but, rather, the campus *and* society both against disruption and violence. This report is concerned with the campus version of this common problem. *[Exhibit 11: National Commission on the Causes and Prevention of Violence: Violence in the United States; Exhibit 12: Attitudes of Undergraduates, Graduate Students, and Faculty, for All Institutions (table); Exhibit 13: Faculty and Graduate Student Attitudes Toward the Emergence of Radical Student Activism, by Carnegie Commission Typology of Institutions (table)]*

Great variety marks higher education in both its students and its faculty members. College students and faculty generally consider themselves more liberal politically than the public at large, but a sizable portion of both students and faculty consider themselves middle-of-the-road or conservative. They spread over the same broad spectrum of political ideology as the general public. *[Exhibit 14: Political Ideology of Undergraduates, Graduate Students, and Faculty in All Institutions, and of the United States Public (table)]*

Great variety also marks youth throughout the nation. Young

---

[1] We estimate that not more than 1 percent of students have participated in disruption against the campus or society or both. Within this 1 percent, a much smaller number are fully committed to participate regularly in disruptive or violent actions against the campus or society or both.

EXHIBIT 11

National Commission on the Causes and Prevention of Violence: Violence in the United States

Violence in the United States has risen to alarmingly high levels. Whether one considers assassination, group violence, or individual acts of violence, the decade of the 1960s was considerably more violent than the several decades preceding it and ranks among the most violent in our history. The United States is the clear leader among modern, stable democratic nations in its rates of homicide, assault, rape, and robbery, and it is at least among the highest in incidence of group violence and assassination.

This high level of violence is dangerous to our society. It is disfiguring our society—making fortresses of portions of our cities and dividing our people into armed camps. It is jeopardizing some of our most precious institutions, among them our schools and universities—poisoning the spirit of trust and cooperation that is essential to their proper functioning. It is corroding the central political processes of our democratic society—substituting force and fear for argument and accommodation.

We have endured and survived other cycles of violence in our history. Today, however, we are more vulnerable to violence than ever before. Two-thirds of our people live in urban areas, where violence especially thrives. Individual and group specializations have intensified our dependence on one another. Men are no longer capable of solitary living and individual self-defense; men must live together and depend upon one another to observe the laws and keep the peace.

The American people know the threat. They demand that violence be brought to a halt. Violence must be brought under control—to safeguard life and property, and to make possible the creation of the understanding and cooperation needed to remedy underlying causes. No society can remain free, much less deal effectively with its fundamental problems, if its people live in fear of their fellow citizens; it is ancient wisdom that a house divided against itself cannot stand.

SOURCE: National Commission on the Causes and Prevention of Violence, *To Establish Justice, To Insure Domestic Tranquility*, 1969.

people with no college education are politically more conservative than young people with some college education. Young people with less than college education, for example, showed greater preference for George C. Wallace as a presidential candidate in 1968 and more disapproval of legal protest marches than did the college-educated. Youth, both inside college and outside college, is very heterogeneous. It is a basic error to treat this age group as a homogenized mass. [*Exhibit 15: Educational Level and 1968 Vote Prefer-*

EXHIBIT 12

Attitudes of Undergraduates, Graduate Students, and Faculty, for All Institutions Toward Means of Achieving Change and Political Goals

	Under-graduates	*Graduate students*	*Faculty*
Meaningful social change cannot be achieved through traditional American politics			
Strongly agree	16%	11%	11%
Agree with reservations	37	26	23
Disagree with reservations	36	38	39
Strongly disagree	11	25	27
TOTAL	100%	100%	100%
*In the U.S.A. today there can be no justification for using violence to achieve political goals**			
Strongly agree	46%		49%
Agree with reservations	29		25
Disagree with reservations	20		18
Strongly disagree	6		8
TOTAL	100%		100%

* Question not asked of graduate students.
SOURCE: Carnegie Commission survey of undergraduates, graduate students, and faculty in 1969–70.

ence among Young People Aged 18 to 24 (table); Exhibit 16: Educational Status and Attitudes toward Protest: National Sample of 21- to 30-Year-Olds, 1968 (table)]

We conclude that students and faculty members are divided, as is American society, about means and ends; but they stand predominantly, as does American society, against disruption and violence and for ordered change.

MANY
CAMPUSES

A campus is a particularly sensitive institution where both its own problems and those of society are constantly under discussion and scrutiny. A campus may become troubled not only when its own members are discontented with academic life, but also when they are dissatisfied with policies or events in society. This has been true throughout American history—at the time of the War of Independence, of the Civil War, of the movement for women's suffrage, and of the Great Depression. Campuses have been centers of discussion and protest during each of these periods of national turmoil, sometimes to a greater extent than society itself.

Campuses are now once again centers for dissent in the nation. The great majority of protest activities on the campuses in recent years, as in earlier times, have been nondisruptive and nonviolent. Even after the Cambodian incursion and the deaths at Kent and Jackson State in spring 1970—which gave rise to the most extensive campus demonstrations in American history—only 4 percent of the campuses experienced violent protests, and in many cases by a small minority of students. [*Exhibit 17: Number of United States Institutions Experiencing Incidents of Violent or Disruptive Protests: 1968–69 Academic Year (table); Exhibit 18: Percent of Institutions Experiencing Various Reactions to the Cambodia Incursion and Kent State and Jackson State Shootings, by Type of Institution (table)*]

There are many campuses in the United States—over 2,500 total—which differ from each other in such characteristics as size, location, selectivity in admissions policies, educational style, and types of degrees offered. About one-half of these institutions have experienced some organized dissent, but only about 5 percent have experienced any violence or terrorism in any recent year.

Students and faculty members vary greatly in their beliefs and actions; and campuses vary greatly in the amount of dissent and disruption that occurs upon them. To judge many or all members of the campus, or many or all campuses, because of the behavior of a few is poor judgment. The many who may be punished in the process of penalizing the few may become embittered and lose confidence in American society's ability to handle problems justly. Generalized repression and retaliation should be opposed with the same resolution as disruption itself. A shotgun approach is as unwise here as in any other area of our national life where individual and small-group behavior is involved.

Therefore, we conclude that actions by society in response to coercion and violence be undertaken only with reference to those specific individuals and groups who engage in it. A campus as a whole, or a system as a whole, or higher education as a whole, should not be penalized.

EXHIBIT 13

Faculty and Graduate Student Attitudes Toward the Emergence of Radical Student Activism, by Carnegie Commission Typology of Institutions*

| | | Doctoral-granting institutions | | | |
| | | | | | |
Attitude	*All insti-tutions*	*Heavy emphasis on research*	*Moderate emphasis on research*	*Moderate emphasis on doctoral programs*	*Limited emphasis on doctoral programs*
Faculty:					
Unreservedly approve	2%	3%	2%	3%	3%
Approve with reservations	38	47	39	40	46
Disapprove with reservations	42	39	42	40	35
Unreservedly disapprove	18	11	17	17	16
Total percent	100%	100%	100%	100%	100%
Graduate students:†					
Unreservedly approve	3%	7%	3%	3%	3%
Approve with reservations	30	41	33	31	28
Disapprove with reservations	41	34	40	40	42
Unreservedly disapprove	26	18	24	26	27
Total percent	100%	100%	100%	100%	100%

*For a description of the Carnegie Commission typology of institutions, see Appendix C.
† Not applicable to last three types of institutions.
SOURCE: Carnegie Commission survey of faculty and graduate students in 1969–70.

Nondoctoral: liberal arts and occupational		Liberal arts colleges		Two-year colleges	Schools of engineering, technology
Compre-hensive programs	Limited programs	I	II		
3%	2%	4%	2%	2%	3%
38	34	48	43	31	23
44	46	37	40	44	43
15	18	11	15	23	31
100%	100%	100%	100%	100%	100%
1%	1%				
29	24				
42	46				
28	29				
100%	100%				

EXHIBIT 14

Political Ideology of Undergraduates, Graduate Students, and Faculty in All Institutions, and of United States Public

	Campus		
Political ideology*	*Under-graduates*	*Graduate students*	*Faculty*
Left	5%	5%	5%
Liberal	38	36	39
Middle-of-the-road	35	27	26
Moderately conservative	16	26	24
Strongly conservative	2	4	3
Don't know or no answer	4	2	3
TOTAL	100%	100%	100%

* Response to the question "How would you characterize yourself politically at the present time (left, liberal, middle-of-the-road, moderately conservative, or strongly conservative)?"

† Response to the question "How would you describe yourself (very liberal, fairly liberal, middle-of-the-road, fairly conservative, or very conservative)?"

SOURCE: (1) *Campus opinion:* Carnegie Commission survey of undergraduates, graduate students, and faculty in 1969–1970. (2) *Public opinion:* Gallup poll from November 1970.

Public	
Political ideology†	*U.S. Public*
Very liberal	5%
Fairly liberal	16
Middle-of-the-road	36
Fairly conservative	30
Very conservative	9
Don't know or no answer	4
TOTAL	100%

EXHIBIT 15

**Educational Level and 1968 Vote Preference among Young People
Aged 18 to 24**

	Non-high school graduates	High school graduates	Some college	College graduates	Student
Wallace	39%	32%	21%	8%	7%
Humphrey	11	18	13	29	19
Nixon	31	33	39	42	37
None	19	17	28	22	38
Number	(173)	(452)	(261)	(119)	(395)

SOURCE: Seymour Martin Lipset and Earl Raab, *The Politics of Unreason,* Harper & Row, Publishers, Incorporated, New York, 1970.

The challenge to the campuses is how to reform themselves in a manner that will discourage disruption, protect dissent, and better serve both the students and society. It is important to recognize, nevertheless, that a campus itself does not have the power to solve all the problems of which disruption is a reflection. Many protests are directed toward societal problems over which a campus has no direct control, and thus a campus is caught between the protesters and the objects of their protests.

We believe that the following three sets of actions are essential:[2]

1 Development of a bill of rights and responsibilities for *all* members of institutions

2 Development of consultation processes and contingency planning for emergency situations on the campuses

3 Development of fair, equitable, and effective procedures to handle violations of campus rules

---

[2] The Commission, as noted earlier, will also issue reports on campus governance and academic reform. We note now, however, that it must be recognized that the very process of reform, however essential the reforms, may engender dissatisfaction and dissent, and, thus, that the process of reform, in the short run, may increase unrest. Nevertheless many reforms are both necessary and desirable. They should be undertaken on their merits and not as a short-term cure for unrest.

Many campuses are now in a new situation. The old informal consensus no longer exists; the tradition of gradual change is met by sudden confrontation; and the private word of advice or admonition is no longer sufficient in the handling of what are often now deliberate violations. Thus many campuses need a new constitution in place of the old consensus, quick action in certain situations instead of delayed collegial unanimity, and formal discipline as well as friendly guidance. This all may be greatly regretted, but it also has become greatly required.

EXHIBIT 16

Educational Status and Attitudes Toward Protest: National Sample of 21- to 30-Year-Olds, 1968

Attitude toward taking part in protest meetings or marches that are permitted by the local authorities

Education	Percent disapprove	N
Less than H.S. grad	54	56
H.S. grad	45	100
Some college	37	82
College grad	16	45
Total 21- to 30-year-olds	40	283

SOURCE: Data from Survey Research Center, University of Michigan, 1968 Election Study.

EXHIBIT 17

Number of United States Institutions Experiencing Incidents of Violent or Disruptive Protests: 1968–69 Academic Year

Protest incident	*Number of sample institutions at which protest occurred*	
1. *Burning of building by protestors*	11	
2. *Breaking or wrecking of building or furnishings*	18	
3. *Destruction of records, files, papers*	5	
4. *Campus march, picketing, or rally with physical violence*	18	
5. *One or more persons killed*	2	
6. *Some persons injured*	14	
Total of institutions experiencing violent protests (1 through 6 above)		41
7. *Building or section of building occupied*	62	
8. *Entrance to building barred by protestors*	27	
9. *Officials held "captive" by protestors*	7	
10. *Interruption of school function (e.g., classes, speech or meeting)*	59	
11. *General campus strike or boycott of school function*	37	
Total of institutions experiencing disruptive protests (1 through 11 above)*		125

* Included in the disruptive protest category are strikes and boycotts of classes, which would not necessarily be considered disruptive according to the definitions in this Carnegie Commission report.

SOURCE: Alan E. Bayer and Alexander W. Astin, "Violence and Disruption on the U.S. Campus, 1968–69," *Educational Record,* fall 1969, vol. 50, no. 4.

Estimated number of institutions in the population at which protest incident occurred	Percent of institutions in the population at which protest incident occurred
43	1.8
80	3.4
21	0.9
62	2.6
8	0.3
45	1.9
145	6.2
275	11.7
83	3.5
24	1.0
260	11.1
141	6.0
524	22.4

EXHIBIT 18

Percent of Institutions Experiencing Various Reactions to the Cambodia Incursion and Kent State and Jackson State Shootings, by Type of Institution

Reaction	All institutions N = 1,856*	Public four-year colleges N = 255	Public universities N = 114
Student/staff strike, one day or longer	14	13	28
Efforts by students to communicate with local citizens about the war and the campus reaction	40	45	71
Essentially peaceful demonstrations	44	54	76
Demonstrations causing damage to persons or property	4	5	28

*The number of cases does not sum to 1,856 because private two-year colleges and most special-purpose institutions are represented only in the total column.

SOURCE: Carnegie Commission survey of 1,856 college and university presidents conducted in July 1970.

Independent four-year colleges N = 198	Independent universities N = 37	Catholic institutions N = 227	Protestant institutions N = 338	Public two-year colleges N = 477
27	41	10	7	8
61	89	37	35	27
62	89	41	38	32
3	16	2	1	1

4. A Bill of Rights and Responsibilities for Members of the Campus

Campuses, historically, have had few explicit guidelines for the rights and responsibilities of all their members. They have operated, instead, on the basis of certain principles and relationships affecting separately each of their constituent groups. Increasingly, however, these traditional arrangements are no longer fully effective in some places. Among the traditional guidelines are the following:

1 One set of principles, pursued particularly by the American Association of University Professors, has sought to protect academic freedom from attacks by trustees, administrators, legislators, and the general public. Academic freedom, however, is now under attack from within the campuses as well as from outside. *(Exhibit 19: American Association of University Professors: Academic Freedom, 1940)*

2 There has been a series of regulations, campus by campus, governing academic requirements and the social conduct of students. Students now want to be *within* the academic community and to take part in decisions which affect them, not merely to be *under* the rules of a campus. Moreover, as the campuses have given up their roles *in loco parentis,* many regulations have come to be inappropriate although they still exist in fact.

3 There have been the largely unwritten but shared understandings among faculty members and administrators about the nature of academic life and desirable conduct within it. These understandings have mainly involved collegial consensus about professional ethics and full tolerance toward the individual faculty member in his own teaching and research endeavors. Faculty members no longer share all the same understandings; in particular, there are disagreements over what constitutes appropriate political activity by and within the institution.

These three sets of principles and relationships have left certain gaps:

- Faculty responsibilities — perhaps particularly the greater responsibilities of faculty members with tenure, since they have greater security, authority, and status — have been less clearly set forth than faculty rights.

- Student rights have often been less carefully established than student responsibilities.

- The appropriateness of political action on a campus, by whomever, but particularly by the institution and its component parts, has not been sufficiently defined.

- Too much has been left to oral tradition. More people need to know more precisely what is expected of them.

- Disruption and violence, from whatever source, have not been adequately defined and proscribed.

We believe the time has come for campuses to develop bills of rights and responsibilities for *all* their members. As participants

EXHIBIT 19

American Association of University Professors: Academic Freedom, 1940

(a)   The teacher is entitled to full freedom in research and in the publication of the results, subject to the adequate performance of his other academic duties; but research for pecuniary return should be based upon an understanding with the authorities of the institution.

(b)   The teacher is entitled to freedom in the classroom in discussing his subject, but he should be careful not to introduce into his teaching controversial matter which has no relation to his subject. Limitations of academic freedom because of religious or other aims of the institution should be clearly stated in writing at the time of the appointment.

(c)   The college or university teacher is a citizen, a member of a learned profession, and an officer of an educational institution. When he speaks or writes as a citizen, he should be free from institutional censorship or discipline, but his special position in the community imposes special obligations. As a man of learning and an educational officer, he should remember that the public may judge his profession and his institution by his utterances. Hence he should at all times be accurate, should exercise appropriate restraint, should show respect for the opinions of others, and should make every effort to indicate that he is not an institutional spokesman.

SOURCE: Excerpt from 1940 *Statement of Principles on Academic Freedom and Tenure,* American Association of University Professors.

in the educational process in a particular institution, individuals share certain basic rights and responsibilities regardless of their roles in the institution. The consensus and selective rules of the past have too often become the confusion of the present. Reforms which are needed on campuses can be undertaken more successfully if there are broad prior agreements about the rights and responsibilities of any and all members of the institution. There are explicit codes of conduct as well as checks on the behavior of individuals in other institutions in society, and there is a need for them now in campus communities.

The process of formulating such agreements should be so structured that it will give rise to the greatest of understanding and the widest acceptance of the results. The process can be as important as the formal results. Guidelines for the conduct of all members of a campus should, consequently, be developed by each campus through wide consultation and discussion. Each major group has an important and distinct role to play. Students should have full rights of initiation of proposals and of consultation. The faculty has a particular role to play in its own right but also through its dual relationship to the students and to the administrators and trustees. Presidents bear the greatest burden of leadership. Trustees have, however, the ultimate responsibility for adoption of guidelines as policy.

We agree with the Scranton Commission, which has also suggested the need for a set of guidelines on conduct, that in adopting them:

The opinions of all segments of the university should be sought. The justification for such openness goes far beyond the need to establish "credibility." Different parts of the university community have different values and interests which can be reconciled in a code of discipline only if all factions have the opportunity to be heard. The extent of direct participation of university members in these processes will vary from one institution to another, and will in any event depend on their good faith and willingness to work for the common good of the university.

We also agree that, in the end, there must be a document, whether a code of discipline as they recommend, or a bill of rights and responsibilities as we recommend, or both. In the words of the Scranton Commission:

We emphasize that the community cannot allow itself to be paralyzed by the failure of all segments of the university to agree on a disciplinary code. Agreement is desirable, but even in its absence there must be a code.

Thus, agreement of all elements of a campus should be the goal, but tacit acceptance may be the best that can be obtained in some circumstances. One way or another, there needs to be a setting forth of rights and responsibilities. Not every specific act which would violate rights and responsibilities can be covered in any bill or code; therefore rights and responsibilities, as well as codes of conduct, must be broadly stated and then reasonably interpreted.

The Commission has prepared an example or model of such a bill of rights and responsibilities, intended to apply to a *whole* campus: faculty, students, administrators, staff, and trustees. It incorporates minimal principles which should guide behavior in the academic community if the campus is to serve its essential purposes—to pursue knowledge and to teach in an atmosphere conducive to the free exchange of ideas. While members of campuses have other special obligations because of their particular roles in the institution, *all* members share the common rights and obligations described below.

We hope that each campus, if it has not already done so, will develop its own bill of rights and responsibilities, perhaps using as one basis the guidelines that follow. The bill itself cannot, of course, guarantee that there will be no disruptive or violent behavior on a campus. A campus is particularly vulnerable to disruption and violence because so many different people come and go almost around the clock in a free-flowing sort of way. No other institution in society is so open to so many people so much of the time—not the factory or store, not the office or service shop, not the government bureau or high school. Disruption, also, can result from the actions of very small numbers of persons, and terrorism from even fewer. But the process of developing the bill, and the principles embodied in it, may help to create an atmosphere in which such behavior is less likely to occur and can better be met if it does.

The Commission's bill of rights and responsibilities is intended as a working document which campuses may use in developing their own bills. Because of the great diversity in higher education in the United States, the principles set forth here are necessarily general, and individual institutions would need to adapt them according to their own particular circumstances.

We see at least three merits in the general approach of this model bill:

1 It treats rights and responsibilities simultaneously—one person's rights are only effective as other people recognize them and accept responsibility to guarantee them.

2 It approaches a total campus community as a single entity. Too often, in the past, faculty members have set rules for the students but not for themselves; or trustees have set rules for the faculty but not for themselves. We believe the time is appropriate for certain rights and responsibilities to be applied equally to all members of a campus.

3 It establishes the principle that the greater the privileges of members of the institution, the more responsible they should be for maintenance of high standards of conduct and an environment conducive to extending, sharing, and examining knowledge and values. Thus faculty members with tenure, as well as trustees and administrators, all of whom have substantial authority and security, should not inhabit protected enclaves above and beyond the rule of law nor be shielded from the legitimate grievances and requests of other elements of a campus.

We see the academic process essentially as a means to ascertain truth as against falsity, to gain knowledge as against ignorance, to improve intellectual excellence as against shoddiness. Thus procedural values are of the highest importance. A campus is not and must never become a place for any means to any self-chosen end. This is the central theme of this proposed bill.

A BILL OF RIGHTS AND RESPONSIBILITIES FOR MEMBERS OF THE INSTITUTION: FACULTY, STUDENTS, ADMINISTRATORS, STAFF, AND TRUSTEES

Preamble

Members of the campus have an obligation to fulfill the responsibilities incumbent upon all citizens, as well as the responsibilities of their particular roles within the academic community. All members share the obligation to respect:

- The fundamental rights of others as citizens.
- The rights of others based upon the nature of the educational process.
- The rights of the institution.
- The rights of members to fair and equitable procedures for determining when and upon whom penalties for violation of campus regulations should be imposed.

1 *As citizens, members of the campus enjoy the same basic rights and are bound by the same responsibilities to respect the rights of others, as are all citizens.*

Among the basic rights are freedom of speech; freedom of press; freedom of peaceful assembly and association; freedom of political beliefs; and freedom from personal force and violence, threats of violence, and personal abuse.

Freedom of press implies the right to freedom from censorship in campus newspapers and other media, and the concomitant obligation to adhere to the canons of responsible journalism.

It should be made clear in writings or broadcasts that editorial opinions are not necessarily those of the institution or its members.

The campus is not a sanctuary from the general law.

The campus does not stand *in loco parentis* for its members.

Each member of the campus has the right to organize his or her own personal life and behavior, so long as it does not violate the law or agreements voluntarily entered into, and does not interfere with the rights of others or the educational process.

Admission to, employment by, and promotion within the campus shall accord with the provisions against discrimination in the general law.

2 *All members of the campus have other responsibilities and rights based upon the nature of the educational process and the require-*

ments of the search for truth and its free presentation. These rights and responsibilities include:

Obligation to respect the freedom to teach, to learn, and to conduct research and publish findings in the spirit of free inquiry.

Institutional censorship and individual or group intolerance of the opinions of others are inconsistent with this freedom.

Freedom to teach and to learn implies that the teacher has the right to determine the specific content of his course, within the established course definition, and the responsibility not to depart significantly from his area of competence or to divert significant time to material extraneous to the subject matter of his course.

Free inquiry implies that (except under conditions of national emergency) no research, the results of which are secret, is to be conducted on a campus.

Obligation not to interfere with the freedom of members of a campus to pursue normal academic and administrative activities, including freedom of movement.

Obligation not to infringe upon the right of all members of a campus to privacy in offices, laboratories, and dormitory rooms and in the keeping of personal papers, confidential records and effects, subject only to the general law and to conditions voluntarily entered into.

Campus records on its members should contain only information which is reasonably related to the educational purposes or safety of the campus.

Obligation not to interfere with any member's freedom to hear and to study unpopular and controversial views on intellectual and public issues.

Right to identify oneself as a member of the campus and a concurrent obligation not to speak or act on behalf of the institution without authorization.

Right to hold public meetings in which members participate, to post notices, and to engage in peaceful, orderly demonstrations.

Reasonable and impartially applied rules designed to reflect the educational purposes of the institution and to protect the safety of the campus shall be established regulating time, place, and manner of such activities and allocating the use of facilities.

Right to recourse if another member of the campus is negligent or irresponsible in performance of his or her responsibilities or if another member of the campus represents the work of others as his or her own.

Right to be heard and considered at appropriate levels of the decision-making process about basic policy matters of direct concern.

Members of the campus who have a continuing association with the institution and who have substantial authority and security have an especially strong obligation to maintain an environment conducive to respect for the rights of others and fulfillment of academic responsibilities.

Tenured faculty should maintain the highest standards in performance of their academic responsibilities.

Trustees have a particular responsibility to protect the integrity of the academic process from external and internal attacks and to prevent the political or financial exploitation of the campus by any individual or group.

3 *The institution, and any division or agency which exercises direct or delegated authority for the institution, has rights and responsibilities of its own. The rights and responsibilities of the institutions include:*

Right and obligation to provide an open forum for members of the campus to present and debate public issues.

Right to prohibit individuals and groups who are not members of the campus from using its name, its finances, and its physical and operating facilities for commercial or political activities.

Right to prohibit members of the campus from using its name, its finances, or its physical and operating facilities for commercial activities.

Right and obligation to provide for members of the campus the use of meeting rooms under the rules of the campus, including use for political purposes such as meetings of political clubs; to prohibit use of its rooms on a regular or prolonged basis by individual members or groups of members as free headquarters for political campaigns; and to prohibit use of its name, its finances, and its office equipment and supplies for any political purpose at any time.

Right and obligation not to take a position, as an institution, in electoral politics or on public issues, except on those issues which directly affect its autonomy, the freedom of its members, its financial support, and its academic functions.

Right and obligation to protect the members of the campus and visitors to it from physical harm, threats of harm, or abuse; its property from damage and unauthorized use; and its academic and administrative processes from interruption.

Right to require that persons on the campus be willing to identify themselves by name and address, and state what connection, if any, they have with the campus.

Right to set reasonable standards of conduct in order to safeguard the educational process and to provide for the safety of members of the campus and the institution's property.

Right to deny pay and academic credit to members of the campus who are on strike,[1] and the concomitant obligation to accept legal strikes legally conducted without recourse to dismissal of participants.

4   *All members of the campus have a right to fair and equitable procedures which shall determine the validity of charges of violation of campus regulations.*

The procedures shall be structured so as to facilitate a reliable determination of the truth or falsity of charges, to provide fundamental fairness to the parties, and to be an effective instrument for the maintenance of order.

All members of the campus have a right to know in advance the range of penalties for violations of campus regulations. Definition of adequate cause for separation from the campus should be clearly formulated and made public.

Charges of minor infractions of regulations, penalized by small fines or reprimands which do not become part of permanent records, may be handled expeditiously by the appropriate individual or committee. Persons so penalized have the right to appeal.

In the case of charges of infractions of regulations which may lead to notation in permanent records, or to more serious penalties such as suspension or expulsion, members of the campus have a right to formal procedures with adequate due process, including the right of appeal.

Members of the campus charged or convicted of violations under general law may be subject to campus sanctions for the same conduct, in accord with campus policies and procedures, when the conduct is in violation of a campus rule essential to the continuing protection of other members of the campus or to the safeguarding of the educational process.

---

[1] In case of total or partial closures due to strikes, we suggest immediate cessation of pay and academic credit for those directly participating. The campus should not make claim to be the only area of society where strikes are cost-free to their participants. Workers uniformly forego their pay as they withdraw their services. They are subject to the costs of strikes as well as the potential benefits. Persons on campus can hardly expect the one and only "free ride." A cost-free strike, also, is not an effective means of demonstrating moral conviction.

Exhibits for "A Bill of Rights and Responsibilities for Members of the Campus"

American Association of University Professors: Freedom and Responsibility *(Exhibit 20)*

American Association of University Professors: Statement on Professional Ethics *(Exhibit 21)*

American Association of State Colleges and Universities: Academic Freedom, Responsibility, and Tenure, 1970 *(Exhibit 22)*

University of California: Restrictions on the Use of University Resources and Facilities for Political Activities *(Exhibit 23)*

American Council on Education: Tax-exempt Status of Universities—Impact on Political Activities by Students, June 19, 1970 *(Exhibit 24)*

University of Michigan: Faculty Pay Policy During Strike *(Exhibit 25)*

American Civil Liberties Union: Academic Due Process *(Exhibit 26)*

American Bar Association Commission on Campus Government and Student Dissent: University Disciplinary Procedures *(Exhibit 27)*

Relevant Appendixes

Appendix E: American Civil Liberties Union—Academic Freedom and Civil Liberties of Students in Colleges and Universities

Appendix F: Cuyahoga Community College—Rights and Responsibilities of the College Community

Appendix G: Harvard University—Universitywide Statement on Rights and Responsibilities

Appendix H: The University of North Carolina—Policies, Procedures, and Disciplinary Actions in Cases of Disruption of Educational Process

Appendix I: University of Washington—Rules of Conduct on Campus

Appendix J: Joint Statement on Rights and Freedoms of Students

Appendix K: American Bar Association Law Student Division Committee on Student Rights & Responsibilities—Model Code for Student Rights, Responsibilities & Conduct

Appendix L: Cleveland State University—Policy on Maintenance of the Educational Environment and Student Bill of Rights and Responsibilities

Appendix M: The National Union of Students and The National Council for Civil Liberties (Great Britain)—Academic Freedom and the Law, 1970

Appendix N: University of Oregon—Student Conduct Program

Appendix O: University of California—Interim Report of the State-wide Academic Council

Appendix P: University of Illinois at Urbana-Champaign—Faculty Senate Statement on Faculty Responsibility and Academic Freedom

Appendix Q: Oregon State Board of Higher Education—Statement Relating to Faculty Conduct, 1970

Appendix R: Stanford Chapter of the American Association of University Professors—Report on Faculty Self-Discipline, January 1971

Appendix S: American Association of State Colleges and Universities—Basic Rights and Responsibilities for College and University Presidents, 1970

EXHIBIT 20

American Association of University Professors:
Freedom and Responsibility

A Statement of the Association's Council, October 31, 1970

For more than half a century the American Association of University Professors has acted upon two principles: that colleges and universities serve the common good through learning, teaching, research, and scholarship; and that the fulfillment of this function necessarily rests upon the preservation of the intellectual freedoms of teaching, expression, research, and debate. All components of the academic community have a responsibility to exemplify and support these freedoms in the interests of reasoned inquiry.

The 1940 *Statement of Principles on Academic Freedom and Tenure* asserts the primacy of this responsibility. The 1966 *Statement on Professional Ethics* underscores its pertinency to the individual faculty member and calls attention to his responsibility, by his own actions, to uphold his colleagues' and his students' freedom of inquiry and to promote public understanding of academic freedom. The *Joint Statement on Rights and Freedoms of Students* empha-

EXHIBIT 20—continued

sizes the shared responsibility of all members of the academic community for the preservation of these freedoms.

Continuing attacks on the integrity of our universities and on the concept of academic freedom itself come from many quarters. These attacks, marked by tactics of intimidation and harassment and by political interference with the autonomy of colleges and universities, provoke harsh responses and counter-responses. Especially in a repressive atmosphere, the faculty's responsibility to defend its freedoms cannot be separated from its responsibility to uphold those freedoms by its own actions.

I

Membership in the academic community imposes on students, faculty members, administrators, and trustees an obligation to respect the dignity of others, to acknowledge their right to express differing opinions, and to foster and defend intellectual honesty, freedom of inquiry and instruction, and free expression on and off the campus. The expression of dissent and the attempt to produce change, therefore, may not be carried out in ways which injure individuals or damage institutional facilities or disrupt the classes of one's teachers or colleagues. Speakers on campus must not only be protected from violence, but given an opportunity to be heard. Those who seek to call attention to grievances must not do so in ways that significantly impede the functions of the institution.

Students are entitled to an atmosphere conducive to learning and to even-handed treatment in all aspects of the teacher-student relationship. Faculty members may not refuse to enroll or teach students on the grounds of their beliefs or the possible uses to which they may put the knowledge to be gained in a course. The student should not be forced by the authority inherent in the instructional role to make particular personal choices as to political action or his own part in society. Evaluation of students and the award of credit must be based on academic performance professionally judged and not on matters irrelevant to that performance, whether personality, race, religion, degree of political activism, or personal beliefs.

It is a teacher's mastery of his subject and his own scholarship which entitle him to his classroom and to freedom in the presentation of his subject. Thus, it is improper for an instructor persistently to intrude material which has no relation to his subject, or to fail to present the subject matter of his course as announced to his students and as approved by the faculty in their collective responsibility for the curriculum.

Because academic freedom has traditionally included the instructor's full freedom as a citizen, most faculty members face no insoluble conflicts between the claims of politics, social action, and conscience, on the one hand, and the claims and expectations of their students, colleagues, and institutions, on the other. If such conflicts become acute, and the instructor's attention to his obligations as a citizen and moral agent precludes the fulfillment of substantial academic obligations, he cannot escape the responsibility of that choice, but should either request a leave of absence or resign his academic position.

II

The Association's concern for sound principles and procedures in the imposition of discipline is reflected in the 1940 *Statement of Principles on Academic Freedom and Tenure,* the 1958 *Statement on Procedural Standards in Faculty Dismissal Proceedings,* the 1968 "Recommended Institutional Regulations on Academic Freedom and Tenure," and the many investigations conducted by the Association into disciplinary actions by colleges and universities.

The question arises whether these customary procedures are sufficient in the current context. We believe that by and large they serve their purposes well but that consideration should be given to supplementing them in several respects:

First, plans for ensuring compliance with academic norms should be enlarged to emphasize preventive as well as disciplinary action. Toward this end the faculty should take the initiative, working with the administration and other components of the institution, to develop and maintain an atmosphere of freedom, commitment to academic inquiry, and respect for the academic rights of others. The faculty should also join with other members of the academic community in the development of procedures to be used in the event of serious disruption, or the threat of disruption, and should ensure its consultation in major decisions, particularly those related to the calling of external security forces to the campus.

Second, systematic attention should be given to questions related to sanctions other than dismissal, such as warnings and reprimands, in order to provide a more versatile body of academic sanctions.

Third, there is need for the faculty to assume a more positive role as guardian of academic values against unjustified assaults from its own members. The traditional faculty function in disciplinary proceedings has been to assure academic due process and meaningful faculty participation in the imposition of discipline by the administration. While this function should be maintained, faculties should recognize their stake in promoting adherence to norms essential to the academic enterprise.

Rules designed to meet these needs for faculty self-regulation and flexibility of sanctions should be adopted on each campus in response to local circumstances and to continued experimentation. In all sanc-

EXHIBIT 20—continued

tioning efforts, however, it is vital that proceedings be conducted with fairness to the individual, that faculty judgments play a crucial role and that adverse judgments be founded on demonstrated violations of appropriate norms. The Association will encourage and assist local faculty groups seeking to articulate the substantive principles here outlined or to make improvements in their disciplinary machinery to meet the needs here described. The Association will also consult and work with any responsible group, within or outside the academic community, that seeks to promote understanding of and adherence to basic norms of professional responsibility so long as such efforts are consistent with principles of academic freedom.

EXHIBIT 21

American Association of University Professors:
Statement on Professional Ethics

From its inception, the American Association of University Professors has recognized that membership in the academic profession carries with it special responsibilities. The Association has consistently affirmed these responsibilities in major policy statements, providing guidance to the professor in his utterances as a citizen, in the exercise of his responsibilities to students, and in his conduct when resigning from his institution or when undertaking government-sponsored research. The *Statement on Professional Ethics* that follows, necessarily presented in terms of the ideal, sets forth those general standards that serve as a reminder of the variety of obligations assumed by all members of the profession. For the purpose of more detailed guidance, the Association, through its Committee B on Professional Ethics, intends to issue from time to time supplemental statements on specific problems.

In the enforcement of ethical standards, the academic profession differs from those of law and medicine, whose associations act to assure the integrity of members engaged in private practice. In the academic profession the individual institution of higher learning provides this assurance and so should normally handle questions concerning propriety of conduct within its own framework by reference to a faculty group. The Association supports such local action and stands ready, through the General Secretary and Committee B, to counsel with any faculty member or administrator concerning questions of professional ethics and to inquire into complaints when local consideration is impossible or inappropriate. If the alleged offense is deemed sufficiently serious to raise the possibility of

EXHIBIT 21—continued

dismissal, the procedures should be in accordance with the 1940 *Statement of Principles on Academic Freedom and Tenure* and the 1958 *Statement on Procedural Standards in Faculty Dismissal Proceedings.*

I. The professor, guided by a deep conviction of the worth and dignity of the advancement of knowledge, recognizes the special responsibilities placed upon him. His primary responsibility to his subject is to seek and to state the truth as he sees it. To this end he devotes his energies to developing and improving his scholarly competence. He accepts the obligation to exercise critical self-discipline and judgment in using, extending, and transmitting knowledge. He practices intellectual honesty. Although he may follow subsidiary interests, these interests must never seriously hamper or compromise his freedom of inquiry.

II. As a teacher, the professor encourages the free pursuit of learning in his students. He holds before them the best scholarly standards of his discipline. He demonstrates respect for the student as an individual, and adheres to his proper role as intellectual guide and counselor. He makes every reasonable effort to foster honest academic conduct and to assure that his evaluation of students reflects their true merit. He respects the confidential nature of the relationship between professor and student. He avoids any exploitation of students for his private advantage and acknowledges significant assistance from them. He protects their academic freedom.

III. As a colleague, the professor has obligations that derive from common membership in the community of scholars. He respects and defends the free inquiry of his associates. In the exchange of criticism and ideas he shows due respect for the opinions of others. He acknowledges his academic debts and strives to be objective in his professional judgments of colleagues. He accepts his share of faculty responsibilities for the governance of his institution.

IV. As a member of his institution, the professor seeks above all to be an effective teacher and scholar. Although he observes the stated regulations of the institution, provided they do not contravene academic freedom, he maintains his right to criticize and seek revision. He determines the amount and character of the work he does outside his institution with due regard to his paramount responsibilities within it. When considering the interruption or termination of his service, he recognizes the effect of his decision upon the program of the institution and gives due notice of his intentions.

V. As a member of his community, the professor has the rights and obligations of any citizen. He measures the urgency of these obligations in the light of his responsibilities to his subject, to his students, to his profession, and to his institution. When he speaks or

EXHIBIT 21—continued

acts as a private person he avoids creating the impression that he speaks or acts for his college or university. As a citizen engaged in a profession that depends upon freedom for its health and integrity, the professor has a particular obligation to promote conditions of free inquiry and to further public understanding of academic freedom.

SOURCE: *AAUP Bulletin,* vol. 55, pp. 86–87, spring 1969.

EXHIBIT 22

American Association of State Colleges and Universities: *Academic Freedom, Responsibility, and Tenure,* 1970

The purpose of this statement is to promote public understanding and support of academic freedom and tenure and agreement upon procedures to assure them in colleges and universities. Institutions of higher education are conducted for the common good and not to further the interest of either the individual teacher or the institution as a whole. The common good depends upon the free search for truth and its free exposition.

INSTITUTIONS OF HIGHER EDUCATION ARE COMMITTED TO THE SOLUTION OF PROBLEMS AND CONTROVERSIES BY THE METHOD OF RATIONAL DISCUSSION. ACTS OF PHYSI-CAL FORCE OR DISRUPTIVE ACTS WHICH INTERFERE WITH UNIVERSITY ACTIVITIES, FREEDOM OF MOVEMENT ON THE CAMPUS, OR FREEDOM FOR STUDENTS TO PURSUE THEIR STUDIES ARE THE ANTITHESIS OF ACADEMIC FREEDOM AND RESPONSIBILITY AS ARE ACTS WHICH IN EFFECT DENY FREEDOM OF SPEECH, FREEDOM TO BE HEARD, AND FREE-DOM TO PURSUE RESEARCH OF THEIR OWN CHOOSING TO MEMBERS OF THE ACADEMIC COMMUNITY OR TO INVITED VISITORS TO THAT COMMUNITY.

ACADEMIC FREEDOM IS THE RIGHT OF SCHOLARS IN IN-STITUTIONS OF HIGHER EDUCATION FREELY TO STUDY, DISCUSS, INVESTIGATE, TEACH AND PUBLISH.

Academic freedom (is-essential-to-these-purposes-and) applies to both teaching and research. Freedom in research is fundamental

NOTES:

1. Capital letters indicate revision or addition to the 1940 American Association of University Professors statement.

2. Material in parenthesis and lined-through indicates suggested omissions from the 1940 statement.

EXHIBIT 22—continued

to the advancement of truth. Academic freedom in its teaching aspect is fundamental for the protection of the rights of the teacher in teaching and of the student to freedom in learning. It carries with it duties correlative with rights.

ACADEMIC FREEDOM   (a)   The teacher is entitled to full freedom in research and in the publication of the results, subject to the adequate performance of his other academic duties; but research for pecuniary return should be based upon an understanding with the authorities of the institution. (b)   The teacher is entitled to freedom in the classroom in discussing his subject; but he should be careful to PRESENT THE VARIOUS SCHOLARLY VIEWS RELATED TO HIS SUBJECT AND AVOID PRESENTING TOTALLY UNRELATED MATERIAL. Limitations of academic freedom because of religious or other aims of the institution should be clearly stated in writing at the time of the appointment.

(*)ACADEMIC RESPONSIBILITY   THE CONCEPT OF FREEDOM SHOULD BE ACCOMPANIED BY AN EQUALLY DEMANDING CONCEPT OF RESPONSIBILITY. The college or university teacher is a citizen, a member of a learned profession, and an officer of an educational institution. When he speaks or writes as a citizen, he should be free from institutional censorship or discipline, but his special position in the community imposes special obligations. As a man of learning and an educational officer, he should remember that the public may judge his profession and his institution by his utterances. Hence he should at all times be accurate, should exercise appropriate restraint, should show respect for the opinions of others, and should make every effort to indicate that he is not an institutional spokesman.

ACADEMIC TENURE   (*)/   Tenure is a means to certain ends; specifically: (1) Freedom of teaching and research and of extramural activities and (2) a sufficient degree of economic security to make the profession attractive to men and women of ability. Freedom and economic security, hence, tenure, are indispensible to the success of an institution in fulfilling its obligations to its students and to society./ (a)   After the expiration of a probationary period, FULL-TIME teachers or investigators should have permanent or continuous tenure, and their service should be terminated only for adequate cause, except in the case of retirement for age, or under extraordinary circumstances because of financial exigencies.

(*)   Title inserted. Originally Item (c) under Academic Freedom section.
(*)   This paragraph (within the slant lines) was originally paragraph 3 of the introductory section of the 1940 statement.

EXHIBIT 22—continued

In the interpretation of this principle it is understood that the following represents acceptable academic practice:

(1)   The precise terms and conditions of every appointment should be stated in writing and be in the possession of both institution and teacher before the appointment is consummated.

(2)   Beginning with appointment to the rank of full-time instructor or a higher rank, the probationary period should not exceed seven years, including within this period full-time service in all institutions of higher education; but subject to the proviso that when, after a term of probationary service of more than three years in one or more institutions, a teacher is called to another institution it may be agreed in writing that his new appointment is for a probationary period of not more than four years, even though thereby the person's total probationary period in the academic profession is extended beyond the normal maximum of seven years. Notice should be given at least one year prior to the expiration of the probationary period if the teacher is not to be continued in service after the expiration of that period.

(3)   During the probationary period a teacher should have the academic freedom that all other members of the faculty have.

(***) (4)   CONTINUATION OF ACADEMIC TENURE INVOLVES MAINTENANCE OF COMPETENCE AS A TEACHER AND SCHOLAR.

(⊬) (5)   Termination for cause of a continuous appointment, or the dismissal for cause of a teacher previous to the expiration of a term appointment, should, if possible, be considered by both a faculty committee and the governing board of the institution, WHEN REQUESTED BY THE PERSON AFFECTED. In all cases where the facts are in dispute, the accused teacher should be informed before the hearing in writing of the charges against him and should have the opportunity to be heard in his own defense by all bodies that pass judgment upon his case. He should be permitted to have with him an adviser of his own choosing who may act as counsel. There should be a full stenographic record of the hearing available to the parties concerned. In the hearing of charges of incompetence the testimony should include that of teachers and other scholars, either from his own or from other institutions. Teachers on continuous appointment who are dismissed for reasons not involving moral turpitude should receive their salaries for a year from the date of notification of dismissal whether or not they are continued in their duties at the institution.

(†) (6)   Termination of a continuous appointment because of financial exigency should be demonstrably bona fide.

(***)   New Item.
(⊬)   Originally Item 4 under Academic Tenure in the 1940 statement.
(†)   Originally Item 5 under Academic Tenure in the 1940 statement.

University of California: Restrictions on the Use of University Resources and Facilities for Political Activities

The following basic guidelines, effective immediately, constitute Presidential policies governing the use of resources and facilities for political purposes or activities:

1. The name, insignia, seal, or address of the University or any of its offices or units shall not be used for or in connection with political purposes or activity except as consistent with University regulations.

2. In correspondence, statements, or other material relating to political activities or issues, the University title of a faculty or staff member shall be used only for identification; if such identification might reasonably be construed as implying the support, endorsement, advancement, or opposition of the University with regard to any political activity or issue, the identification shall be accompanied by an explicit statement that the individual is speaking for himself and not as a representative of the University or any of its offices or units.

3. University equipment, supplies, and services—duplicating machines, telephones, mail and messenger service, vehicles, computers, stationery, and other equipment, supplies, or services—shall not be used for or in connection with political purposes or activities. (This does not prohibit the incidental use of resources, e.g., sound equipment, in connection with permitted use of University facilities.)

4. No University facility shall be used for political activities other than those open discussion and meeting areas provided for in campus regulations.

5. No display or distribution of political materials, such as posters, notices, handbills, and banners, shall be permitted except as specifically authorized by campus regulations concerning the time, place, and manner of exercising rights of speech and advocacy.

6. Nonmembers of the University community shall not be permitted to engage in political activities on University grounds or in University buildings and other facilities except as specifically provided by campus regulations concerning the invitation of non–University speakers to address meetings on campus.

SOURCE: President's Office, University of California, 1970.

EXHIBIT 24

American Council on Education: Tax-exempt Status of Universities—
Impact of Political Activities by Students, 1970

Recent activities on college campuses have given rise to expressions of concern within colleges and universities and on the part of members of Congress and others that institutions of higher education may inadvertently or otherwise involve themselves in political campaigns in such a way as to raise questions as to their entitlement to exemption under Section 501 (c) (3) of the Internal Revenue Code and as to liability under other provisions of Federal law. Activities which would bring into serious question the entitlement of a college or university to tax exemption could undermine the private support of higher education as a whole, so essential to the very existence of many such institutions. For this reason, educational institutions benefiting from the tax exemption should be aware of the problem and exercise care to make certain that their activities remain within the limits permitted by the statute.

Exemption of colleges and universities from Federal income taxes is dependent upon their qualifying as institutions organized and operated *exclusively* for religious, charitable, or educational purposes described in Section 501 (c) (3) of the Internal Revenue Code. For some years that section has provided that "no substantial part of the activities of" an exempt institution may be "carrying on propaganda, or otherwise attempting, to influence legislation" and further, that an exempt institution may "not participate in, or intervene in (including the publishing or distributing of statements), any political campaign on behalf of any candidate for public office."

By the Tax Reform Act of 1969, the last-quoted prohibition was incorporated in companion provisions of the Internal Revenue Code dealing with the deduction of contributions for income, gift, and estate tax purposes. As interpreted, this provision would deny exempt status to institutions engaging in legislative activities which are *substantial* in the light of all facts and circumstances. Additionally, it *absolutely* proscribes participation in or intervention by an exempt institution in any "political campaign on behalf of any candidate for public office."

The mere rearrangement of an academic calendar for the purpose of permitting students, faculty and other members of the academic community to participate in the election process, without more, would not be deemed intervention or participation by the institution itself in a campaign on behalf of a candidate. Nor does it constitute proscribed legislative activity. This assumes that the recess period is in fact a substitute for another period which would have been free of curricular activity, and that the university itself does not otherwise intervene in a political campaign. During the period of the recess, members of the academic community should be entirely free to participate in the election process or not as they choose and should be so advised. The case may be different if the academic calendar, in fact, is shortened rather than rearranged for the purpose of permitting students, faculty and other members of the academic community to participate in the election process. In that case the question might be raised whether releasing faculty and staff members from normal duties, with pay, to participate in the process represents an indirect participation by the institution itself in a political campaign on behalf of a candidate for public office. Presumably those whose employment obligation is not limited to or governed by the academic year could be permitted to adjust their vacation period to permit time off during a political campaign in lieu of a vacation at another time. (Shortening of the calendar could also generate complaints that the institution is not providing a full term of instruction.)

Educational institutions traditionally have recognized and provided facilities on an impartial basis to various activities on the college campuses, even those activities which have a partisan political bent, such as for example, the Republican, Democratic and other political clubs. This presents no problem. However, to the extent that such organizations extend their activities beyond the campus, and intervene or participate in campaigns on behalf of candidates for public office, or permit nonmembers of the university community to avail themselves of university facilities or services, an institution should in good faith make certain that proper and appropriate charges are made and collected for all facilities and services provided. Extraordinary or prolonged use of facilities, particularly by nonmembers of the university community, even with reimbursement, might raise questions. Such organizations should be prohibited from soliciting in the name of the university funds to be used in such off-campus intervention or participation.

Every member of the academic community has a right to participate or not, as he sees fit, in the election process. On the other hand, no member of that community should speak or act in the name of the institution in a political campaign.

In order to assure compliance with the requirements of Section 501 (c) (3), universities in their corporate capacities should not intervene or participate in any campaign by endorsing or opposing a candidate or taking a position on an issue involved in the campaign for the purpose of assisting or opposing a candidate. Those who in their official capacity frequently speak for the university should undertake to make it clear when expressing individual views that they are not stating a university position. Whether or not a university has participated in or intervened in a campaign within the meaning of the Internal Revenue Code can be determined only by looking at

EXHIBIT 24—continued

all past and present facts and circumstances relevant to the question.

We would make three further observations:

1.   Colleges and universities may be subject to restraints of the Corrupt Practices Act which forbid corporations or labor unions from making direct or indirect contributions in connection with political campaigns (including primaries). Adherence to the Internal Revenue Code restrictions discussed above should eliminate any questions in connection with this Act.

2.   State law governing all of the above may be more stringent and should be examined.

3.   There may be special restrictions on the use of facilities provided in whole or in part with Federal funds.

EXHIBIT 25

University of Michigan: Faculty Pay Policy during Strike

The following policy has been agreed to by the faculty, the administration and the Regents.

The University cannot make payments of wages and salaries to individuals who choose to withhold the services for which they are employed. In the event of a strike, it is possible that some individuals will decide to withhold all or part of their services, in which case the following general rules will apply:

1.   Any faculty member who participates in such a strike by withholding his services has an affirmative obligation to communicate this to the supervisor of his administrative unit. The supervisor will then inform the faculty member that his salary will be discontinued until such time as the faculty member returns to work.

2.   Allegations that a faculty member has withheld his services during a strike will be referred to the unit supervisor for appropriate action. In the event that the supervisor of a given administrative unit finds that a faculty member has withheld his services because the faculty member is engaged in a strike, the supervisor shall promptly contact the faculty member and inform him that his salary is being discontinued until such time as the faculty member returns to work.

3.   A faculty member whose salary is discontinued under these rules

EXHIBIT 25—continued

may appeal the determination through the grievance procedures applicable to his school or college, and, subject to the rules governing appeals thereto, to the Senate Advisory Review Committee.

SOURCE: Office of the President, University of Michigan, 1970.

EXHIBIT 26

American Civil Liberties Union: Academic Due Process

1. Minor infractions of college regulations, penalized by small fines or reprimands which do not become part of a student's permanent record, may be handled summarily by the appropriate administrative, faculty, or student officer. However, the student should have the right to appeal.

2. In the case of infractions of college regulations which may lead to more serious penalties, such as suspension, expulsion, or notation on a student's permanent record, the student is entitled to formal procedures in order to prevent a miscarriage of justice.[1]

    These procedures should include a formal hearing by a student-faculty or a student judicial committee. No member of the hearing committee who is involved in the particular case should sit in judgment.

    Prior to the hearing the student should be:

    a. advised in writing of the charges against him, including a summary of the evidence upon which the charges are based.

    b. advised that he is entitled to be represented and advised at all times during the course of the proceedings by a person of his own choosing, including outside counsel.

    c. advised of the procedures to be followed at the hearing.

    At the hearing, the student (or his representative) and the member of the academic community bringing charges (or his representative) should each have the right to testify, although the student should not be compelled to do so, and each should have the right to examine and cross-examine witnesses and to present documentary and other evidence in support of respective contentions. The college administration should make available to the student such authority as it may possess to require the

EXHIBIT 26—continued

presence of witnesses and the production of documents at the hearing. A full record should be taken at the hearing and it should be made available in identical form to the hearing panel, the administration and the student. After the hearing is closed, the panel should adjudicate the matter before it with reasonable promptness and submit its finding and conclusions in writing. Copies thereof should be made available in identical form, and at the same time, to the administration and the student. The cost should be met by the institution.

3. After completion of summary or formal proceedings, the right of appeal should be permitted only to the student. On appeal, the decision of the hearing Board should be affirmed, modified or reversed but the penalty, if any, not increased.

DOUBLE PENALTIES Respect for the presumption of innocence requires that a college not impose academic sanctions for the sole reasons that a student is or has been involved in criminal proceedings.

A student charged with or convicted of a crime should not be subject to academic sanctions by the college for the same conduct unless the offense is of such a nature that the institution needs to impose its own sanction upon the student for the protection of other students or to safeguard the academic process. Where there is a possibility that testimony and other evidence at a college hearing would be subject to disclosure by way of subpoena in a subsequent court proceeding, college disciplinary hearings should be postponed to safeguard the student's right to a fair determination in the criminal proceeding.

[1] A student may be suspended only in exceptional circumstances involving danger to health, safety or disruption of the educational process. Within twenty-four hours of suspension, or whenever possible prior to such action, the student should be given a written statement explaining why the suspension could not await a hearing.

SOURCE: American Civil Liberties Union: *Academic Freedom and Civil Liberties of Students in Colleges and Universities,* New York, 1970.

**American Bar Association Commission on Campus Government and
Student Dissent: University Disciplinary Procedures**

The Commission is concerned exclusively with appropriate procedures in cases where a substantial sanction, such as suspension or expulsion, may be imposed for alleged misconduct by a student. The recommendations of the Commission are not intended to apply to purely academic decisions by a university, nor do they apply to cases in which the penalties involved are not serious. Furthermore, the Commission recognizes that a student, with knowledge of his rights, may prefer and may choose to accept informal procedures for the determination of guilt or the imposition of a sanction.

For reasons stated previously, no attempt shall be made to suggest a model of universal utility. Instead the Commission recommends that institutions of higher learning structure their disciplinary proceedings in a manner reasonably calculated to accomplish several goals. The procedures established should facilitate a reliable determination of the truth or falsity of the charges. They should provide fundamental fairness to the parties, and they should be an effective instrument for the maintenance of order. The Commission rejects the proposition that one of the purposes of university disciplinary proceedings is to provide a forum to politicize a campus.

1.   Principles for Achieving Reliability and Fundamental Fairness

   a.   The Need for Rules

   A number of colleges and universities have instituted disciplinary proceedings against students on the basis of their "inherent authority" to maintain order on campus, in spite of the absence of any rule forbidding the particular conduct which formed the basis of the charge. Where the particular conduct involved substantial disruption and was otherwise of such a nature that the students could not reasonably have supposed that it would be condoned by the institution, the university's authority to proceed simply on the basis of its inherent authority has generally been upheld by the courts. On the other hand, one federal court of appeals has recently rejected the view that inherent authority alone is a sufficient basis for serious disciplinary action, further observing that the doctrines of vagueness and overbreadth that other courts have applied to invalidate certain university rules applicable to political activity "presuppose the existence of rules whose coherence and boundaries may be questioned."

   Given the unsettled state of the law and the reasonableness of competing points of view on this subject, the Commission is not

EXHIBIT *27—continued*

inclined to recommend either that a university may never act against a student other than pursuant to a published rule clearly furnishing the basis for a specific charge or that it may freely act against the student even in the absence of any clearly applicable and previously published rule. Rather, the Commission believes it more useful to state the various considerations according to which an institution may better determine what fundamental fairness may require in the circumstances of a given case:

(1) A college or university ought not be expected to formulate elaborately detailed codes of conduct comparable to the consolidated criminal statutes of a state. An attempt to differentiate among all possible offenses in comparable refinement is not within the resources of many colleges, it may detract from the educational character of an academic institution, and it may inadvertently encourage an adversary relationship in which professional quibbling is substituted for fundamental fairness.

(2) For most purposes, however, it is feasible for a college or university to describe its standards with sufficient clarity and to publish those standards in a form readily available to its students in a manner which, while not exaggerated in length, detail, or complexity, will provide fair notice of what is expected and what is forbidden.

(3) While it might be helpful to designate a responsible person or group of persons to furnish an authoritative advisory opinion upon inquiry by those wishing to know whether a proposed course of conduct would be deemed to violate a rule that is somewhat vague, or would be deemed to be inconsistent with the institution's inherent power to maintain order on campus, the value of such a procedure should be seen as complementary to published rules and not as a general substitute for rules.

(4) Where a rule has been adopted which is applicable to behavior involving some aspect of freedom of speech, association, or assembly, there is a special obligation that the rule be stated with clarity and precision.

b. The Scope of Rules

The Commission elsewhere in this Report records its view that university rules may appropriately overlap certain state and federal statutes, and that the concept of double jeopardy does not limit the scope of a university's rules. Thus, a student who disrupts a classroom in a manner that subjects him to a general statute applicable to assault and battery may also appropriately be subject to university disciplinary processes as well. Conversely, the fact that certain student conduct is not necessarily subject to any state or federal statute does not make it inappropriate for a college to forbid such conduct, as may ordinarily be true of cases of cheating on examinations or plagiarism. The relation of college rules to general laws is therefore largely coincidental, and the scope of university rules is appropriately determined by the announced objectives of the university and the extent to which it has reasonably determined that certain rules are fairly related to the accomplishment and protection of those objectives. Given the diversity of our institutions of higher learning and the fact that they are not all established for identical purposes, it is consequently not possible to describe uniform outside limits on the nature and scope of the rules that each may choose to maintain.

At the same time, the Commission recommends that a college or university ought not proliferate its rules beyond the point of safeguarding its own stated objectives. In this respect, a college rule that does no more than to duplicate the function of a general statute and to multiply the individual's punishment under general law without vindicating any distinct and separate concern of the academic community may be seen by many as a form of double punishment and lead to bitterness and recrimination. The Commission emphasizes, therefore, that the scope of university rules ought to be determined by each institution with reference to its own needs and objectives, and not with reference to the scope of state or federal jurisdiction.

c. Equality of Enforcement

The university has an obligation to apply its rules equally to all students who are similarly situated. This does not mean, however, that a university is required to refrain from prosecuting some offenders because there are other offenders who cannot be identified or who are not presently being tried for some other valid reason. In the absence of evidence of discriminatory enforcement, the university may properly try those offenders against whom charges have been brought although it is clear that there are other offenders who are not before the tribunal.

d. Impartiality of the Trier of Fact

The truth or falsity of charges of specific acts of misconduct should be determined by an impartial person or group. Fundamental fairness does not require any particular kind of tribunal or hearing committee, nor does it necessarily require that the finder of fact comes from or (in the case of a group) be composed of any particular segments of the university community.

EXHIBIT 27—continued

e. Notice of the Charge

A student accused of specific acts of misconduct should receive timely notice of the specific charge against him. The charge should be sufficiently precise to enable the student to understand the grounds upon which the university seeks to justify the imposition of a sanction and to enable him adequately to prepare any defense which may be available to him.

f. Information Concerning the Nature of the Evidence in Support of the Charge

If a student denies the facts alleged in the charges, he should be informed of the nature of the evidence on which the disciplinary proceeding is based. He should either be given the right to confront the witnesses against him or be provided with the names and statements of the witnesses who have given evidence against him. In cases where credibility is involved, fundamental fairness may require that a student be provided the opportunity to question his accusers.

g. Opportunity to be Heard

The student should be given an opportunity to respond to the evidence against him. He should be able to present his position, make such denial or explanation as he thinks appropriate, and testify or present such other evidence as is available to him. The technical rules of evidence applicable to civil and criminal trials are not applicable. A student may waive his right to a hearing either expressly or by his failure to appear without justification at the time set. Failure to appear without justification may itself be made punishable.

h. Basis of Decision

The trier of fact before whom the hearing is conducted should base its decision on the evidence presented at the hearing. A finding of guilt and the imposition of a sanction should be based on substantial evidence.

i. Representation of Accused

A student should have the right to be represented at the hearing by any person selected by him, such as a fellow student, a faculty member, a lawyer, or a friend from outside the university community.

The Commission understands the doubts of those who are concerned that the participation by a lawyer may make some disciplinary procedures unworkable, especially where the trier of fact is not a lawyer and legal counsel for him is unavailable.

The Commission agrees that it would be most unfortunate if university disciplinary proceedings were to be conducted in the atmosphere sometimes characteristic of criminal trials. It also recognizes, however, that a hearing on charges of misconduct is an adversary proceeding in the sense that the university is seeking to impose a sanction of substantial severity upon the student, and the student is seeking to avoid the imposition of the sanction. Frequently, there will be sharp controversy over questions of fact, under circumstances in which a young student may lack the expertise to investigate effectively or be too inarticulate to present his case adequately without professional assistance. In many cases there will be a need for counsel for the same reasons that counsel is needed in civil and criminal cases, juvenile proceedings, administrative hearings, or negotiations between private persons.

In complex cases where a student is represented by counsel, it may be essential to have a law trained hearing officer, and on occasion it may also be desirable for the university to present its case through counsel. It may be necessary for the university to utilize the services of members of a law school faculty, local attorneys in private practice, its general counsel, or lawyer alumni to meet such needs.

j. Interim Suspension

As a general rule the status of a student should not be altered until the charges brought against him have been adjudicated. Experience has shown, however, that prompt and decisive disciplinary action may be required in extreme cases before there is an opportunity to conduct a hearing, as in cases in which a student's continued presence on campus constitutes an immediate threat or injury to the well-being or property of members of the university community, or to the property or the orderly functioning of the university. The imposition of interim suspension should entitle the suspended student to a prompt hearing on the charges against him. Fundamental fairness may require an informal review of the decision to impose interim suspension in the absence of a prompt hearing on the charges.

SOURCE: *Report of the American Bar Association Commission on Campus Government and Student Dissent,* Chicago, 1970.

5. Consultation and Contingency Planning

Campus governance has been devised historically for gradual change based upon protracted consultation and full faculty consensus. The problems of today often call for more immediate action. A campus must, consequently, prepare in advance to seek to prevent and to deal with emergency situations. Its aims should be to respond to legitimate grievances insofar as these are directed toward the campus itself; to maintain itself as an ongoing center of learning; to protect dissent; to prevent coercive interference; to prevent coercive interference from becoming violent; and to prevent violence from escalating to greater violence. To accomplish these ends requires care, openness, effective leadership, contingency planning, and machinery to deal promptly with different types of situations.

In general, we see the following as difficulties in handling emergency situations by many campuses:

- Grievance procedures are often too slow or even nonexistent. The process needs to be improved and speeded up.

- Rules governing protest activities have often been unwise or imprecise or both.

- Too many members of the campus have been reluctant to give up the myth of uninterrupted serenity, and thus too few campuses have adequately thought through the handling of emergencies. No adequate machinery for quick consultation has existed.

- Alternative procedures have been too little considered in advance.

- The view that a campus is some kind of sanctuary from the law has been held for too long by too many.

- Police relations have been treated on an arm's-length basis that encourages improvisation, rather than accepted as an essential part of campus life, as they are elsewhere in society.

· Campuses have often failed to consider temporary closure in emergency situations.

Too many campuses have faced the inevitable as though it were the impossible; have acted impetuously where the most careful advance thought is essential; and have stayed with traditional approaches despite quite new conditions.

No one set of new policies or procedures is appropriate for all institutions or even for a single institution. The particular context of each event may suggest a somewhat different response. But the range of alternatives available and the actions necessary to implement them need to be examined ahead of time.

GRIEVANCES   To handle grievances which are directed at the campus itself, every institution should have a well-publicized procedure. In large institutions, it may be helpful to have an individual or agency to inform members of the campus of the appropriate agency to hear their individual complaints and suggestions, and to assist them in being heard; ombudsmen or hearing committees composed of faculty, students, and administrators can serve this function. When the complaints are responded to, both the response and the rationale behind it should be made widely known. Wherever possible, wide consultation with the relevant segments of a campus should be undertaken before decisions are made. Such actions may encourage the greater use of regular channels and thus help to prevent disruption.

We recommend that regular procedures and channels for hearing grievances and suggestions directed to a campus be established and be well publicized; that decisions be based on wide consultation with those segments of the campus affected by them; and that decisions and the rationale behind them be made widely known.

RULES   Organized protest activity has become a frequent form of dissent on many campuses. In order to help assure that protest actions will be peaceful and to discourage disruptive interference with the educational process, campuses should formulate rules regulating the time, place, and manner of such activities. These rules should give wide latitude for assembly and dissent. Their purposes should be the observance of law, the protection of the rights of others, and the orderly continuation of the educational process.

In institutions where such protest actions are common, a group of faculty and student marshals might be formed to monitor them. This group could observe the actions, advise participants of their rights and responsibilities, and report both on violations of campus rules and on excessive actions by law enforcement officers; it should not have law enforcement responsibilities. The impartiality of such marshals is essential. They should organize themselves to perform their duties on a regular basis.

The Commission recommends that campus rules be formulated which regulate the time, place, and manner of peaceful assemblies.

On campuses where organized protest does occur, faculty and student marshals might be available to monitor these events and to report on violations of campus rules and excessive actions by law enforcement officers. The marshals should be organized so that they are available on a regular, ongoing basis.

AUTHORITY
AND CON-
SULTATION
The president of the campus must have the full power to deal with crisis situations. The trustees should clearly delegate this authority to him. They should not interfere during the crisis itself. They have full right, however, to review his conduct subsequently. To assist the president in the conduct of his authority, there should be consultative machinery readily available—an executive committee representing the faculty and an executive committee representing the students, or an executive committee representing a joint council of faculty and students. *(Exhibit 28: Edward Shils: The Hole in the Centre and University of Chicago—Consultation)*

During any situation of disruption, the administration should keep the campus and its trustees informed of its actions and the rationale behind them. This communication function is essential if members of the campus are to base their evaluations and subsequent behavior on full knowledge of the situation; in the past this function has frequently been inadequately fulfilled. Daily newsletters or other publications issued by the administration may help to prevent escalation of the crisis. Use of a campus radio

EXHIBIT 28

**Edward Shils: The Hole in the Centre and University of
Chicago—Consultation**

The American universities were not prepared for the disorders which
have occurred in so many of them over the past five years. I do not
refer here to any deficiencies of sympathy with the student body
or with the demands put forward by it or to any failure to appreciate
the alleged idealism of the new generation of students. Nor do I refer
to the incapacity of their senior members to foresee the outburst
before it occurred. It is probably true that many or most university
teachers are not sympathetic to the exorbitant demands of most of
the student agitators—although enough of them are to shatter the
ranks of the teaching staff—and it is certainly true that the disorders
were not foreseen. They are not to be criticised on these accounts.
Much more serious has been the unpreparedness of the machinery of
university government to deal with the university-wide problems
created by the promulgation of demands and the taking of radical
action to enforce them. Had the machinery of university decision-
making been in better order, the students' demands and actions could
have been dealt with without convulsions. And as long as the machinery for decisions on university-wide issues remains as it is in
most American universities, such issues will arise. If the rate of increase in financial support declines, these issues will precipitate
rancour within the teaching and research staffs of the universities. . . .

Between the greatly strengthened independence of departments
and of individuals within departments, and the weakened authority of
president and trustees, there came into existence within the university a no-man's land, where the writ of "legitimate" authority did
not run. It was an area once dominated by presidents and deans and
now dominated by no one. It was the area of decisions affecting or
involving the entire university. No machinery of collective self-
government was developed there but since decisions still had to be
made—even if they were no more than formal ratifications of what
had been decided by departments—presidents, trustees and deans
still made the decisions. They did so however only on sufferance and
as long as they did not interfere with what was really important,
i.e., the research and teaching concerns of departments and individuals. Decisions as to the size of the entire university or the size
of constituent units and the existence of new units tended to be made
either by the market forces of effective external demand or by negotiation between department and individuals and the deans and president; intermediate deliberative and decision-making organs did not
develop in the area left by the gradual ebbing of autocratic presidential power and the gradual swelling of departmental and individual
power. University-wide matters such as disciplinary regulations,
admissions, rules which had to be applied uniformly over the whole

university and which were peripheral to the interests of departments and individuals, etc., were neglected in this process and they remained accordingly in the hands of the president's agents, the deans and other members of "the administration". The active sector of the university paid as little attention to this part of the university structure as they did to the maintenance and procurement sides. They were classed as "administration" and as of very marginal significance in what was important in the university. . . .

The no-man's land is a lacuna of thought and organisation which must be repaired. The crisis of the American universities, which has variously been said to consist of the attack by the students from within and by a disillusioned public and its political leaders from without, is to a much greater extent a crisis of the disaggregation of the university through departmental and individual centrifugality limited only by the limits of financial resources.

SOURCE: Edward Shils: "The Hole in the Centre: University Government in the United States," *Minerva*, January 1970.

[The 1944 Laird Bell proposals at the University of Chicago are] a model which American universities could do well to follow as a way out of the crisis which I have recently described as "The Hole in the Centre". The solution propounded is a simple one: through the system of a representative "committee of the council", consisting of seven elected council members, which meets weekly with the president of the university, and a council of the senate, consisting of 51 members, which meets with the president at least once a month, a pattern of consultation has been developed. The senate meets annually, but its main function is the election of 17 members of the teaching staff each year for a three-year term. The record of the deliberations and decisions are circulated to all members of the teaching staff. A combination of university self-government and presidential authority has in this manner become so firmly established that the cleavage between "administration" and "faculty", so common throughout the American university system, has been largely avoided.

SOURCE: Edward Shils: "Presidents and Professors in American University Government," *Minerva*, July 1970.

station can also be helpful. *(Exhibit 29: Eric Ashby and Mary Anderson: Aggressive Tolerance)*

We recommend that Presidents be given the authority to deal with emergency situations, and that they seek advice from pre-existing consultative groups drawn from the campus community.

We also recommend that the administration keep the campus and its trustees informed of the decisions it makes and the rationale behind them.

THE RANGE OF ALTERNA-TIVES If and when disruption does occur on a campus, the administration should consider the whole range of responses open to it. For nonviolent incidents, such as disruptive but nonviolent interference with classes or occupation of buildings, peaceful procedures internal to the campus should be used initially. These include seeking to persuade the participants to desist and then warning them of consequences if they do not. If the persuasion and warning do not suffice, then penalties — including injunctions and arrests — become necessary, but nonviolent actions should be met to the maximum extent possible by responses other than force.

The Commission recommends that in cases of nonviolent disruption, to the extent possible, procedures internal to a campus be used initially and nonviolent actions be met by responses which do not use force.

Violent actions, involving injury to persons or more than incidental damage to property, should be met immediately by enforcement of the law, using internal and external personnel to the full extent necessary.

The Scranton Commission has enumerated successive options which an administration should move through in preventing or ending disruptive interference. We endorse these suggestions:

1 Negotiation

2 Wait out a nonviolent incident to see if it dissipates on its own

3 The use of injunctions, particularly in static situations like building occupations

4 Disciplinary and judicial procedures

5 Closing the campus in the face of continued violence or unrelenting and potentially dangerous nonviolent disruption.

Whereas the First Amendment expressly protects the freedoms of speech, press, assembly and petition, no federal statute yet provides

EXHIBIT 29

Eric Ashby and Mary Anderson: Aggressive Tolerance

The cascade of propaganda which issues from duplicators during sit-ins may be—it usually is—composed of lies, innuendo, and the stale rhetoric of revolt. But it is a mistake to dismiss it as harmless trash. It puts the Establishment on the defensive and if the Establishment responds with nothing but silence or pompous resolutions, the thoughtful critical student may well begin to wonder whether the Establishment has a convincing defence to put up. The New Left declare that tolerance is repressive; their aim is to provoke an act of intolerance. Silence from the Establishment may create the impression that tolerance is weak. The proper response is not intolerance; it is (if we can give it a label) *aggressive* tolerance. Aggressive tolerance means that a university, threatened with some act of disruption, does not suppress it by force but by moral condemnation. This of course takes time. The prime tactic is to circulate continually, to staff and students, accurate and uncoloured facts, and also frank comment, preferably written by young members of staff known to have liberal views, about the relation between disruption and the articles of faith of a liberal university. The most notable example of this technique comes from the University of Chicago, which had a serious disruption in 1969. The university had not renewed the contract of one of its assistants (who was not on tenure) in sociology. It was alleged that this decision had been prejudiced by the assistant's political views. On 30 January students occupied the administration building and issued demands to the president, including one for the immediate re-hiring of the assistant, and one which read "Amnesty [for themselves] with the understanding that we consider our actions legitimate and not subject to discipline." The same day, and almost every day thereafter until the sit-in was over, the university issued an hour-by-hour "Chronology of developments", reporting, in flat black and white, what the sitters-in were doing, what various committees were doing, what disciplinary steps were being taken. Everyone on the campus was aware (for instance) that by 10 p.m. on 30 January 115 students had been summoned to attend the disciplinary committee; that at 6 p.m. on 2 February demonstrators in the administration building elected a new steering committee; that at 10 a.m. on 12 February a thirty-page report was issued on the case which had precipitated the sit-in; and that at 4:50 p.m. that day "four truck loads of garbage were removed from the administration building, on grounds that the garbage constituted a fire hazard". This bulletin neutralised much of the material being published from the demonstrators. But this was not all. Almost every day flysheets were issued, written by members of the staff or groups of students, commenting on the affair. Thus, as a riposte to the demand for amnesty,

EXHIBIT 29—continued

the chapel deans and the chaplains of the Episcopal, Roman Catholic and Methodist churches signed a flysheet with these words:

When Martin Luther King, Jr. supported civil disobedience, he did so by reminding us that ". . . an individual who breaks a law that conscience tells him is unjust . . . willingly accepts the penalty. . . ." We do not find this spirit prevailing in the present call for amnesty. On the contrary, the demand for amnesty indicates a lack of moral seriousness about the relation between acts and their consequences.

Other flysheets critical of amnesty were issued by members of the teaching staff. The demand for amnesty was (wrote O. J. Kleppa) "a confession of moral impotence, an unwillingness to accept one of the basic ingredients of adult life"; and H. S. Bennett, in another flysheet, wrote ". . . I have recollections of the loud and heroic sounding trumpetings from persons entering the administration building for the sit-in. . . . Now they whine for amnesty, implying that they want to do away with all risk." The cumulative effect of these flysheets and the daily chronology was to cut the demonstrators down to size, so that they appeared to be adolescents seeking a painless martyrdom; to reassure the public that the university had never lost the initiative, to minimise the risk of an emotional right-wing backlash (a danger in British universities too); and to build up a conviction in the minds of staff and students that tolerance, which allowed the students to occupy a building for over two weeks, without ejection by force and without calling in the police, was not a negative thing, an absence of convictions: it was a passionately held faith in human values. At the end of the affair the disciplinary committee announced its unanimous decisions over 126 students summoned to appear before it, and the *Chicago Tribune* ran a leading article headed "A great university is true to itself".

SOURCE: Eric Ashby and Mary Anderson: *The Rise of the Student Estate in Britain*, Macmillan & Co., Ltd., London, 1970.

effective remedies against private acts which violate these rights. We agree with the National Commission on the Causes and Prevention of Violence that:

Obstructions to peaceful speech and assembly—whether by public officials, policemen, or unruly mobs—abridge the fundamental right to free expression. On the other hand, speech, assembly, and other forms of conduct that become coercive or intimidating invade the fundamental First Amendment rights of other citizens. When a mob forces a university to suspend

EXHIBIT 30

American Bar Association Commission on Campus Government and Student Dissent: Injunctions

A number of institutions have sought injunctive relief for the purpose of quelling campus disturbances, with varying degrees of success. Some courts have granted injunctions upon the theory that the presence of an immediate threat to property or persons or a significant interference with the educational mission of the university constitutes a threat of irreparable harm justifying injunctive relief. In at least one state, it is no longer necessary to allege that irreparable injury is threatened if the court finds that "a state of emergency exists or is imminent within the institution." In most instances, universities have been able to obtain a temporary restraining order upon an *ex parte* application by counsel.

There are a number of advantages to the use of injunctions in cases of student disorders: An injunction can be narrowly drafted to deal with a specific disturbance with much more precision than a general statute, thus responding more effectively to the disruption while avoiding unduly broad limitations upon freedom of expression. The injunction constitutes a public declaration by the courts of the unlawful nature of the actions taken or threatened by the disrupting students. The issuance of an injunction may generate a favorable public reaction to the position of the university. It may persuade moderate students to refrain from participating in the disruption. It imposes restraint upon the disrupting students by a non-university governmental entity. Students may obey a court order when they would ignore the orders of a university official. The injunction may provide students with an opportunity to end a disruption without losing face. If contempt proceedings are instituted to enforce the injunction, the hearing of the contempt citation will generally be accelerated on the court's docket, thus resulting in a speedier determination than might have occurred if the criminal processes had been utilized.

There are also disadvantages. It is frequently necessary to utilize local law enforcement officers to serve process. In most states, the injunction is not self-enforcing, although at least one state statute makes a violation of an injunction a crime in itself. Enforcement of an injunction through court proceedings may involve some of the same problems as those presented when police are used to quell a disturbance. A university that is not prepared to enforce the injunction through contempt proceedings should not seek one. To obtain an injunction in such a situation might permit a court decree to be flouted by students with impunity.

There may be significant procedural problems involved in establishing proof of notice of the injunction when the defendant is brought before the court in contempt hearings. There may be sub-

EXHIBIT 30—continued

stantial problems of identification when large numbers of students are involved. Where the evidence is insufficient, there is a possibility that an acquittal may have the effect of re-enforcing the status of the offenders within the campus community. An improvidently secured injunction may have the effect of polarizing resistance to university discipline. Improper resort to the injunction for the purposes of restraining the exercise of First Amendment freedoms may result in lower court denials or appellate court reversals embarrassing to the university, and may contribute to the arguments of dissidents that the university does not respect basic constitutional rights.

In determining whether to seek injunctive relief, a university may wish to consider other factors as well. Violation of an injunction may be punishable even in circumstances where the injunction should not have been granted, but enforcement of the sanction of contempt in such a case may in practice contribute to a disrespect for the law. Indiscriminate use of injunctions may encourage disruptions if students conclude that they can engage in disruptive activity without fear of arrest or university disciplinary proceedings as long as they are prepared to yield to a court order when the university seeks injunctive relief. Certainly no institution should depend upon the injunctive relief as the sole remedy to assist it in dealing with disruptions or threats of disruptions.

It has been suggested that a statute conferring jurisdiction upon federal district courts to issue injunctions in cases of some campus disturbances would be desirable. A federal statute would provide a uniform procedure for the use of injunctions throughout the country. Necessarily, however, federal courts would be required to rely in the first instance upon the relatively small contingent of United States marshalls to enforce their orders.

The Commission has reached no conclusion on the desirability of such a statute. If such a statute is enacted, however, the Commission believes that it should not preempt state jurisdiction and should not be aimed at students exclusively. Such a statute should follow the model suggested by the National Commission on the Causes and Prevention of Violence, authorizing universities, along with other affected persons, to obtain federal court injunctions against willful private acts of physical obstruction that prevent other persons from exercising their First Amendment rights of speech, peaceable assembly, and petition for the redress of grievances.

SOURCE: *Report of the American Bar Association Commission on Campus Government and Student Dissent,* Chicago, 1970.

classes, the rights of teachers to teach and students to learn are abridged; when a speaker is shouted down or forced from a platform, he is deprived of freedom to speak, and the great majority of the audience is deprived of freedom to listen. . . .

. . . Although these rights are expressly safeguarded by the federal Constitution, the existing remedies available to aggrieved persons are not adequate. *(Exhibit 31: National Commission on the Causes and Prevention of Violence: Keeping Open the Channels of Peaceful Protest)*

EXHIBIT 31

National Commission on the Causes and Prevention of Violence: Keeping Open the Channels of Peaceful Protest

We have pointed out the fundamental distinction between protest and violence, the fact that there is no necessary connection between them, and the need to vindicate the former while opposing the latter. As we have noted, the First Amendment to the Constitution protects freedom of speech, freedom of the press, and the "right of the people peaceably to assemble and to petition the government for a redress of grievances." In the Supreme Court's words, the First Amendment entails a "profound national commitment to the principle that debate on public issues should be uninhibited, robust and wide open."*

Obstructions to peaceful speech and assembly—whether by public officials, policemen, or unruly mobs—abridge the fundamental right to free expression. On the other hand, speech, assembly and other forms of conduct that become coercive or intimidating invade the fundamental First Amendment rights of other citizens. When a mob forces a university to suspend classes, the rights of teachers to teach and students to learn are abridged; when a speaker is shouted down or forced from a platform, he is deprived of freedom to speak, and the great majority of the audience is deprived of freedom to listen.

Society's failure to afford full protection to the exercise of these rights is probably a major reason why protest sometimes results in violence. Although these rights are expressly safeguarded by the federal Constitution, the existing remedies available to aggrieved persons are not adequate. The only approximation to an effective remedy at the federal level is a court injunction authorized under 42 U.S.C. sec. 1983, a Reconstruction era civil rights statute that creates a private cause of action for the "deprivation of any rights, privileges, or immunities secured by the Constitution" by any person acting "under color of" state law. The relative ineffectiveness of this private remedy is indicated by the rarity with which injunctions have been sought in the thirty years since the statute was first interpreted to apply to interference with First Amendment rights. Moreover, state officials acting under color of state law are not alone in posing

EXHIBIT 31 — continued

threats to First Amendment rights; on college campuses, for example, the protesters themselves have obstructed free speech and peaceful assembly. No present federal law affords a remedy for private abridgement of First Amendment rights.**

Accordingly, we recommend that the President seek legislation that would confer jurisdiction upon the United States District Courts to grant injunctions, upon the request of the Attorney General or private persons, against the threatened or actual interference by any person, whether or not under color of state or federal law, with the rights of individuals or groups to freedom of speech, freedom of the press, peaceful assembly and petition for redress of grievances.

Under present law private citizens can seek federal injunctions in instances where the complainant alleges unreasonable denial of permits for parades or meetings by state or federal officials or their issuance only on excessively restrictive conditions. Private persons can also obtain federal injunctive relief on proof of suppression by government agencies or their employees of publications or communications (including the seizure or destruction of newsmen's cameras or film) or the use by law enforcement officials of excessive or unauthorized force to arrest or disperse individuals who seek to make lawful expressions of their views. Our proposal would authorize the Attorney General, as well as private persons, to initiate such proceedings in appropriate cases involving state or federal action. It would also authorize suits for injunctions, both by the Attorney General and by private persons, against private obstruction of the exercise of free expression by pushing speakers off platforms, by the making of deliberately excessive noise, or by seizure of or denial of access to buildings or other facilities, streets and public areas — a type of interference with First Amendment rights not now covered by any federal statute.

The statute should also authorize suits for either damages or an injunction by the persons aggrieved and allow the Attorney General to intervene in such suits on request of the parties or the court or on his own motion. State and federal courts should be given concurrent jurisdiction to enforce the statute.

Our proposal suggests a greater federal role in preserving freedom of expression. We do so because federal district courts, which often deal with somewhat comparable provisions in other areas of federal law, are experienced in handling requests for injunctions expeditiously and fashioning careful and effective decrees. The use of federal court injunctions would also provide for greater uniformity in the judicial treatment of those infringing the constitutional rights of others. It would increase the likelihood that the experience of one community or institution would be readily available and useful in handling subsequent problems elsewhere.

State remedies against private misconduct involving infringement of First Amendment rights are usually based not on the First Amendment but on trespass statutes or disorderly conduct ordinances. Such laws were not written to deal with acts of physical obstruction, particularly those committed for demonstrative purposes, and are not always effective in handling such conduct. Moreover, where acts of violence or obstruction are committed in the name of righting fundamental grievances, those engaging in such conduct may find it harder to justify disobedience of court orders issued to uphold the First Amendment than would be true of orders based upon the laws against trespass and disorderly conduct.

In recent legislation, Congress has given the Attorney General an increasingly active role in protecting certain vital individual rights. This approach seems particularly appropriate for the protection of First Amendment rights, since the mechanism of peaceful dispute, debate, compromise, and change is so essential to the preservation of a just and orderly society and since private persons are often unable to protect their First Amendment rights without some assistance.

* *New York Times v. Sullivan*, 376 U.S. 254.

** The Supreme Court has suggested that federal statutory remedies against such private acts of interference are constitutional but that no statute yet enacted provides them. *United States v. Guest*, 383 U.S. 745.

SOURCE: National Commission on the Causes and Prevention of Violence, *To Establish Justice, To Insure Domestic Tranquility*, 1969.ʳ

One approach to expanding the remedies available for violations of First Amendment rights is contained in the Hruska-Hart Bill (First Amendment Freedoms Act) that grew out of the deliberations of the National Commission on the Causes and Prevention of Violence. *(Exhibit 32: First Amendment Freedoms Act)*

We recommend that it should be unlawful to interfere in any way with any person's exercise of his constitutional rights. Aggrieved persons should be able to bring civil action for appropriate relief, and United State district courts should be given original jurisdiction to grant permanent or temporary injunctions, temporary restraining orders, or any other orders, and to award damages.[1]

[1] We recognize that there is a question of the constitutionality of the provision that private individuals or groups may bring civil action if they claim interference with their First Amendment rights.

First Amendment Freedoms Act

91st Congress
2d Session

S.3976

_____

IN THE SENATE OF THE UNITED STATES

June 16, 1970

Mr. Hruska (for himself and Mr. Hart) introduced the following bill; which was read twice and referred to the Committee on the Judiciary

_____

A BILL

To make it unlawful to interfere in any way with any person's exercise of his constitutional rights of religion, speech, press, assembly, or petition.

Be it enacted by the Senate and House of Representatives of the United States of America in Congress assembled,

SHORT TITLE

Section 1. This Act may be cited as the "First Amendment Freedoms Act."

CERTAIN CONDUCT UNLAWFUL

Sec. 2. It shall be unlawful for any person or group, except as authorized by law, to interfere, either willfully by the use of physical force, by the use of disruptive noise with specific intent to interfere, or by the unreasonable withholding or limitation under color of Federal or State law of any required permit, license, or other permission—

(1) with the orderly conduct of any meeting, address, discussion, worship, or other assembly, or with the free passage of persons or

the conduct of business or research in any street, building, or other place incidental to the exercise of the constitutional rights of religion, speech, press, assembly, or petition; or

(2) with the exercise by any person or group, by demonstration, picketing, publication, or other means, of the rights of free speech, free press, peaceable assembly, or petition to the Government for redress of grievances.

ENFORCEMENT BY PERSONS AGGRIEVED

Sec. 3. (a) Any individual, group, institution, or other public or private person who claims to have been injured, or who believes that he will be irreparably injured, by conduct in violation of section 2 of this Act, may bring a civil action for appropriate relief.

(b) The United States district courts shall have original jurisdiction of civil actions under this Act. A civil action under this Act may be brought without regard to the amount in controversy in the United States district court for the district in which the unlawful conduct is alleged to have occurred or to be about to occur.

(c) In any civil action under this Act, the district court may grant as relief, as it deems appropriate, any permanent or temporary injunction, temporary restraining order, or other order, and may award damages together with court costs.

(d) Upon timely application in any civil action under this Act brought in a United States district court, the court shall permit the Attorney General to intervene if he certifies that the case is of general public importance.

ENFORCEMENT BY THE ATTORNEY GENERAL

Sec. 4. Whenever the Attorney General has reasonable cause to believe that any person or group is engaged in a pattern or practice of resistance to the full enjoyment of any of the rights secured by this Act, or that any group has been or is about to be denied any of the rights secured by this Act and such denial raises an issue of general public importance, he may bring a civil action in any appropriate United States district court by filing a complaint setting forth the facts and requesting such preventive relief, including an application for a permanent or temporary injunction, restraining order, or other order against the person or persons responsible for such pattern or practice, or denial or threatened denial of rights, as he deems necessary to insure the full enjoyment of the rights secured by this Act.

EXHIBIT 32—continued

MEDIATION BY THE COMMUNITY RELATIONS SERVICE

Sec. 5. In addition to its other functions specified in title X of the Civil Rights Act of 1964 (42 U.S.C., ch. 21, subch. VIII), the Community Relations Service shall, in the manner provided by law, assist States, localities, public and private agencies or institutions, and persons or groups of persons in resolving disputes, disagreements, or difficulties relating to conduct prohibited by section 2 of this Act.

EFFECT OF STATE LAWS

Sec. 6. Nothing in this Act shall be construed to invalidate or limit any law of a State or political subdivision of a State, or of any other jurisdiction in which this title shall be effective, that grants, guarantees, or protects the same rights as are secured by this Act.

A CAMPUS IS
NOT A
SANCTUARY

A campus is not and should not be a sanctuary from the law, a place where the outside police may under no circumstances enter. The view that it should be a sanctuary began when the universities of the late middle ages were part of the church, and the church and state shared authority over society; thus the universities were partly immune from kingly and princely powers. The church had its own laws. Henry VIII ended this arrangement in England. Then the universities became part of the aristocratic enclave in society, standing substantially above the law which was meant for the lower and lesser classes. Concomitantly and subsequently, *in loco parentis* on campus meant, among other things,[2] that a campus disciplined its own students and dispensed with outside authority except over major crimes. Society tacitly recognized campuses as mini-sanctuaries where the outside police did not normally intervene so long as nothing important happened of an illegal nature. *(Exhibit 33: Margaret Chase Smith: Sanctuary)*

In the modern United States, a campus is not part of the church; nor does it carry the immunities of an aristocratic class; nor is it any longer so largely, if at all, engaged in personal control *in loco parentis*. Illegal acts by students and faculty members have occurred on many campuses. Increasingly, also, nonstudents, who

[2] Historically it has also meant that academic institutions had the responsibility to preserve the public and private morals of the students.

are not subject to campus discipline, have been deeply involved; the rise of contiguous youth communities of "nonstudents" or "street people" blurs the old and clear distinction between "town and gown"; a campus is no longer so much an "ivory tower" on the periphery of society. Thus the mini-sanctuary status of many campuses no longer has an adequate basis in student and faculty conduct, or in the confinement of actions on campus to members of the institution. Nor can the mini-sanctuary status of a campus be accepted as extending to the youth community that has come to surround many campuses. [*Exhibit 34: University of California, Berkeley: Arrest Statistics, 1970 (table)*]

While a campus does have authority over its academic processes, it is not a sanctuary standing beyond the laws of the democratic state. Nor should it ever be. The mistaken myth that it has historically been a total sanctuary in the United States and the view that it should be one now only cause misconceptions and disappointments. This myth and this view are too subject to exploitation to be allowed to stand as accepted academic doctrine. *(Exhibit 35: American Civil Liberties Union: Law Enforcement on the Campus)*

A campus cannot have it both ways. It cannot both give up *in*

EXHIBIT 33

Margaret Chase Smith: Sanctuary

For an overwhelming majority of Americans believe that:

Trespass is trespass—whether on the campus or off.

Violence is violence—whether on the campus or off.

Arson is arson—whether on the campus or. off.

Killing is killing—whether on the campus or off.

The campus cannot degenerate into a privileged sanctuary for obscenity, trespass, violence, arson and killing with special immunity for participants in such acts.

Criminal acts, active or by negligence, cannot be condoned or excused because of panic, whether the offender be a policeman, a National Guardsman, a student, or one of us in this legislative body.

Ironically, the excesses of dissent on the extreme left can result in repression of dissent. For repression is preferable to anarchy and nihilism to most Americans.

SOURCE: Speech to the United States Senate, June 1, 1970.

EXHIBIT 34

University of California, Berkeley: Arrest Statistics, 1970[1]

Total arrests on campus,[2] 1970

Students	138	Adults	687
Not students	799	Juveniles	250
TOTAL	937	TOTAL	937

Of the 937 arrests, the total number for disruptive kinds of activities on campus, 1970, was 240 (includes assault, trespassing, failure to disperse, malicious mischief, possessing and carrying weapons, disturbing the peace of the campus).

Students	60
Not students	180
TOTAL	240

[1] The total number of students enrolled at the University of California, Berkeley, is approximately 28,000.

[2] These data report number of arrests; the actual number of different *persons involved* would be lower because some people were arrested more than once.

SOURCE: Berkeley, University of California Police.

EXHIBIT 35

American Civil Liberties Union: Law Enforcement on the Campus

Police presence on the campus is detrimental to the educational mission of the university and should be avoided if at all possible. In those last-resort situations, where all efforts to resolve campus disorders internally have failed, the institution may have to invite police to the campus to maintain or restore public order.

Guidelines and procedures for summoning off-campus law enforcement authorities should be established by a committee representing the administration, faculty and students. This committee should also determine the duties and prerogatives of campus security officers.

The proper function of law officers in crime detection cannot be impeded. Members of the academic community, however, should not function surreptitiously on campus as agents for law enforcement authorities. Such action is harmful to the climate of free association essential to a college community.

SOURCE: American Civil Liberties Union, *Academic Freedom and Civil Liberties of Students in Colleges and Universities,* New York, 1970.

loco parentis and then insist on its status as a sanctuary from the general law. In modern times neither *in loco parentis* nor the sanctuary are viable. Students and staff, in escaping from *in loco parentis,* enter the larger society with different restraints but still with restraints. Nor can a campus, or members of it, undertake excursions of an illegal nature into the surrounding community and then retreat back into the campus free of pursuit. There are no one-way streets in a situation of this sort. Once the traffic begins, it, of necessity, flows both ways.

We recommend that the view that a campus is a sanctuary from the processes of the law and law enforcement be totally rejected.

POLICE
RELATIONS

A campus is, however, a special kind of institution where reason is enthroned and violence is abhorred by most of its members, and where some of its members are especially sensitive to involvement by the police and even enraged by their presence. Thus, it is wise for campuses to make a conscious effort to spell out in advance the situations in which they would want and need outside law enforcement assistance.

Traditionally, police have been little needed and little used on campus. There have been small campus police forces for patrolling the campuses against illegal acts, such as petty theft, for handling occasional pranks by students, marshalling crowds, and giving friendly advice to students and visitors. Occasional major crimes such as murder, rape, and bombings have been handled by outside police.

This approach still works well on some campuses. But on many others it has failed. Few campuses are equipped to deal with situations involving mass disruption and violence; thus, in such situations most campuses need help from outside law enforcement personnel. In some cases, no rational response by a campus may succeed in preventing escalation to disruption and violence because some individuals wish to escalate the situation and to polarize both the campus and the wider society. A particularly disturbing aspect of the new situation is how much violence, injury, and destruction can be perpetrated by so few people, often in a secret manner. Some illegal actions by students and nonstudents have gone quite beyond the powers of prevention and control by the campus police force. Outside police have come in, or have been called in, or have been sent in, on an emergency basis, often without prior understanding or any special training. The result has often been a revulsion by a campus community against this intrusion, particularly when the police have used undue force. Friendly rapport between many of the students and faculty members, on the one hand, and their own campus police force, on the other, has sometimes not been maintained. New approaches are necessary.

Given the broad diversity in institutions of higher education, no single arrangement is likely to be best for all institutions. What kind of arrangements a campus makes with police depends on:

- The size, location and composition of the institution

- The likelihood of serious crime and disorder

- The capabilities of an institution's own internal security force

- The nature of overlapping police jurisdiction

(Exhibit 36: University of Michigan: Campus-Police Relations; Exhibit 37: Wayne State University: Campus Police)

We generally endorse the recommendations of the Scranton Commission in their chapter on "The Law Enforcement Response," while noting the variety of situations on different campuses and on the same campus at different moments of time.[3] *(Exhibit 38: Scranton Commission: Dispersal of Crowds on Campus; Exhibit 39: Ending Sit-ins and Occupations of Buildings; Exhibit 40: The Control of Massive Disorders; Exhibit 41: Counteracting Violent Conduct and Gunfire; and Appendix A)*

The Carnegie Commission also recommends that whereas a campus should initially respond internally and peacefully to nonviolent coercive interference, as noted above, it should have immediate recourse to the assistance of outside law enforcement authorities

---

[3] The recommendations in the Scranton Commission chapter on "The Law Enforcement Response" address the following major concerns:

1. THE POLICE:
   Police on Campus. Improving Police Performance: The Need for Professionalism. The Quality of Police Manpower. Consultation and Planning. Police Tactics on the Campus. The State Police.

2. THE NATIONAL GUARD:
   Protective Equipment. Nonlethal Weapons. Lethal Weapons. The Decision to Call Up the Guard. Deployment of the Guard. State and Federal Responsibility.

in situations of potential violence, violence, and terrorism unless its own security force is fully competent to handle the situation.

Campus personnel chosen to communicate with law enforcement agencies should consist of persons who not only can achieve rapport, but also can effectively present the views of the campus community.

Representatives of the administration, the faculty, and the students should participate in establishing guidelines and procedures for relations between a campus and law enforcement authorities. These guidelines should be made public.

EXHIBIT 36

University of Michigan: Campus-Police Relations

Over 20 years ago the University of Michigan decided to have only a small security force serving only nightwatchman and fire protection functions, and to utilize the city of Ann Arbor for its law enforcement needs. The campus fire security force is not armed.

The University has an agreement with the city of Ann Arbor, by which it makes voluntary payments and has the protection of the city police and fire departments. As a consequence, the university has maintained close association with the local police, and the arrangement has been a successful one.

In a crisis there is normally continuous contact and constant assessment by police and the campus, eventuating in a joint decision. The decision of whether police should intervene rests with the president; once a decision is made the police decide how many law enforcement personnel are needed, where they come from, and how they are to be deployed.

Faculty and students, as well as administrators, are involved in assessing a crisis and in making suggestions for its resolution. The Governor is also kept informed throughout the crisis. Two aspects of the University of Michigan arrangements which have also contributed to its success in dealing with a crisis are the frequent contact between police and students in noncritical situations, and the emergency information system. Students and police have had frequent meetings to talk over problems of the campus and law enforcement, which have led to good rapport between them. During a crisis, the administration has been careful to print newsletters daily to supply the campus with information about the status of its response to demands, what behavior it would and would not tolerate, and the status of its discussions with students and police.

SOURCE: Prepared by Carnegie Commission staff.

EXHIBIT 37

Wayne State University: Campus Police

The campus police force at Wayne State University has peace officer status and is approaching the goal of being composed entirely of graduate students currently enrolled at the University. Several officers are instructors in the Academic Law Enforcement program. Until five years ago Wayne State relied upon the Detroit Police Department for its law enforcement needs. When the campus began to close off streets, a case could be made for a professional security force on campus.

All campus police officers are commissioned by the police commissioner of Detroit; to acquire this status they go to the police academy for 18 to 20 weeks, and participate in an eight-week departmental training program. They have the same responsibilities and authority as all police officers. To be on the Wayne force, a man must have a B.A. degree and be a candidate for an advanced degree at Wayne in Police Science or one of the social sciences. Their average age is 25 to 26. The campus police force has full responsibility for the area comprising the campus. Since there is very little housing at Wayne, the officers have almost no responsibility for living quarters. There are 40 student police officers in the campus force. They carry side arms but no long arms. When on patrol they wear regular uniforms, when monitoring at a dance they wear blazers, and when off duty and going to class they wear no uniform.

In addition to the 40 student peace officers there are 13 security guards who are not armed, a complement of technicians, and a parking control group. The cost for one year of operation is just under $500,000—comparable to what it would cost to use the regular Detroit police.

The Wayne force has a working arrangement with the Detroit police that they will come onto campus only when they are called. When students are arrested by the Wayne force, they are taken to a Detroit police station. Although the Detroit police have a technical right to come onto the campus, by arrangement they do not. Thus far the process has worked unusually well. The Detroit police have been called onto the campus only twice in five years.

SOURCE: Prepared by Carnegie Commission staff.

EXHIBIT 38

Scranton Commission: Dispersal of Crowds on Campus

The police cannot disperse or arrest a crowd simply because the university administration wants them to do so. The police enforce the criminal laws, not the university's internal rules. An assembly which violates campus rules may not be illegal. Where it is not, the police have no authority to intervene. Confusion over this point can result in an improper or ineffective law enforcement response on the campus. Such confusion can be avoided through a clear definition of the limits of the authority of the police and the situations in which the university administration may properly seek their assistance—spelled out in the contingency plan.

If it becomes necessary to restore order on the campus during a massive assembly, and the police have authority to act, they are more likely to achieve this objective by dispersing the crowd than by attempting mass arrests. As Thomas Reddin, the former police chief of Los Angeles, told the Commission:

The important thing is to restore order, secure the area . . . not to make arrests. If you dissipate too much of your strength in making arrests you are going to create further incidents and just make it explode even further.

We recommend the following steps in dispersing a crowd:

(a) Every effort should be made to induce the crowd to disperse on its own. If feasible, a university official rather than a police officer should first appeal to the crowd. The official should notify the crowd that they are participating in an unlawful assembly, order them to disperse, indicate the consequences if the request is not heeded, and indicate acceptable routes of dispersal.

(b) If the crowd refuses to disperse, a police officer should repeat this order and related instructions. The police should then respond in a measured fashion. If the crowd is non-violent, the use of well-organized police lines, moving slowly but resolutely, is the safest and most effective dispersal method. When it is necessary to arrest demonstrators who refuse to move, teams should be employed to effect methodical arrest and removal. If serious resistance or violence (short of armed resistance) is encountered, the police commander should discontinue the advance and order the use of nonlethal chemical agents, followed once again by the use of police lines. Under no circumstances should the police attempt to disperse a crowd by firing over it.

EXHIBIT 38— continued

(c)   Escape routes should be left open. Failure to provide avenues of escape increases the risk of injuries and induces members of the crowd to stand and fight. The crowd should always be directed toward areas that facilitate dispersal.

(d)   The leaders of unlawful conduct should be arrested at the first reasonable opportunity, but at a time and place selected to minimize adverse reaction from the crowd. Inasmuch as that may require arrests following the dispersal of the crowd, it is helpful for the police to have a photographic record of the disorder for purposes of identification and evidence. The police should employ the minimum force necessary to make arrests and should avoid hasty arrest procedures, unjustified arrests, and other such unprofessional and provocative conduct.

Commanders must recognize that their conduct and attitude can help minimize tensions and confusions. By maintaining a balanced perspective, they encourage their men, and even members of the crowd, to exercise restraint.

EXHIBIT 39

Scranton Commission: Ending Sit-Ins and Occupations of Buildings

When the police are asked to regain possession of an occupied building, their goal should be to do it with a minimum of injury to persons and property. These guidelines should increase the likelihood of success:

(a)   Before attempting to gain possession, the police should state the nature of their authority and request the occupiers to leave. If possible, this request should be conveyed personally to the leaders.

In rare situations a warning may increase the risk to property or to hostages in a building. In most situations, however, a public announcement provides the occupiers with a last opportunity to avoid arrest. Many may take advantage of the opportunity. But the very existence of this opportunity—even if no one uses it—fixes responsibility for the arrests upon those who persist in staying in the building. The announcement also minimizes the risk that surprise police action will cause a frightened or violent overreaction by the occupiers.

EXHIBIT 39—continued

(b)   After a brief but reasonable interval, persons remaining in the building should be arrested on a systematic and individual basis by specially detailed arrest teams. These arrest teams should use the minimum force necessary to make the arrests. They should be protected and supported by other officers in the unit. The rapid entry of a large number of officers into a building may lead to a chaotic situation, increasing the likelihood of personal injury.

(c)   Police should carefully choose the time when the occupiers are to be removed from the building to reduce the threat of crowd reaction from those outside the building. University officials should be consulted before making the decision.

(d)   The police should encourage a small number of students and faculty who are not involved in the occupation or sit-in to observe their action at as close a range as is practical. Observers can have a quieting influence on both the arrestees and the police; they can also refute false charges or confirm true ones against either the police or the protestors.

EXHIBIT 40

Scranton Commission: The Control of Massive Disorders

Certain procedures for the deployment of police are particularly applicable to campus disorders which have become so intensified and widespread as to require large numbers of officers.

(a)   Mobilized personnel should report directly to a staging or assembly area where they can be formed into squads or other tactical units before deployment to the scene of the disorder. This will enable commanders to establish early control over the operation, which usually cannot be done if officers report directly to the scene of the incident.

(b)   It may often be advisable to seal off all or part of the campus. Such perimeter control limits the numbers of individuals engaged in the disorder, prevents sightseers from exposing themselves to danger or interfering with police activities, and prevents expansion of the disorder from the campus to the neighboring community.

(c)   Police should leave the campus rapidly as soon as the need for their presence has ceased. Although too hasty a with-

EXHIBIT 40—*continued*

drawal of police can lead to a new outbreak of disorder, the continued appearance of a quasi-military occupation after peace has been restored can be equally inflammatory. When their presence is no longer required, officers should proceed to their off-campus command post, to be available for return to the campus if necessary.

EXHIBIT 41

Scranton Commission: Counteracting Violent Conduct and Gunfire

The prevention and control of violent conduct aimed at destroying property or inflicting serious personal injury require special tactics. Above all, police commanders should make sure that their officers respond to such actions in a coordinated manner. The loss of command and control may result in hasty and precipitous action by individual officers, in the use of excessive force, and in the isolation of officers from their units, all of which increase the risk of serious physical harm.

Participants in campus disorders have very rarely fired weapons. However, even the inaccurate report of sniper fire presents a difficult test for effective police command and control. Every police agency must develop guidelines and training procedures to insure a disciplined and orderly response whenever sniper fire is reported or observed.

Only specially trained and disciplined teams should be used in anti-sniper action. The general issuance of shoulder arms, such as shotguns or rifles, is normally not justified, and lethal shoulder weapons should not be carried onto the campus except by these teams. If at all possible, the teams should remain at a command post, out of sight, until ordered to a particular location to respond to reported or observed sniper fire. Only in the event of gunfire beyond the capabilities of these teams should more police be armed with such weapons. They must be subject to the same rigid controls imposed upon the anti-sniper teams.

The following general procedures should be followed when sniper fire is reported:

* The police should take cover and withhold their fire.

* The police should determine the validity of the report. If the report is valid, an anti-sniper team should be called.

EXHIBIT 41— continued

* Persons in the area should be ordered away, and the area or building isolated to prevent escape of the sniper and danger to bystanders.

* If, as the last resort, gunfire is needed to respond to sniper fire, it should be limited and controlled by a supervisor or senior officer. Police must never respond to sniper fire with a broad barrage of gunfire.

Some police forces, such as the Mississippi Highway Safety Patrol, have allowed their officers to use a variety of unofficial weapons and ammunition during disorders. This practice can result in undisciplined fire, and hinders accountability for deaths and injury. It should be ended immediately. Only through the use of specifically controlled weapons can police commanders ensure that officers are trained in their proper use.

CAMPUS CLOSURE Campus closures are repugnant to a campus community; they should be a last resort. But campuses have been closed in their entirety in the past, either by internal or external action, and some may be closed in the future. This may be the surest way under extreme circumstances to avoid continued disruption. Closures have served in a number of situations, both here and abroad, to reduce tensions. If they are to occur, however, understanding should be reached in advance regarding the following:

- Who has the authority? If done internally, we recommend that it be the president with the concurrence of the trustees. If done externally, we recommend that it be the governor of a state, but only after prior consultation with the president of the campus and with provision for immediate appeal to a specified court of law.

- Under what circumstances? We suggest that the circumstances be clear danger of violence to persons or property.

- What happens to faculty and administrative staff pay and student credit? We suggest that no action be taken for closures of short duration. However, if closures are of substantial duration, then pay and credit should be subject to adjustment.

- What activities shall continue? Care of hospital patients and of laboratory animals must, of course, continue. Some research and other activities may well be continued.

(Exhibit 42: Excerpts from the Japanese Law Regarding Student Unrest)

Excerpts from the Japanese Law Regarding Student Unrest

ARTICLE 3   The university president, faculty and other staff members shall desire the normal functioning and improvement of their university, and in case a dispute breaks out, all members of the university shall cooperate and make every effort towards quickly devising a settlement by compromise.

As the person chiefly responsible for his institution, the president of a university where a dispute has occurred shall exercise leadership and unite the staff of the whole institution in seeking to find a settlement for the dispute, determine the policies and measures relating to that settlement and shall work to promote it. At this time, he shall adopt appropriate measures to supervise and preserve the facilities, equipment and other property of the university in question in accordance with its essential purpose.

The president and other officials of a disrupted university shall endeavor to entertain in a reasonable manner the desires and opinions of students of the university in question which are presented at an appropriate place, and shall consider ways of expressing in the measures which are to be taken those hopes and opinions which would contribute to a settlement by compromise of the conflict in the university and to the improvement of its administration.

ARTICLE 7   The president of a disrupted university may, if he deems it necessary to reach a settlement of the dispute, suspend for up to six months all or part of the educational and research facilities of a faculty, an institute or other department or organization (referred to hereafter as "faculties and other departments") in which a dispute has arisen. If conditions warrant, the period may be extended for three months.

If more than nine months have elapsed since the disruption began in a university's faculties or other departments, or in case trouble breaks out again within a year after the dispute has been settled, and continues for more than six months, and when the settlement of the dispute is considered difficult, the Minister of Education may, after hearing the opinion of the university president and consulting the Special Council on University Problems, suspend education and research functions in the faculty or other departments of the university in question. He shall direct the president of the university to take all necessary measures in such cases.

When it is recognized that the dispute has been settled in the faculties and other parts of a disrupted university where the measure of suspension referred to in the previous paragraph has been taken, the Minister of Education must, after hearing the views of the university president, cancel the measures imposed on the faculty or other departments of the school in question.

ARTICLE 8   When a suspension referred to in the second paragraph of the previous article is imposed on a faculty or other part of a disrupted university, the following shall apply until the suspension is lifted:

(1) With respect to staff members of the faculty or other part of the university in question, with certain exceptions, the appointive authority shall suspend them from their duties, the provisions of articles 89 and 91 of the National Civil Servants Law (Law No. 120, 1947) notwithstanding. In this case, the provisions of the Public Education Officials Special Law, article 10, shall not apply. The exceptions referred to above are: (a) Those persons whose work is especially important in dealing with disruption of the university in question, or whose work involves daily supervision or whom it would, because of special conditions, be difficult to suspend immediately. Such persons shall observe the regulations established by directives from the Ministry of Education. (b) Emergency service personnel and (c) Persons who cease work or who are suspended by provisions of another law.

(2) Seventy percent of their salary, family allowance, adjustment allowance, temporary allowance, and bonus shall be paid to persons suspended by the previous provision.

SOURCE: Japanese Law No. 70 (1969), on Provisional Measures Concerning University Administration, promulgated in August 1969.

6. Procedures for Determining Violations of Campus Regulations and Assessing Penalties

Protection of the rights and enforcement of the obligations of members of a campus require a campus response to alleged violations, which is characterized by (1) an impartial hearing leading to (2) a fair decision and to (3) acceptance of the hearing and decision by the members of the campus.

Historically, even in the best circumstances, the following factors have made it difficult for a campus to provide such a response.

- On most campuses, mechanisms have not been provided for impartial hearings for student complaints against faculty members.

- Faculty members seldom, in fact, have rendered judicial judgments against fellow faculty members. This is characteristic of many professions, not just the academic one. Fellow faculty members are colleagues who must be lived with on the same campus for many years; often they are also close friends.

- The administration has often acted at one and the same time as policeman, prosecutor, and judge.

In recent years the process of providing an impartial hearing, leading to an equitable conclusion which is generally acceptable to the campus, has been subject to additional pressures:

- There is less informal consensus on campus about standards of conduct, and thus less agreement about what decisions would be equitable.

- More complaints or alleged violations are now suffused with political content, and thus may lead to repercussions far greater than the importance of the issue in any particular case.

- Political actions much more frequently involve both faculty members and students; and, if faculty members are given, as they often are, a collegial immunity from punishment, then punishment of simultaneously involved students also becomes more difficult.

- Attacks on academic freedom and the academic conduct of academic life now also come from the inside and from the left. Campuses, historically, have been prepared to resist such attacks from the outside and from the right.

- Violations of rules and laws more often involve group or mass behavior, and such cases are inherently harder to handle under any procedure than are cases involving individuals only.

- More outsiders are now involved in campus affairs—in political actions, in petty theft, in drug violations. Since outsiders are not subject to campus discipline, their involvement makes it more difficult to handle, on campus, actions taken by campus members in conjunction with outsiders.

- Challenges to authority, and especially challenges regarding the governance and structure of the university, often make it difficult for some members of the campus to feel that justice has been done, regardless of the nature of specific procedures.

- Faculty members on many campuses have become more reluctant to serve in a judicial capacity than they once were—because of interference with their many other duties, because of the breakdown in faculty consensus, and because of the loss of a sense of faculty authority over students.

- The public is watching on-campus judicial actions with greater intensity than in the past. A campus is no longer hidden behind the ivy-covered walls. It is much more central to the lives of many more citizens; and it is much more in the spotlight of public commentary. Justice on campus is no longer solely a campus affair.

It is largely because of these pressures that in recent years we have seen greater tendencies on campuses to adopt new and often complex judicial procedures. Yet, much of the earlier approach is worthy of preservation, to the extent it can be preserved, because it is consistent with those special characteristics of the academic community which have contributed greatly to the quality of learning and to creativity in the search for truth. Such special characteristics include wide latitude for personal choice, tolerance for the conduct of others, reliance on the power of example and persuasion, reluctance to engage in coercive actions, and a spirit of collegiality (faculty and students are viewed as "members," not "employees" or "customers"). We should be reluctant to move to a

highly legalistic system which would jeopardize these characteristics on those campuses and in those aspects of campus life in
which these characteristics still exist.

Because of the additional pressures referred to above, situations
on many campuses, however, now require more precise rules than
in the past, more formal procedures, and new mechanisms for
clearly impartial judgments. A reexamination of two broad questions now seems appropriate: Where should alleged violations be
handled? And what campus procedures will facilitate impartial
hearings leading to fair decisions which will be generally accepted
by the members of the campus? The suggestions below are offered
for consideration by those campuses whose judicial procedures
have been troublesome or ineffective.

WHERE SHOULD ALLEGED VIOLATIONS BE HANDLED? Serious, violent actions such as physical assault, rape, bombings,
and arson have always been handled by the outside courts. How-
ever, other actions which are in violation of campus rules and which
could also be construed as violations of general law have frequently
been handled only by the campus. The same situation occurs in
the general society. Many offenses are handled inside the family,
or the workplace or the club, without complaints to law enforcement personnel. The number of such cases in the academic community has grown in recent years, particularly in connection with
political protests. This includes cases of interference with the
constitutional rights of others, breaches of the peace, trespass,
and interference with obligations. There is no strong argument
for the campus to handle cases which involve the general law. It
is difficult for the campus to handle such cases effectively for
several reasons. The campus is often quite divided about the
application of rules and laws in situations of political protest;
full amnesty is often demanded and sometimes granted. Faculty
members, some with tenure, are occasionally involved, and faculty
committees have seldom been willing to penalize faculty members.
If participating faculty members are not penalized, then students
can hardly be penalized either. These cases often involve outsiders
as well as insiders. The campus is not generally in a position to
handle cases which turn primarily on legal questions. Consequently, it is generally better to let the law take its course.

If violations are found by the general courts to have taken place,
the campus still retains the right to assess its own penalties, in-

cluding suspension or expulsion, in order to provide for the safety of its members and property and to protect the educational process. Waiting for determination by general courts may, in serious cases, require suspension of students, faculty members, or staff employees, pending final court action.

We recommend that significant actions which could be construed as violations of the general law be handled by the outside courts. A corollary to this is that campus authorities have an obligation to report significant violations of the general law that come to their attention.

Regarding what alleged campus violations should be handled by the campus, we agree with the Scranton Commission that members of the campus ". . . should be held legally accountable only for conduct that they had reason to know was prohibited. The absence of clear, enforceable and enforced rules of conduct can produce confusion and turmoil."

We recommend that members of a campus should be tried or punished only for alleged violations of existing codes or regulations; therefore, these should be regularly reexamined. Such regulations should be consistent with the bill of rights and responsibilities adopted by a campus.

WHAT PROCEDURES SHOULD BE USED BY A CAMPUS? The campus does need its own procedures to handle violations of its codes and regulations. These procedures should be structured so as to facilitate a reliable determination of the truth or falsity of charges, to provide fundamental fairness to the parties, and to be an effective instrument for the maintenance of order. The nature and extent of these procedures must take into consideration the fact that the campus is primarily an educational institution; its members cannot afford to become bogged down in frequent, complicated, and time-consuming judicial machinery.

The procedures used for any particular charge should be related to the nature of the violation and the severity of the penalty that could be imposed.

The general strategy for the future should be to continue to rely on traditional approaches and mechanisms in those instances in which they work well. On most campuses these include:

- The informal handling of minor infringements of standards of personal conduct by advice and admonitions from students, faculty members, department chairmen, deans, and presidents.

- The handling of cases involving infringements of standard operating rules —on dormitory quiet, return of library books, misuse of campus automobiles, and so forth—in an expeditious manner by committees of students or faculty or both.

- The maintenance of traditional standards of academic conduct of students —against cheating and plagiarism, for example—by individual faculty members, or by committees composed of faculty members, or by committees composed of faculty members and students.

- The preservation of freedom of faculty members—to express their opinions in the face of attempted suppression by administrators or trustees or public officials—by faculty committees on privilege and tenure.

The following additional recommendations regarding campus judicial processes are proposed for consideration by campuses where cases arise beyond these four categories and beyond reliance on the general courts for violations of the law. Such cases include those involving:

- Additional penalties beyond those imposed by the courts for violations of the general law which also violate campus rules and regulations.

- Violations of the academic rights and responsibilities of members of the campus community as defined in the Bill of Rights and Responsibilities.

- Violations of the rights and responsibilities of the institution as set forth in the Bill of Rights and Responsibilities.

We suggest the use of both ombudsmen and hearing officers.

A campus ombudsman, or ombudsmen, could be appointed to handle informally complaints made by faculty, students, and administrators; the office would be supplemental to other procedures for resolving dissatisfaction and disagreements on the campus. The ombudsman would independently attempt to resolve both academic and nonacademic grievances, as well as help individulas to use existing avenues for redress of grievances. He could be chosen by a joint committee of faculty, students, and administrators.

A campus hearing officer could be appointed for formal investigation of facts and for provisional decisions in disciplinary cases.

The use of hearing officers may be particularly useful in instances of faculty violations of academic responsibilities, such as withholding grades to students or failing to meet regularly scheduled classes. Any member of a campus community could bring charges to the hearing officer, and the parties themselves, it is hoped, would accept the provisional decision of the hearing officer. Each party, however, would have the right of appeal to a higher tribunal on the merits of the case but would be restricted in the presentation of additional facts to those facts not previously available. The availability of determined facts and of a provisional decision by the hearing officers should greatly reduce the burden on any higher tribunal. The hearing officer could be chosen by the administration from individuals recommended by faculty, faculty-student, or student committees.

A further possibility worthy of serious consideration in hearing officer proceedings, as well as in other formal proceedings, is designation of a "campus attorney" to serve in a capacity similar to that of a district attorney. He would prosecute cases of alleged violations of campus rules so that administrative officers with other responsibilities would not interfere with or endanger the performance of their principal duties by acting as prosecutors as well. The accused would have the right to an attorney of his own, of course, as he would in serious cases if there were no campus attorney. *(Exhibit 43: Cornell University: Judicial Administrator)*

We recommend that careful consideration be given to use of (a) ombudsmen, (b) hearing officers, and (c) campus attorneys.

If the parties do not accept the solutions recommended by the hearing officer, then additional procedures become necessary. Whether faculty, students, and administrators are all to be included in one set of procedures or whether each group should have its own procedures will depend upon the campus and its traditions. In any event, we recommend that the hearing tribunal in cases which could result in suspension or dismissal be composed partially or totally of persons "external" to the case, that is to say, of persons who are not members of the same face-to-face community. Such tribunals might be composed of a mix of faculty and/or student members and outside individuals, preferably with an external person as chairman, or entirely of external persons. External persons might come from other schools within an institution with many schools, from another campus of a multicampus institution,

Cornell University: Judicial Administrator

To place the judicial system on an equitable, efficient and punctual basis, the University should create the position of judicial administrator. He would assume the responsibility of assuring order and freedom within the University community necessary to fulfill its aims and purposes. He would be responsible for the administration of a well-defined procedure for citation of code violations and for the judicial system to insure that all such code violations are processed equitably, efficiently and punctually. This official should report at a very high, if not the highest, administrative level. He should not be in the Dean of Students' office and would eliminate the need for the present position of code administrator. This official should also be responsible for the development of all necessary procedures to avoid campus disorder of any nature. He should be concerned with relations between the University and the town, county, and state officials responsible for the maintenance of order. In administering the code and adjudicatory system, this official must supervise the task of assuring the publication, understanding and support of the system by the University as a whole. It is obvious that this administrative official must be mature, able, and fully qualified to handle the increasingly sensitive responsibilities outlined above. Giving the position substance and dignity will increase support for the entire judicial system.

SOURCE: *The Report of the Special Trustee Committee on Campus Unrest at Cornell,* Ithaca, New York, 1969.

or from other nearby campuses. Lawyers or judges would also be useful external individuals. Such a selection process should add objectivity and fairness to the procedures and relieve fellow members of face-to-face groups from the personal difficulties of service in such cases.

It needs to be recognized quite frankly that no professional group, including professional faculty, penalizes its colleagues except with the greatest of reluctance. Also, face-to-face communities have difficulty living with the personal animosities that result from their own handling of difficult disciplinary cases. The external judicial authority is helpful in handling the most difficult cases within the family and the workplace, and this may also well prove to be true for the campus. Settlement of such cases is better removed from the ongoing relations of the school or the college or the campus. Part of the spirit of the law is that its enforcement be separated from personal considerations.

Selection of an external person or persons should reflect the choices of those against whom charges might be brought. If faculty and administrators use one procedure, for example, then the faculty senate might choose one outside person, the administration one, and then together they might choose one person from a list of possibilities suggested by each. As an alternative, we suggest choice of particular individuals by lot from previously established lists of eligible persons.

We recognize that some campuses, particularly those with long and accepted traditions, may both wish to handle disciplinary matters entirely internally and may be able to do so effectively; but for many campuses we believe that reliance on persons external to the campus can be helpful in cases of special difficulty.

To the extent that higher education moves toward unionization, outside arbitrators or panels are likely to be utilized more often, in any event, for alleged violations of academic rights and responsibilities; unionization makes it less likely that one party, for example, the administration, will agree to judicial procedures which rely wholly on the other, for example, the faculty. For alleged violations which can be construed as violations of external laws, and which may also involve internal penalties, we particularly suggest the use of outside arbitrators or mixed panels.

We agree, additionally, with the recent AAUP statement that in dealing with faculty members, "Systematic attention should be given to questions related to sanctions other than dismissal, such as warnings and reprimands, in order to provide a more versatile body of academic sanctions."

All parties, in the types of cases set forth above, should have appeal available to the board of trustees of the institution.[1] Whatever earlier procedures are used, all individuals who are subject to expulsion do, also, of course, have recourse to the general courts after institutional procedures have been exhausted.

We recommend that in serious cases involving "rights and responsibilities" of members of the campus community and possible campus penalties beyond those for violation of the external law, campus judicial tribunals be composed partially or wholly of external persons, defined as persons drawn from outside the particular school or college or campus whose members are involved in the dispute.

---

[1] Appeal may be made to the board of trustees, a committee of the trustees, or a tribunal designated by the trustees to act on their behalf.

The campus needs to provide evidence—to students, faculty members, administrators, and the general public—that justice will be done. This requires clear rules, expeditious and simple procedures that move quickly from informal to formal procedures, and the availability of independent and impartial tribunals.

7. Concluding Note

The United States, in the past decade, has been in greater internal turmoil than at any time since the period of the Civil War a century ago. The campuses have, in recent years, been in the greatest turmoil in all their history of over three centuries. New directions are required and are being chosen both by the nation and by the campus. It is of the greatest importance that these new directions be charted through democratic processes in an atmosphere of reason. The campus has an essential role to play in this period of historical transition. To be fully effective, for the sake of the nation and for its own welfare, it must protect the expression of dissent, however vigorous, while eliminating disruption, however insistently it may be pursued. This requires, in our judgment, new agreements over the norms governing academic life, new methods to handle emergency situations, and new judicial procedures to assure justice. Campuses across the nation are in the process of meeting these requirements in their highly varied situations. Our discussion in this report and the documents which accompany it are submitted with the hope that they may assist this sometimes tortured adjustment by the campuses to the new circumstances which now surround them externally and characterize them internally.

Appendix A: Summary of Recommendations in Other Commission Reports

The recommendations summarized here are on the following topics:

Relationship between Campus and Larger Society

Legislation in Response to Disruption

Civil Authorities and Campus Disruption

Youth's Role in Its Own Future and Future of Society

Drugs

The Military Draft

Rights and Responsibilities of Members of the Community

Campus Security

Campus Communications

Participation in Campus Decisions

The Commission reports included are:

Final Report of the National Commission on the Causes and Prevention of Violence, 1969.
(Hereafter referred to as Eisenhower Commission.)

Report of the Brock Campus Tour, Congressional Record, June 25, 1969.
(Hereafter referred to as Brock Report.)

First Report of the Temporary Commission to Study the Causes of Campus Unrest, Albany, New York, 1970.
(Hereafter referred to as New York Legislature.)

Report of the American Bar Association Commission on Campus Governance and Student Dissent, 1970.
(Hereafter referred to as American Bar Association.)

Report of the Task Force on Higher Education, 55th Legislative Assembly, Salem, Oregon, 1969.
(Hereafter referred to as Oregon Legislature.)

Final Staff Report: State of Michigan Senate Committee to Investigate Campus Disorders and Student Unrest, 1970.
(Hereafter referred to as Michigan Legislature.)

American Council on Education: Report of the Special Committee on Campus Tensions, 1970.
(Hereafter referred to as American Council on Education.)

The Report of the President's Commission on Campus Unrest, 1970.
(Hereafter referred to as Scranton Commission.)

Interim Report of the Select Committee to Investigate Campus Disturbances to the 108th Ohio General Assembly, 1970.
(Hereafter referred to as Ohio Legislature.)

1. Relationship between Campus and Larger Society

EISENHOWER COMMISSION

The public is urged to recognize that the campus reflects the desires and weaknesses of the larger society. All parties must learn to listen to each other on the problem of the generation gap. All must acknowledge the inevitability of change.

BROCK REPORT

"The crucial factor in the widening gap between students and others is the students' perception of reality. That must be understood by all who seek solutions. This requires of us comprehension, and of the student, understanding." It is unfair to single out the university as the weak link in the educational system. Twelve years precede this; there are imperfections in all phases of our educational system that deserve thorough attention. Open communication is needed between university and government officials, Congress and the public.

NEW YORK LEGISLATURE

The people of New York State should try to understand the problems of the campus. Communication channels between the people and the campus should be open.

The citizenry should use the campus as a local resource—its facilities, services, and cultural events. People should be cautious and use all available information before evaluating campus activities and problems. The public, and especially the parents of students, should sit down with students for candid exchanges of views. Be careful not to base opinions solely on dramatic media. Join with those in the academic community to achieve a better world.

AMERICAN BAR ASSOCIATION

"Responsible citizens should recognize the difficulty of the problem and give great weight to the judgment of the officials who are best able to make the difficult assessments required and who have the responsibility for the welfare of the institution and the maintenance of order."

SCRANTON COMMISSION

"We believe it urgent that Americans of all convictions draw back from the brink. We must recognize even our bitter opponents as fellow Americans with rights upon which we cannot morally or legally encroach and as fellow human beings whom we must not club, stone, shoot, or bomb."

"We urgently call for reconciliation. Tolerance and understanding on all sides must re-emerge from the fundamental decency of Americans, from our shared aspirations as Americans, from our traditional tolerance of diversity, and from our common humanity. We must regain our compassion for one another and our mutual respect."

"Violence must end."

"Understanding must be renewed."

"All Americans must come to see each other not as symbols or stereotypes but as human beings."

"Reconciliation must begin."

"The university is often held responsible for the actions of individuals or groups who are its members. Sometimes this happens even when these political actions are obviously unrepresentative and clearly do not have the support of the institutions involved. We urge everyone — alumni, legislators, and the public at large — to understand that such individual actions are just that, and to refrain from condemning a university or withholding support from it because it protects its members' rights as citizens."

"We urge that the President exercise his reconciling moral leadership as the first step to prevent violence and create understanding. It is imperative that the President bring us together before more lives are lost and more property destroyed and more universities disrupted.

"We recommend that the President seek to convince public officials and protestors alike that divisive and insulting rhetoric is dangerous. In the current political campaign and throughout the years ahead, the President should insist that no one play irresponsible politics with the issue of 'campus unrest.'

"We recommend that the President take the lead in explaining to the American people the underlying causes of campus unrest and the urgency of our present situation. We recommend that he articulate and emphasize those values all Americans hold in common. At the same time we urge him to point out the importance of diversity and coexistence to the nation's health."

"We call upon all members of the university to reaffirm that the proper functions of the university are teaching and learning, research and scholarship. An academic community best serves itself, the country, and every principle to which it is devoted by concentrating on these tasks."

"Students must accept the responsibility of presenting their ideas in a reasonable and persuasive manner. They must recognize that they are citizens of a nation which was founded on tolerance and diversity, and they must become more understanding of those with whom they differ."

"Students must face the fact that giving moral support to those who are planning violent action is morally despicable."

"The Commission has been impressed and moved by the idealism and commitment of American youth. But this extraordinary commitment brings with it extraordinary obligations: to learn from our nation's past experience, to recognize the humanity of those with whom they disagree, and to maintain their respect for the rule of law. The fight for change and justice is the good fight; to drop out or strike out at the first sign of failure is to insure that change will never come."

"The trustees—as well as the regents or governing boards of public universities—have a particular responsibility to mediate between their institutions and alumni, politicians, and the public. They have a continuing duty to explain the institution's values, goals, complexities, and changes. They should, for example, explain why the nature of a university requires it to condone seemingly untoward conduct, such as the espousal of unpopular views by students, teachers, or guest speakers."

"*Alumni* have their own distinctive responsibilities to the institutions at which they were educated:

- "Alumni should refrain from hasty judgments on complex university problems and should avoid stereotyping entire groups because of the actions of a few of their numbers.

- "Alumni should support improvements of American higher education. They should not insist that universities remain changeless, or be surprised if their institutions are not the same as they were when the alumni were students.

- "Constructive criticism and sustained financial support from alumni are essential to the vitality of American colleges and universities. Many of the nation's universities and colleges are in an unprecendented financial squeeze. Disagreement with specific university policies or actions should not lead alumni to withdraw their general support from higher education."

"American universities have special—and sometimes neglected— responsibilities to the communities in which they are located. Especially when they are in or near areas of major economic and social deprivation, universities should carefully examine their existing policies in the light of the following suggestions:

- "Universities should avoid actions that will aggravate existing local problems or create new problems.

- "Plans for university expansion should be implemented only after consultation with the community.

- "In light of existing teaching and research programs, colleges and universities should search for service projects that strengthen the university's basic purposes. Medical education is an example of the fruitful union of direct health services with medical education and research.

- "Universities should also consider providing fieldwork and other 'real world' experience in conjunction with regular academic work in the social sciences and the arts. A model for such a program has been proposed by the National Academy of Sciences and the Social Science Research Council which has suggested creation of multidisciplinary graduate schools of applied behavioral sciences.

- "Universities should make available to members of the local community as many educational and cultural programs as possible within the constraints of its other commitments and responsibilities.

- "Outside practitioners should be more frequently involved in regular academic courses, especially in the social sciences, in order to provide students with the opportunity to compare the practitioner's perspective on the world and on his experience of it with that of the academician.

- "In making decisions, universities should consider giving weight to broad social aims and to specific community needs. For example, some institutions are already acting—although not without considerable complications—as sponsors for federally subsidized housing, while others are developing practices to guarantee equal opportunity to minority group workers and businesses.

- "Universities should set an example of non-discriminatory practices in all areas."

2. Legislation in Response to Disruption

EISENHOWER COMMISSION   Legislation already exists to withdraw financial aid from students engaging in disruption. No useful purpose would be served by more such laws. If aid is withdrawn in a way seen as unjust, many more students may come to regard institutions as unjust.

BROCK REPORT   No repressive legislation. "Any action by the Congress or others which would, for example, penalize innocent and guilty alike by cutting off all aid to any institution which has experienced difficulty would only serve to confirm the cry of the revolutionaries and compound the problem for each university. This holds, also, for any action which would establish mediation or conciliation on the part of the federal government. In our opinion the fundamental responsibility for order and conduct on the campus lies with the university community."

NEW YORK LEGISLATURE   The complexities of the problem cannot be solved merely by legislation, especially some repressive legislation which would only intensify the problem. The Commission recommends no additional legislation by New York State at this time.

AMERICAN
BAR
ASSOCIATION

On proposed legislation to curtail financial assistance to students involved in disruptions of the universities at which they are enrolled: "The Commission views with deep concern these statutes and proposals for terminating financial aid to students who engage in disruptive activities and to the universities which they attend." Such legislation could operate in a discriminatory manner because it applies to those on financial aid—the needy. The American Bar Association Commission agrees with Eisenhower Commission that additional laws along these lines would not accomplish a useful purpose, and might increase the difficulty.

"Legislation has been introduced in the Congress to expand the federal criminal law to encompass specified acts of disruption in federally assisted institutions of higher learning. The Commission is unconvinced that there is need for federal criminal legislation. Internal disciplinary procedures and state and local laws appear to provide effective techniques for the resolution of controversy and the maintenance of order."

OREGON
LEGISLATURE

Legislative intervention in controlling campus disorder is not needed in Oregon at this time; crisis-oriented legislation on student discipline would serve no productive purpose. Statutes, codes, and guidelines already establish rights and responsibilities of students and the authority of institutions. They should be firmly and fairly applied. Enforcement of existing regulations is needed. The action of the administration should make legislative intervention unnecessary in the future.

The legislature should enact legislation relevant to interference of the educational process by nonstudents. A measure should empower the governor to declare a state of emergency on any campus in the state if campus disruption is incurred or threatened. Upon such a declaration the governor should be empowered to bar nonstudents or trouble-makers from the campus, making the violation of the order a misdemeanor.

MICHIGAN
LEGISLATURE

No new laws or modifications of existing laws are necessary either to enumerate new crimes or to make more serious offenses of existing crimes in order to deal with campus disorder.

Publicly endowed scholarship funds should be withdrawn, withheld, or denied only for reasons directly related to scholarly achievement. Political or social views, in thought, word, or deed, are not relevant.

It should be made clear by legislation, if necessary, that campus rules apply to all persons who enter the campus even as visitors.

Legislation about abortions and drugs should be deliberated on the assumption that they are societal issues rather than campus issues.

The legislature should consider a vote of confidence in institutions to manage their own affairs in a proper and desirable manner.

SCRANTON
COMMISSION

"(1) New laws requiring termination of federally funded financial aid to those involved in campus disruption should not be enacted; similar provisions in existing federal law should be repealed or allowed to expire.

"Few of the provisions already enacted clearly define the conditions and conduct that justify withdrawing an individual's financial aid. Each creates substantial administrative difficulties, and the interplay of inconsistent provisions, sometimes applicable to the same student, makes it almost impossible to establish workable guidelines. In many cases, it is unclear whether the termination of financial assistance is automatic (upon conviction of a crime, for example) or at the discretion of the institution. Due process requirements under these statutes, and the duration of the ineligibility they impose, are insufficiently defied. The statutes discriminate against students who receive financial aid because they have no effect on those, often from wealthy families, who do not. Finally, these laws have completely failed to deter campus disruptions. They have only complicated campus disciplinary procedures and, by providing another student grievance, sometimes helped to provoke further disruption.

"(2) Those federal laws which restrict political activities on the campus should not be interpreted or enforced in such a way that the university will not be able to remain a forum for the free expression of ideas.

"Universities as institutions should not take political positions. We support the continuation of a ban on direct institutional involvement in partisan politics. But we feel that provision of university facilities to members of the university on an impartial and reasonable basis should be permitted activity for the university. This is not 'politicizing the university'—it is merely recognizing that the university is a community in which the expression of political ideas should not be hampered.

"(3)   The federal government should not attempt to mediate campus disputes, or bring legal action to enjoin campus disruption.

"Campus officials are well advised to consider using the services of a mediator in resolving campus disputes. But federally sponsored mediation could easily be viewed as unwarranted and even 'repressive' government intervention in the university's affairs. Private mediation services now available to universities should be as useful, and they do not have the disadvantages of government mediation.

"We also oppose legislation that would terminate federal aid to institutions where disruption or violence occurs."

OHIO
LEGISLATURE

It is undesirable for legislatures to try to manage universities. The academic communities themselves should solve what problems they can.

"Financial assistance should not be given to any student guilty of serious misconduct, regardless of his academic standing. . . . further study is needed to determine precisely what legislation may be necessary to effect this policy."

A general statute should be enacted requiring that serious criminal conduct on campus be reported to law enforcement authorities.

Legislation should establish minimum training for campus security officers and provide that the chief of campus security be a professional law enforcement officer. The legislation should also provide that campus security personnel have the same obligation and authority to arrest as other law enforcement officers; and should encourage cooperation between local government and university authorities. ". . . but it should be clear that campus authorities have no authority to hinder or prevent local law enforcement officers from enforcing the law within their jurisdictions, including on campus."

Legislation is needed to clarify the jurisdiction on state university campuses of various law enforcement agencies; it should clarify duties and authority when more than one agency is involved and should require coordination by advance planning.

"The Committee recommends legislation to control trespass upon university property, for use as a law enforcement tool in denying access to campuses to persons having no legitimate business there."

3. Civil Authorities and Campus Disruption

EISENHOWER COMMISSION

"The Commission recommends that the President seek legislation that would confer jurisdiction upon the United States District Courts to grant injunctions, upon the request of the Attorney General or private persons, against the threatened or actual interference by any person, whether or not under color of state or federal law, with the rights of individuals or groups to freedom of speech, freedom of the press, peaceful assembly and petition for redress of grievances." (Introduced by Senators Hruska and Hart, June 1970, S.3976)

AMERICAN BAR ASSOCIATION

There is no Commission recommendation on Hruska-Hart type bill. If enacted, Commission recommends that it should not preempt state jurisdiction and should not be aimed at students exclusively.

Many problems about extent and form of civil intervention on campus are foreseeable. Plans can be developed to deal with contingencies. "The advice of university counsel, prior consultation with local police and public officials, informing members of the university community of what action will be taken in different situations, can go far towards minimizing the adverse effects that sometimes have accompanied recourse to civil authority in the past." Universities must establish contact with civil authorities and develop understandings about when to intervene and the manner in which they will act if intervention is necessary.

For training university security personnel, funds should be made available, and the programs should aim to make officers sensitive to the aspirations and tactics of student groups.

With an eye toward legislative action: A statewide definition of "peace officer" is needed by all law enforcement agencies and should be spelled out; campus security officers having essentially police functions should be given "peace officer" status (in this case, full authority to enforce state statutes); campus security officers should also be deputized under the state police so that they may function on all campuses of the state in time of emergency. It is urgently recommended that minimum hiring and training standards for all law enforcement agencies within the state be established and enforced; certainly, campus security officers should have training equivalent to that of the state police, and after such training they should receive compensation commensurate with that training. Legislation should be considered that would allow the state police to be the first outside force called to assist campus security officers when extra manpower is needed and to provide that any additional police agencies called to the campus would be under unified state police command or, alternatively, all forces would be under the unified command of the chief executive of the college or university.

"Maintaining a regular campus police force may be appropriate on a large campus which is in effect a community separate from that of any neighboring town. For most colleges and universities, however, the cost of such a force is prohibitive and can seldom be justified if local police are available and if good relations can be established between the locality and the university. The large majority of institutions will be adequately protected by security personnel not enjoying peace officer status, or by the services of regular county or municipal officers."

"We . . . urge that peace officers be trained and equipped to deal with campus disorders, firmly, justly and humanely. They must avoid both uncontrolled and excessive response."

"We recommend the development of joint contingency plans among law enforcement agencies. They should specify which law enforcement official is to be in command when several forces are operating together."

"Shoulder weapons (except for tear gas launchers) are very rarely needed on the college campus; they should not be used except as emergency equipment in the face of sniper fire or armed resistance justifying them."

"We recommend that National Guardsmen receive much more training in controlling civil disturbances. During the last three years, the Guard has played almost no role in Southeast Asia, but has been called to intervene in civil disorders at home more than 200 times."

"We urge that the National Guard be issued special protection equipment appropriate for use in controlling civil disorders. We urge that it have sufficient tactical capability and nonlethal weaponry so that it will use deadly force only as the absolute last resort."

"The police cannot prepare to deal with campus disorder without extensive consultation and joint planning with the university itself. In most cases, the relations between university officials and the police do not extend beyond what is needed to handle minor problems in normal times. This is not enough to meet the problems of a campus disruption. Developing a capacity to deal with disruption requires a continuing relationship between the university and the police. We recommend several measures to help achieve this."

"The university and police must consult with one another at the first hint of a threatening situation.

"But even early consultation is not enough. Public agencies and universities must develop relations of a far more regular kind. Long before the threat of a crisis, the highest officials of the university and the city or town in which it is located should arrive at some understanding about law enforcement and protest on the campus: specifically, they should agree upon the circumstances in which the police are to be called onto the campus."

"A joint contingency plan should identify a university official (and his deputy) responsible for maintaining liaison with the police. It should define the circumstances under which the university is likely to call in the police. It should describe the degree of force and types of weapons likely to be used under different contingencies. It should determine the circumstances in which university observers and student marshals will be used.

"The plan should address itself to the question of command among all possible participating law enforcement agencies and the National Guard."

"As part of a joint plan, a notebook should be prepared for each university. The notebook should include detailed maps of the campus and the immediate vicinity, designating the location of critical on-campus areas, sites for the location of a command post, staging areas for personnel and equipment, and power and communication sources."

"The joint contingency plan should include arrest policies and procedures, and it should provide for the presence of the District Attorney or his assistant to give legal guidance."

"In addition to the joint contingency plan, each law enforcement agency should have its own, more detailed, internal contingency plan."

"The internal plan should provide for the organizational structure and chain of command necessary to meet a situation of campus disorder."

"In advance of massive assemblies, or ones that appear to present some risk of violence, university officials should inform the police of the circumstances and seek their advice about how to prepare for them. A foolproof system of rapid communication between police, university officials, and leaders of the demonstration should be set up."

"We urge each governor to assess the capabilities of the police force of his state, and to prepare that force for a role in controlling campus disorders."

"We recommend that additional training in the control of civil disorders be given National Guardsmen during their six-month basic training program and their annual two-week summer training period, and that the federal government provide the states with funds to pay for additional disorder control training."

"We recommend that the Department of the Army ensure that all senior Guard officers attend the Civil Disturbance Orientation Course and that it encourage participation by junior officers in annual field training exercises with police agencies. We also recommend that university administrators be invited to attend the course and observe the exercises."

"We recommend that the Department of the Army assign a high

priority to the provision of protective equipment for guardsmen detailed to civil disturbance duty."

"Effective nonlethal weapons are urgently needed by the Guard, so that M-1 rifles or other lethal weapons will not be improperly used in campus disorders again.

"The need for something more effective than tear gas and less deadly than bullets is greater than ever before. We recommend that the federal government actively continue its research to develop nonlethal control devices for use in civil and campus disorders."

"We recommend that the states forbid guardsmen to carry rifles, shotguns and sidearms on the campus, except as follows:

"First, until nonlethal devices and protective gear are available to guardsmen, it may be necessary, as a last resort, to issue unloaded shoulder arms for defensive and crowd control purposes. But we reiterate that nonlethal devices and protective gear must be made available immediately.

"Second, squad or detail leaders trained in the use of sidearms should carry them holstered while on the campus. This creates little risk and affords a measure of protection to the squad or detail in the face of an emergency.

"Third, if the command officer is convinced there is a risk of sniper fire, he should deploy specially trained anti-sniper teams operating under guidelines similar to those set forth for the police earlier . . . .

"Only in the event of armed resistance for which anti-sniper teams are inadequate is it proper to deploy disciplined fire teams, armed with appropriate weapons. They must operate under controls similar to those imposed on anti-sniper squads. They should be available for immediate deployment but held until that time at nearby locations."

"We recommend that state National Guard organizations adopt and strictly adhere to standards of restraint for the use of deadly force in campus disorders which at a minimum conform to those promulgated by the Department of the Army."

"To facilitate the decision as to whether and when the Guard should be committed, every state should adopt a formal set of guidelines, preferably in the form of a statute or an executive order, setting forth the circumstances that justify the use of the Guard."

"In any event, the order activating the Guard should spell out clearly the command responsibility if it has not been previously established. Inappropriate or confused command can prolong or intensify a disorder."

"We recommend that each state review its laws concerning Guard call-up, and amend them to give the governor sole authority to activate the Guard. Of course, it is extremely important that the governor consult university, local government, and law enforcement officials before making that decision."

OHIO
LEGISLATURE

The strength of the Highway Patrol should be expanded. Legislation is needed to expand its jurisdiction to permit its effectiveness in campus disorders.

4. Youth's Role in Its Own Future and Future of Society

EISENHOWER
COMMISSION

Lower the voting age to 18. At least one person under 30 should be appointed to each local draft board.

BROCK
REPORT

Lower the voting age to 18. Encourage student participation in politics; most students currently have low regard for institutions, including the political parties.

NEW YORK
LEGISLATURE

Lower the voting age and make corresponding changes in the laws affecting legal maturity.

5. Drugs

EISENHOWER
COMMISSION

"The National Institutes of Health, working with selected universities, greatly expand research on the physical and psychological effects of marijuana use. Federal and state laws make use and incidental possession of marijuana no more than a misdemeanor until more definitive information about marijuana is at hand and the Congress and state legislatures have had the opportunity to revise the permanent laws in light of this information."

NEW YORK
LEGISLATURE
A crash research program should be instituted to see whether marijuana is harmful. Meanwhile penalties for possession and use should be changed.

OHIO
LEGISLATURE
An intensive program to eliminate drug abuse should be begun on all campuses, stressing instruction on signs of abuse, dangers, treatment facilities, and necessity for reporting use and traffic to authorities.

6. The Military Draft

EISENHOWER
COMMISSION
Reform the draft to a lottery system at age 19, taking the youngest first so that the years of prime vulnerability are reduced. Build a greater measure of due process into the exercise of draft board discretion. Give youth a role on local draft boards, by the President naming at least one person under 30 to each local draft board.

BROCK
REPORT
Reform along the lines of the Nixon lottery system.

SCRANTON
COMMISSION
"As long as there are undergraduate deferments, college serves as a haven for young men. As long as there is a draft at all, young men are obviously limited in the choice they can make. And it is also clear that none of the federal programs we have proposed to widen the range of choice for young people will work if our society continues to expect all young people to attend college and to penalize those who do not meet that expectation."

7. Rights and Responsibilities of Members of the Community

EISENHOWER
COMMISSION
A broad consensus should be achieved among faculty, students, and administrators about the permissible methods of presenting ideas, proposals, and grievances and about the consequences of going beyond them. Where agreed-upon and explicit codes of student conduct and procedures for student discipline are lacking, they should be adopted. Where they exist, they should be reviewed and, if necessary, improved.

Students have a right to due process and to participate in making decisions that directly affect them, but these cannot be so extensive that they paralyze the disciplinary process itself.

Disciplinary codes should stress the power of the institution to maintain order and should encourage punishment when it is deserved. The criminal laws of society should be recognized on campus.

NEW YORK LEGISLATURE The definition of community includes the dual concepts that all must be ensured the right to realize in a responsible manner their objectives without risk or fear of unwarranted interruption or reprisal; and all must be guaranteed full equality of access to due process. "Definitive procedures for uncovering and remedying conditions which violate these concepts must be clear and accessible."

AMERICAN BAR ASSOCIATION "Affiliation of a voluntary student organization with extramural organizations is not by itself a sufficient reason to deny that student association the use of campus facilities, although reasonable provisions may be made to safeguard the autonomy of a campus organization from domination by outside groups."

"Modes of speech or assembly that are manifestly unreasonable in terms of time, place, or manner may be forbidden by clear and specific university rules. Such rules are a condition rather than a limitation of freedom within the university."

The classroom is for study of described subject matter for which the instructor has professional responsibility and institutional accountability. Control of order in the classroom rests with the instructor, free of distraction or disruption by those who disagree. It is the obligation of students to respect the rights of others in maintenance of classroom order.

Disciplinary proceedings should be structured so that they "facilitate a reliable determination of the truth or falsity of the charges. They should provide fundamental fairness to the parties, and they should be an effective instrument for the maintenance of order."

As a general rule the status of a student should not be altered until charges are adjudicated. But when a student's continued presence on campus is an immediate threat or injury to the well being or property of members of community or property or orderly functioning of the university, interim suspension may be required.

"The fact that a student has been subject to university disciplinary proceedings does not in any way preclude a subsequent trial of the student for the same conduct by public authorities if his conduct violated the laws of the jurisdiction. Likewise the fact that a student has been tried in the criminal courts does not preclude the assertion of an appropriate disciplinary sanction against him by the university. There is no legal basis for the claim of 'double jeopardy' in either case."

OREGON
LEGISLATURE

Students enjoy the same rights and freedoms as citizens of the general community. The student is subject to certain responsibilities and obligations as a member of the academic community. A student is not entitled to special consideration or immunity from the authorities of the general community. ". . . college and university discipline must be limited to student misconduct which distinctly and adversely affects the academic community in pursuit of its goals."

The university community should enforce its stated policy to regulate student conduct in campus disturbances and therefore make externally imposed forces unnecessary. Students who are found guilty of acts that disrupt, disturb, and interfere with the educational process are subject to sanctions in existing rules, including expulsion. This must be enforced.

A small minority of faculty use the classroom to encourage and promote by words, actions, or conduct the disruption of the educational process; they should "either 'shape up or ship out.'" The administration should require this.

"Individuals known to use the classroom as a platform to advocate and promote student participation in disruption of the academic community should not be employed as teaching assistants; those teaching assistants who so use the classroom should be dismissed."

MICHIGAN
LEGISLATURE

All possible steps should be taken to eliminate the concept that a campus is a sanctuary, in the minds of persons on and off campus.

The primary function of law enforcement is to promote order, not to mete out punishment; judgment and punishment are judicial functions.

There must be a clear channel for just and adequate redress of grievances. Due process should include judgment by peers and provision for appeal.

The goals the institution is trying to attain and to which all may subscribe should be specified in order to get collaboration to improve the entire institution.

AMERICAN COUNCIL ON EDUCATION

Students must recognize and respect the rights and privileges of fellow students and seek the same for themselves, including the First Amendment, rights of free speech and assembly, right to pursue without hindrance one's course of study, and privilege of experimenting with ways of thinking. Threats, violence, coercive disruption of classes, etc., tread on rights and are intolerable.

As *in loco parentis* is given up, students must know that they cannot be shielded from violations of societal laws.

To a great extent an institution's functioning depends on voluntary self-discipline of the students. But in circumstances where internal mechanisms fail, e.g., destructive effects on disciplinary proceedings, a new kind of judicial authority may be required.

Universities should regularly review practices of confidentiality about students and privacy of living quarters, and due process for disciplinary proceedings. The option of formal proceedings should be open to any student whose future could be affected by the outcome of a disciplinary decision.

SCRANTON COMMISSION

"The university should be an open forum where speakers of every point of view can be heard. The area of permitted speech and conduct should be at least as broad as that protected by the First Amendment."

"The university should promulgate a code making clear the limits of permissible conduct and announce in advance what measures it is willing to employ in response to impermissible conduct. It should strengthen its disciplinary process. It should assess the capabilities of its security force and determine what role, if any, that force should play in responding to disorder."

"The university's internal disciplinary code should define clearly the limits of lawful protest activity. People must be informed of the university's rules so that they can conduct themselves accordingly; they should be held legally accountable only for conduct that they had reason to know was prohibited. The absence of clear, enforceable and enforced rules of conduct can produce confusion and turmoil. Further disorder can result from the unexpected imposition of sanctions."

"We recommend that universities make well known their willingness to file criminal charges in appropriate cases, and their intention to cooperate actively with public officials in their prosecution. Students know that serious felonies are prohibited on the campus as elsewhere, but they are often unaware of the broad range of state laws that apply to campus disturbances. Some are under the mistaken impression that the university campus is a sanctuary from most of the laws of civil society. Where this ignorance is widespread, resort to the courts and the use of police carry the risk of sparking further protest and disruption. We agree with the National Commission on the Causes and Prevention of Violence that members of the university community 'cannot argue that of all Americans they are uniquely beyond the reach of the law.'"

"Private as well as public universities should, therefore, take the First Amendment as a guide to what is permissible on their campuses. They should not impose restrictions on meetings or rallies or marches that almost any court would strike down, such as bans on 'subversive' speakers or on those 'who advocate overthrow of the government by force and violence,' or a recently voided rule denying students the right 'to celebrate, parade or demonstrate on the campus at any time without the approval of the [college] President.' Above all, universities must staunchly preserve and defend an atmosphere in which all points of view may be freely expressed."

"Obviously, all members of the academic community, as individuals, should be free to participate actively in whatever campaigns or causes they choose. But universities as institutions must remain politically neutral, except in those rare cases in which their own integrity, educational purpose, or preservation are at stake."

"The university must honestly and forcefully reiterate its first principles and must clearly distinguish between those forms of protest which it will permit and defend, and those it will prohibit."

"Faculty members must realize that they have a shared interest and responsibility in the university community as a whole. They must act on that responsibility not only when their own work is disrupted, but also whenever any part of the university is threatened."

"Above all, the faculty—the chief beneficiary of academic freedom—must be a vigilant defender of this freedom within the university community."

"Faculty members who engage in or lead disruptive conduct have no place in the university community."

"What universities should attempt, however, is to create a climate—a sense of community and of common purpose—in which widely shared agreement on the fundamental mission and values of the university itself will deter the destructive forms of protest. To create such a climate, the university will have to demonstrate, both to students and to the larger society, that its values are worthy of support, and that its policies and programs reflect an authentic commitment to those values."

"In the end, it rests with individual institutions to decide which political issues have direct bearing on higher education and warrant taking institutional positions. We recommend, in general, that such institutional positions be taken infrequently: only when there is clear evidence concerning the direct effects of government policies on higher education; only after considering other possible actions short of taking institutional positions; and only following a full appraisal of the consequences for academic freedom which could flow from taking such a stand. Even then, institutional positions should be taken when possible by many institutions acting in concert, rather than by single universities acting alone. Even more important, the frequent assumption of political positions by universities, as institutions, reduces their ability to pursue their central missions."

"Despite . . . inherent problems the university needs an internal disciplinary process to deal with disruption as much as it needs one to deal with cheating on examinations and other academic infractions. The university should have a means by which to express institutional disapproval of harmful conduct. Moreover, a disciplinary system offers a flexibility in the imposition of sanctions that exclusive reliance on the criminal courts does not permit. Finally, the university must have a procedure for removing, temporarily or permanently, those whose presence poses a danger to its members or processes."

"The question of student and faculty participation in disciplinary proceedings has been a matter of serious concern on many campuses. In attempting to legitimate student tribunals, some universities have selected members by election. This process facilitates the politicization of tribunals and should be discouraged. A tribunal with a broad base of participation—including both student and faculty members—is more likely to gain the community's consent to the process and to assure the tribunal's freedom from improper influence. On the other hand, students and faculty at some institutions seem unwilling to impose appropriate sanctions against disrupters."

"Finally, faculty members should not be able, as they apparently are on many campuses, to perform disruptive acts with impunity. Universities should establish a code and procedures for disciplining faculty members—including those with tenure—who behave impermissibly. We recognize the difficulty of designing appropriate mechanisms for this purpose and of gaining acceptance for them. Nevertheless, we think it essential that efforts be made to rectify a situation that is harmful to the institution and is rightly perceived by students to be unfair."

"For such [defense] research to be academically productive, however, it must be readily available and subject to use and criticism by other scholars. Because classified research does not meet this crucial criterion, we recommend that universities avoid acceptance of new classified projects and terminate existing classified projects unless it is clear that the undesirable results of undertaking such a project are outweighed by compelling advantages."

OHIO
LEGISLATURE
A code of minimum standards of conduct and discipline for all students in state or state-supported universities should be adopted. It should specify standards, the range of possible sanctions, and

model disciplinary procedures. Adoption of the code may be by direct legislative action, by the Board of Regents, or by the universities submitting proposed codes to the Board of Regents for final approval for purposes of standardization.

A similar code of minimum standards of professional conduct and discipline for faculty should be adopted, with the same possible channels for adoption as the student code. It should state the obligations of faculty members to their schools, especially regarding teaching obligations and guidance to students. "Such code should also reflect the fact that the personal behavior of faculty members cannot be entirely disassociated from their professional lives."

"The code of faculty conduct and discipline should provide that whether an offender is tenured or not is irrelevant to the imposition of appropriate sanctions for misconduct."

"The Committee recommends legislation to control trespass upon university property, for use as a law enforcement tool in denying access to campuses to persons having no legitimate business there."

8. Campus Security

EISENHOWER COMMISSION

Universities should prepare and review contingency plans for dealing with campus disorders. There should be advance plans stating the circumstances under which the university will use campus discipline, campus police, court injunctions, other court sanctions, and civil police. It is essential to have a definite plan flexibly employed in a crisis. The university should make clear that it will not hesitate to call civil police when the circumstances dictate and should review with the police in advance the degrees of force that are suitable for particular occasions.

AMERICAN BAR ASSOCIATION

Many problems about the extent and form of civil interaction on campus are foreseeable. Plans can be developed to deal with contingencies. "The advice of university counsel, prior consultation with local police and public officials, informing members of the university community of what action will be taken in different situations, can go far towards minimizing the adverse effects that sometimes have accompanied recourse to civil authorities and develop understandings about when to intervene and the manner in which they will act if intervention is necessary."

For training university security personnel, funds should be made available, and the programs should aim to make officers sensitive to the aspirations and tactics of student groups.

"The interests of the public and higher education will be best served by entrusting the primary responsibility for the maintenance of order on the campus to the universities when they are willing and able to perform the function."

MICHIGAN LEGISLATURE

Two distinct categories of campus security personnel must be made on every campus:

(1) those having police functions
(2) those having essentially watchman functions

The chief of campus security should be made responsible to the internal affairs officer of each institution.

AMERICAN COUNCIL ON EDUCATION

The administration needs to deal with civil authorities' plans for handling crises. The plans must define the division of responsibility between campus and civil authorities and provide for effective communication.

SCRANTON COMMISSION

"Every institution should examine the capability of its internal force, determine what its role should be, and take the necessary steps to bridge the gap between capability and expected performance."

"If a university is to maintain a professional police force, however, it must establish salary levels and recruitment procedures capable of producing a force of men with sufficient emotional control and intelligence to deal with unlawful behavior effectively and without antagonizing members of the university community. The university must also provide proper training for its officers, who should attend a good police training center. Officers must be familiarized with campus problems and university regulations, preferably through a training program supervised by university administrators."

"Many universities place their campus security forces under the direction of a business manager or treasurer. This is appropriate where the force performs only watchman functions, but not where it acts as a police force. The expertise and other duties of business personnel are unrelated to the problems and conflicts that might lead to the involvement of a university force. Universities should place campus forces that perform police functions under the immediate control of a well-trained and experienced chief. He, in turn, should be accountable to a high administrative officer or dean whose other responsibilities put him in close contact with the social and political issues that affect the university's day-to-day life."

"Where university police have primary responsibility for maintaining peace on the campus, its uniformed officers may be required to perform conventional law enforcement duties that make it appropriate for them to carry sidearms, batons, or nonlethal chemical weapons. Obviously, only well-trained personnel should be permitted to carry weapons, and strict guidelines should be adopted for their use."

"Finally, a university's campus police force should enter into a clear jurisdictional understanding with local law enforcement authorities and should establish a working arrangement and channels for the regular exchange of information."

"We disagree with those who have suggested that watchman security forces should perform a law enforcement role in situations of disruption. Only a well-trained, professional police force can handle such situations without serious danger to all concerned."

"The key to the effectiveness of [faculty and student] marshals seems to be their neutrality. The administration should resist the temptation to organize marshals, for the necessary neutrality will vanish if either students or faculty feel the marshals are agents of the administration. The impetus to form a marshal force must come from within student or faculty groups."

"When the university is faced with clear acts of criminal violence, such as arson or bombing, its officials should promptly call for the assistance of outside law enforcement agencies which have the experience and the expertise to deal with crime."

"When the conduct is disruptive but not violent, the initial response should generally be internal. The administration must know and understand the range of available choices. It must choose a course of action and pursue it in a measured fashion, with full awareness of the nature of the disorder and the makeup of the participants."

"For example, the university's objective in responding to an obstructive sit-in must be to restore the occupied building or classroom to its normal university use. It is often both possible and wise to begin with discussion or even negotiation of the protestors' grievances, by calling attention to the applicability of internal disciplinary and external criminal sanctions, and by stating when these will become effective. If persuasion fails and the university cannot 'wait it out,' it may be necessary to resort to more direct measures—injunctions, for example, or the use of police. Here again, it is almost always desirable to give advance notice of the university's intended action in order to provide the disrupters with the opportunity to desist voluntarily."

"Thus, even when a university chooses to 'wait it out,' it should take whatever measures are necessary—and they are often costly and cumbersome—to identify the participants and to be prepared to deal with them appropriately."

"In advance of any disturbance, a university should prepare guidelines specifying the circumstances under which an injunction will be sought. It should determine the court in which to file suit; know what facts are required to maintain the suit; and prepare a contingency file containing the necessary legal forms, leaving only the particulars to be completed in the event of disruption."

"The university should make it known in advance if it is considering closing the campus. Only in this way can those faculty and students who regard campus disruptions as a form of spectator sport be made to consider seriously the costs of disorder and thus ultimately assume some of the responsibility for reaffirming and supporting the values of academic life."

"The administration should also make physical provision for the functioning of the university during disorder. Confidential files and sensitive areas, such as telephone switchboards and computation centers, can often be made more secure."

OHIO
LEGISLATURE
Legislation should establish minimum training for campus security officers and provide that the chief of campus security be a profes-

sional law enforcement officer. The legislation should also provide that campus security personnel should have the same obligation and authority to arrest as other law enforcement officers, and should encourage cooperation between local government and university authorities. ". . . but it should be clear that campus authorities have no authority to hinder or prevent local law enforcement officers from enforcing the law within their jurisdictions, including on campus."

Each campus should evaluate campus security and consider adding officers. Pay scales should be competitive with other law enforcement personnel.

Campus security forces should maintain photographers on call to aid in subsequent identification of offenders.

9. Campus Communications

EISENHOWER
COMMISSION

Faculty leaders and the administration need to put more effort toward improving communications with members of the campus, with alumni, and with the general public. Campus authorities have a responsibility to see that a balanced picture of the campus is presented in the media.

AMERICAN
BAR
ASSOCIATION

It might be helpful to designate a responsible person or group to give an authoritative, advisory opinion to those wanting to know whether a proposed course of conduct would violate a campus rule that is vague.

MICHIGAN
LEGISLATURE

Non-crisis communication channels must be constructed and sustained. They should be informal and formal. Verbal or written communication will fail unless there is mutual respect; therefore the climate must be provided. There must be physical availability for direct communication with some recognized symbol of authority, preferably the president. Extraordinary avenues are needed to deal with the exceptional case, e.g., an ombudsman.

Establish communication-facilitating groups and individuals such as campus-wide senates and ombudsman. These would act as advisory.

Trustees must take the initiative in establishing formal and informal contacts with on-campus groups.

The administration should meet frequently with faculty and student groups to listen and make known their thinking on basic issues.

The administration's urgent responsibility is to ensure open avenues of communication. There should be accessibility and also positive explanations of plans and policies to appropriate constituencies.

Students, faculty, and others should be informed of how decisions are made and the reasons for policies. Boards should make this public. There must be well-publicized rules governing the submission of petitions.

Boards should have special committees to communicate with students and faculty.

"We recommend that every institution have, as part of its administrative structure, a group that will be responsible for keeping the administration aware of developing campus issues, rumors, and activities that require reply or action; for drawing up plans to deal with disruption; and for putting those plans into effect when necessary."

"The team should consult formally with designated representatives of the university's major constituencies. Institutional arrangements for this must be made in advance; the middle of a crisis is not the time to summon a constitutional convention, hold a mass meeting, or conduct a plebiscite."

"Students and faculty should not lend support to those few among them who, for whatever purposes, would subvert and destroy the central values of the university. Sometimes these persons, because they are vocal, assume leadership roles when in fact they speak for scarcely anyone but themselves. By the same token students should overcome their reluctance to inform authorities of those within their midst whom they know to be plotting or to have committed acts of violence and destruction. This is essential not only to protect lives and property, but also to reduce the need for intelligence activities by law enforcement agencies."

"The administration must accept primary responsibility for the management of the campus in times of crisis. But the best of administrators cannot operate without the support of the university's other major constituencies—the students, faculty, and trustees. This support often has not been forthcoming."

OHIO
LEGISLATURE

"The Committee recommends that universities immediately evaluate the effectiveness of their respective policies, methods, and procedures in regard to the accessibility to students of not only faculty members but administrators at all levels, for guidance and consultation. Every effort should be made to maintain a high level of personal contact and to provide students with as much personal attention as possible."

Administrators should "use all the methods, techniques, and media at their disposal to see that faculty members and students are regularly and reliably informed of policies, decisions, and work in progress on issues and problems of importance to the academic community." Administrators should not be secretive in responding to faculty and student requests for information. Students and faculty should actively and responsibly inform administrators of problems and needs.

10. Participation in Campus Decisions

EISENHOWER
COMMISSION

Procedures for governance and reform should allow for more rapid and effective decision making. The best guarantee of academic freedom is that the faculty be the controlling agent for education and research. Students should learn who has power in given areas so that they direct their demands for change to the appropriate group.

Faculty have a special obligation to organize themselves more effectively, to create representative groups with the power to act, and to maintain constant and systematic lines of communication with students. They should be ready to meet challenges to educational integrity.

Students should have a meaningful role in the governance of all non-educational and non-research functions. They should serve on committees dealing with educational and related questions, exercising their right to be heard so long as the faculty remains paramount.

BROCK REPORT — Size affects responsiveness, communications, and many other needs. "The challenge is to find ways to preserve the benefits of size while overcoming its disadvantages. We must seek ways to strengthen the ability of our universities to provide close personal relationships and the experiences available in small group settings. Greater development of community colleges, and even cluster colleges around the large university, can also play an important part in 'rehumanizing' the learning process."

NEW YORK LEGISLATURE — College and university trustees and administrators should rid themselves of the image of the sanctuary; open doors and resources to the outside community, including specialized services and facilities, make the necessary reforms in terms of faculty and student freedoms, including sharing in governance; take leadership about ethnic group contributions into curriculum; open all lines of communication between all constituents of the academic community; encourage dialogue with those outside, especially parents; and establish formal grievance machinery, safeguarded with due process.

The Board of Regents should expand the process of involving students and teachers in a wide variety of educational policy-making activities at all appropriate levels.

Students should accept the legitimacy of institutions of higher education; reject violence as a means to solve problems; work jointly with all; and use all existing channels to fullest extent. The commission wholeheartedly supports the rights of all students to participate fully and responsibly in making decisions affecting them within the academic community in an environment free from intimidation from other elements of the community.

AMERICAN BAR ASSOCIATION — "Given the fact that the classroom may not be utilized to ventilate grievances relevant even to the conduct of the class itself, at least when the instructor indicates his reluctance to depart from the assigned materials, universities should provide some orderly means outside of the classroom for the review and disposition of such grievances. Where such means are provided, or where students otherwise express their grievance with the conduct of a given course without disrupting the classroom itself, they should not be subject to instructional reprisal or punitive grading for doing so. To safeguard these prerogatives as well as to protect students from instructional evaluation based on political bias, individual prejudice, or other considerations not reflecting a professional assessment of educational performance, provision should be made for an orderly procedure of appeal from instructional evaluations allegedly reached on nonacademic grounds."

OREGON
LEGISLATURE

Failure to respond to students' legitimate concerns is a cause of unrest and frustration. Students should be included in both discussion and decision making with faculty and administration. Students are and should be included in determining policy matters relating to student welfare. Opinions should be sought from disinterested and disaffected as well as elected student leaders. This would be a contribution and a learning experience. Students should evaluate undergraduate teaching. Student involvement in policy-making decisions should be related to matters which directly affect their welfare.

MICHIGAN
LEGISLATURE

The role of the president should be carefully redefined at all colleges. Fund raising and authority for the daily operation of the campus should be functions of two different positions (people).

The role, function, and status of anyone performing the tasks of a public information officer must be delineated clearly. He must be well informed and entrusted to speak promptly and clearly for the institution.

Look into the ad hoc committee concept whereby a committee is appointed to do a single job and then disbands. Ad hoc committees tend to minimize the importance of professional campus politicians and draw those interested in the particular problem.

Every publicly supported institution is a regional campus. New programs must be developed to make the urban university equivalent to the land-grant college.

Greater consistency and rationality of programs should be sought through contact between junior and senior colleges and universities.

AMERICAN
COUNCIL ON
EDUCATION Institutions must define who is responsible for what. The administration should be accountable only within the limits of its responsibilities and power to act.

It is an administrative responsibility to see that rules of governance and disciplinary procedures receive continuing assessment.

Every institution needs bylaws, subject to periodic reexamination, setting forth the board's essential authority and responsibility and defining procedures about size, selection and appointment, term of office, composition.

All constituencies should be involved in the reform of the college.

The performance of administrative officers should be subject to periodic review and their roles should be reexamined. Advisory and disciplinary functions should be separated.

The consequences of weakening the authority of the president should be considered. Bylaws should clearly state the president's responsibility and authority. Fixed terms of office should be considered.

A lay board is preferable to other methods. Reform of organization and procedures is needed.

Diversity of age, occupation, etc., should be sought on the board. Adding students and faculty from the same or other institutions might be considered. To avoid a conflict of interest, representatives from other institutions might be preferred.

The faculty should take a more active role in guiding change and examining the institution's goals. Many conceive the role narrowly as training an intellectual elite and they resist reform.

Students who want to propose changes in an institution's policies should learn the process involved and consult with faculty and administration.

Students rightly expect administrators to take the initiative in proposing educational change, but they must recognize that the administration is responsible to widely divergent campus groups and is accountable to a governing board. Attempts to circumscribe freedom to initiate, guide, negotiate, and make decisions will either reinforce the status quo or create chaos.

Students should have substantial autonomy in nonacademic activities and should also participate in matters of general educational policy, especially curricular affairs. Students should serve in a variety of roles on committees that make decisions or recommendations. This will improve the quality of decisions and ensure acceptability to the student body.

"Increased participation of students, faculty, and staff in the formulation of university policies is desirable.

"However, universities are not institutions that can be run on a one-man one-vote basis or with the participation of all members on all issues.

"Competence should be a major criterion in determining involvement in the university decision-making process.

"Another criterion for involvement in decision making should be the degree to which decisions affect any given group. Changes in regulations concerning student life should be made with the involvement of students; changes in faculty policies should obviously be made with faculty involvement.

"Procedures for electing representatives of university constituencies should be carefully designed to guarantee true representativeness, perhaps by having representatives elected by small departmental or residential units, or by establishing quorum requirements to encourage participation and to enhance the legitimacy of the election result.

"Reforms of governance should not undermine administrative leadership. On the contrary, they should be designed to produce policies and leaders who will have the broad support of the community, especially in times of campus crisis.

"Once basic policy decisions are made, their execution should be left to expert administrative hands. Administrators must, of course, remain ultimately accountable to the various constituencies of the university— trustees, students, faculty, alumni, and the general public. But their actions should not be constantly overseen by any of these groups. The involvement of nonadministrators in the daily operations and minor policy decisions of the university erodes the effectiveness and sense of responsibility of administrators."

"We . . . recommend that faculty members assume much greater responsibility for self-regulation and for the welfare of their university community in the following ways:

- "Many faculty members know very little about the operation of their universities. They should inform themselves about the principles, mechanisms, and constraints that are involved in decision making, rather than simply demand dramatic changes without demonstrating how they can be achieved.

- "Faculty committees should be established to evaluate and guide the teaching performance of faculty members.

- "Limitations on the outside service commitments of faculty members should be made explicit and should be enforced by faculty committees.

- "Because faculties are often wedded to the status quo, university administrators must provide much of the leadership for reform."

- "Administrators, principally the president, must bear most of the burden of defending the university against attacks from the outside and of articulating the university's needs and purposes to the public.

- "Above all, the administrator must keep open every possible channel of talk with students. He must have an open mind, for much that students say is valuable; he must have a cryptographers's mind, for much that they say comes in code words and postures; he must have an honest mind, for the worst crime in dealing with the young is to lie to them; he must have a tough mind, for he will frequently, for reasons either invisible or simply unintelligible to his hearers, have to say 'No.' Above all he must have a compassionate spirit—for youth is neither a disease nor a crime, though to its elders it may be one of the world's major puzzles."

- "Trustees have a particular responsibility to interpret and explain their institution to the larger society. They should attempt to inform the public about the institution's values, goals, complexities, and changes. They should defend academic freedom and the right of students, teachers, and guest speakers to espouse unpopular views. They should attempt to help the public understand the underlying causes of student unrest, and to prevent punitive or counterproductive public policies toward higher education.

- "Trustees have an equally important responsibility to assure that their university maintains its central commitments in teaching, to research, and to the preservation of academic freedom against internal erosion. Specifically, this means discouraging excessive service commitments by the university, resisting internal politicization of the university, supporting academic reform, and encouraging improvement in university governance.

- "To be effective in these difficult roles, trustees must be familiar with the institution they oversee and with the concerns of its constituents. They should read campus publications and be in contact with students, faculty members, and administrators. Those unable to find time for these activities will be unable to perform their role well."

"The trustees must exercise the greatest care in making their most important decision—the choice of the university president. He must possess, in addition to more traditional attributes, the qualities of leadership necessary to steer the institution through crisis and disorder. He must have the courage to tell students clearly and honestly when he cannot meet their demands, and he must have the consideration to explain why the answer must be 'no.' Having found such a man, the trustees should permit him (and his administration) to administer the university without undue interference and should support him in times of stress."

Appendix B: Additional Data on Campus Attitudes and Protest Activity

Table 1: Recent College Alumni—Attitudes toward Campus Protests
and Political Activity

Statement	Agree strongly or somewhat
This country would be better off if there were less protest and dissatisfaction coming from college campuses	52%
The protests of college students are a healthy sign for America	51%
	Against student involvement
The college should take the responsibility to see that students do not break the law (Agree)	55%
Students should have the right to protest against recruiters on campus if the students think the recruiters are helping to carry out immoral practices (Disagree)	47%
The college should not try to stop students from taking part in political activity (Disagree)	17%

SOURCE: Joe L. Spaeth and Andrew M. Greeley, *Recent Alumni and Higher Education,* McGraw-Hill Book Company, 1970.

Table 2: Campus Reaction to the Cambodia Incursion and Kent State and Jackson State Shootings, by Institutional Selectivity (Four-year Colleges and Universities only)

	Freshmen mostly from top 10% of high school class (N = 135)	*Freshmen mostly from top 40% of high school class (N = 598)*	*Essentially open admissions (N = 297)*
Student/staff strike, one day or longer	35%	16%	9%
Efforts by students to communicate with local citizens about the war and the campus reaction	80	53	33
Essentially peaceful demonstrations	79	58	41
Demonstrations causing damage to persons or property	9	6	5

SOURCE: Carnegie Commission Survey of College Presidents, July 1970.

Table 3: Campus Reaction to the Cambodia Incursion and the Kent State and Jackson State Shootings, by Institutional Size

	Less than 1,000 (N = 722)	*1,000 to 5,000 (N = 757)*	*5,000 to 12,000 (N = 231)*	*More than 12,000 (N = 138)*
General student/staff strike, one day or longer	10%	13%	17%	29%
Efforts by students to communicate with local citizens about the war and the campus reaction	29	42	54	69
Essentially peaceful demonstrations	28	48	67	75
Demonstrations causing damage to persons or property	1	2	6	30

SOURCE: Carnegie Commission Survey of College Presidents, July 1970.

Table 4: Student Attitudes, May 1970

"Basic changes in the system will be necessary to improve the quality of life in America."	76%
Disagree *that "colleges and universities are too important to our society to be continually disrupted by protests and demonstrations."*	56%
Support of the goals of the May protests (among respondents at colleges experiencing protests in May).	75%
Participation in the May protests (among respondents at colleges experiencing protests).	58%
"School authorities are right to call in police when students occupy a building or threaten violence."	70%
Do not accept "violence as an effective means of change."	68%
Respondent identified self as "radical or far left."	11%

SOURCE: *The Report of the President's Commission on Campus Unrest* (September 1970), based on a special Harris poll conducted in May 1970 at 50 four-year colleges and universities.

Table 5: Institutional Selectivity and Incidence of Violent and Nonviolent Disruptive Protest by Type of Institution (Weighted Population Estimates)

| | | *Universities* | |
*Selectivity level**	N	*Percent with violent protest*	*Percent with nonviolent disruptive protest†*
Low	72	0	0
Low intermediate	51	12	6
High intermediate	124	19	53
High	58	40	45
TOTAL	305	17	31

*Selectivity based on admissions test scores of entering students at each college.

† Included in the nonviolent disruptive category are strikes and boycotts of classes, which would not necessarily be considered "disruptive" according to the definitions in this Carnegie Commission report.

SOURCE: Alan E. Bayer and Alexander W. Astin, "Violence and Disruption on the U.S. Campus, 1968–69," *Educational Record,* vol. 50, no. 4, fall 1969.

Table 6: Institutional Size and Incidence of Violent and Nonviolent Disruptive Protest* by Type of Institution (Weighted Population Estimates)

| | | *Universities* | |
Enrollment	N	*Percent with violent protest*	*Percent with nonviolent disruptive protest*
Under 500	54	0	0
500–999			
1,000–5,000	29	14	69
Over 5,000	222	22	34†
TOTAL	305	17	31

*Included in the nonviolent disruptive category are strikes and boycotts of classes, which would not necessarily be considered "disruptive" according to the definitions in this Carnegie Commission report.

† The 34% figure is correct here. The 42% figure reported in the *Educational Record* is a misprint.

SOURCE: Alan E. Bayer and Alexander W. Astin, "Violence and Disruption on the U.S. Campus, 1968–69," *Educational Record,* vol. 50, no. 4, fall 1969.

	Four-year Colleges			Two-year Colleges	
N	Percent with violent protest	Percent with nonviolent disruptive protest	N	Percent with violent protest	Percent with nonviolent disruptive protest
307	4	14	608	3	5
362	5	7	150	4	0
454	4	28	6	0	0
150	12	37			
,273	5	20	764	3	4

	Four-year Colleges			Two-year Colleges	
N	Percent with violent protest	Percent with nonviolent disruptive protest	N	Percent with violent protest	Percent with nonviolent disruptive protest
129	3	5	224	0	0
394	3	18	169	0	0
591	5	24	303	4	3
159	14	24	68	16	35
,273	5	20	764	3	4

Table 7: Undergraduate Political Ideology and Participation in Demonstrations, for All Institutions

Participation,† since entering college, in:	Total under-graduates	Political ideology*			
		Left	Liberal	Middle-of-the-road	Moderately or strongly conservative
A demonstration against U.S. military policy at their college					
Percent who participated	19	69	30	7	4
Percent who did not participate	81	31	70	93	96
TOTAL	100	100	100	100	100
A demonstration against U.S. military policy elsewhere					
Percent who participated	14	63	22	3	2
Percent who did not participate	86	37	78	97	98
TOTAL	100	100	100	100	100
A demonstration against administrative policies of a college at their college					
Percent who participated	17	44	24	10	7
Percent who did not participate	83	56	76	90	93
TOTAL	100	100	100	100	100
A demonstration against administrative policies of a college elsewhere					
Percent who participated	2	8	2	1	0.4
Percent who did not participate	98	92	98	99	99
TOTAL	100	100	100	100	100
A demonstration against existing ethnic or racial policies at their college					
Percent who participated	7	34	10	2	1
Percent who did not participate	93	66	90	98	99
TOTAL	100	100	100	100	100

		Political ideology*			
Participation,† since entering college, in:	*Total under- graduates*	*Left*	*Liberal*	*Middle-of- the-road*	*Moderately or strongly conservative*
A demonstration against existing ethnic or racial policies elsewhere					
Percent who participated	6	31	8	1	0.5
Percent who did not participate	94	69	92	99	99
TOTAL	100	100	100	100	100
At least one demonstration at their college or elsewhere against U.S. military policy, existing ethnic or racial policies, or *administrative policies of a college*					
Percent who participated	31	87	48	17	11
Percent who did not participate	69	13	52	83	89
TOTAL	100	100	100	100	100

* Response to the question "How would you characterize yourself politically at the present time (left, liberal, middle-of-the-road, moderately conservative, or strongly conservative)?"

† Participated in or helped organize or lead.

SOURCE: Carnegie Commission survey of undergraduates in 1969–70.

Table 8: Political Ideology of Undergraduates, by Carnegie Commission
Typology of Institutions*

		Percent of undergraduates		
		Doctoral-granting institutions		
Political ideology	*All institutions*	*Heavy emphasis on research*	*Moderate emphasis on research*	*Moderate emphasis on doctoral*
Left	5	12	8	6
Liberal	39	49	40	43
Middle-of-the-road	37	26	32	35
Moderately conservative	17	12	17	15
Strongly conservative	2	1	3	1
TOTAL	100	100	100	100

*For a description of the Carnegie Commission typology of institutions, see Appendix C.

SOURCE: Carnegie Commission survey of undergraduates, 1969–70.

Limited emphasis on doctoral	Nondoctoral: liberal arts and occupational		Liberal arts colleges		Two-year colleges
	Comprehensive programs	Limited programs	I	II	
6	5	2	8	5	4
39	42	42	51	39	34
36	34	41	26	37	42
18	18	14	13	17	18
1	1	1	2	2	2
100	100	100	100	100	100

Table 9: Profile of Undergraduates in All Institutions—Political Ideology and Participation in at Least One Demonstration

Political ideology* and participation†	Percent of undergraduates‡
Left and participated	5
Left and did not participate	1
Liberal and participated	19
Liberal and did not participate	21
Middle-of-the-road and participated	6
Middle-of-the-road and did not participate	30
Moderately or strongly conservative and participated	2
Moderately or strongly conservative and did not participate	16
TOTAL	100

*Political ideology: response to the question "How would you characterize yourself politically at the present time (left, liberal, middle-of-the-road, moderately conservative, or strongly conservative)?"

† Participation: participated in or helped organize or lead at least one demonstration since entering college, at their college or elsewhere, against United States military policy, existing ethnic or racial policies, *or* administrative policies of a college.

‡ Percentages may vary up to two percentage points from figures in other tables because of omission of "no opinion" responses, and because of rounding.

SOURCE: Carnegie Commission survey of undergraduates in 1969–70.

Table 10: Percentages of Different Types of Institutions Reporting
Some Incidence of Organized Student Protest in Relation to 27 Issues
(1967–68)

	All N = 859	Public 4-year college N = 97	Public university N = 144
Instruction			
Undergraduate classes typically too large, instruction too impersonal	03%	04%	09%
Senior faculty not sufficiently involved in undergraduate instruction	02	00	06
Poor quality of instruction—in general or specific instances	13	14	15
Generally prevailing system(s) of testing and/or grading	12	13	17
Curriculum inflexibility	15	12	18
Faculty			
Academic freedom for faculty—in principle	04	05	09
Faculty tenure policies, e.g., "publish or perish"	04	05	07
Controversy surrounding a particular faculty member	20	21	28
Freedom of Expression			
"Censorship" of certain publications, e.g., student newspaper	10	08	16
Campus rules regarding speeches, appearances by "controversial" persons	08	04	18
Actual appearance by a particular person of leftist persuasion	05	03	08
Actual appearance by a particular person of rightest persuasion	04	02	09
Student-administration			
Dormitory and other living-group regulations, e.g., women's hours	34	26	35
Food service	25	26	21
Dress regulations	20	15	12
Policies, regulations regarding student drinking	11	05	10
Policies, regulations regarding student use of drugs	05	04	08
Disciplinary action against particular student(s)	16	11	17

Independent 4-year college N = 146	Independent university N = 58	Catholic institutions N = 143	Protestant institutions N = 191	Teachers college N = 53	Technical institutions N = 27
03%	05%	01%	01%	02%	00%
01	03	01	01	00	00
14	10	15	12	08	11
12	12	13	10	08	15
14	19	17	11	11	19
02	03	03	03	04	04
02	05	02	04	04	04
18	29	14	18	25	07
03	09	12	11	06	11
03	09	10	07	02	00
01	03	07	04	04	04
03	03	03	03	02	04
39	36	27	36	28	41
21	29	29	31	15	33
19	10	31	24	13	19
10	09	10	17	06	11
07	07	02	05	02	04
14	20	17	21	08	04

Table 10 *(cont.)*

	All N = 859	*Public 4-year college* N = 97	*Public university* N = 144
Alleged racial discrimination: in admissions, nonaction on fraternity discrimination, etc.	18	13	35
Student-administration communication; students unable to voice grievances	19	15	20
Insufficient student participation in establishing campus policies	27	26	31
Off-campus Issues *Civil rights: local area (off-campus) — protest and/or work*	29	19	35
The draft	25	22	36
On-campus recruiting by one or another of the armed services	25	27	42
On-campus recruiting by any other firm or agency, e.g., Dow, CIA, etc.	20	19	50
U.S. policies regarding Vietnam	38	31	53
Classified defense and related research on campus	04	02	11

SOURCE: R. E. Peterson, *The Scope of Organized Student Protest in 1967–68.* Copyright © 1968 by Educational Testing Service. Reproduced by permission. (Based on a survey of 859 accredited four-year institutions.)

Independent 4-year college N = 146	*Independent university* N = 58	*Catholic institutions* N = 143	*Protestant institutions* N = 191	*Teachers college* N = 53	*Technical institutions* N = 27
17	41	04	14	15	07
20	26	25	17	08	07
25	41	28	24	19	19
34	40	31	24	21	22
27	55	15	20	06	19
32	48	13	16	06	15
13	60	10	04	02	26
44	68	28	30	21	33
01	16	03	02	02	00

Table 11: College Students' Ratings of American Institutions

	Excellent	*Good*	*Favorable (excellent or good)*
Universities	12%	56%	68%
Family	23	35	58
Business	12	44	56
Congress	7	49	56
Courts	6	40	46
Police	6	34	40
High schools	4	33	37
Organized religion	7	26	33
Political parties	2	16	18

SOURCE: *Newsweek,* December 29, 1969 (poll of 1,092 students on 57 campuses conducted in November 1969). A poll compiled by the Gallup Organization. Copyright *Newsweek,* 1969.

Table 12: Faculty Attitudes toward and Participation in Protest Activity, by Carnegie Commission Typology of Institutions*

		Doctoral-granting institutions		
	All institutions	*Heavy emphasis on research*	*Moderate emphasis on research*	*Moderate emphasis on doctoral programs*
Attitude toward most recent campus protest incident†				
Approve of aims and methods	28%	18%	26%	21%
Approve of aims, not methods	25	30	24	25
Disapprove of aims	27	35	30	28
Uncertain	19	16	17	23
Indifferent	1	1	3	3
Total percent‡	100%	100%	100%	100%

*For a description of the Carnegie Commission typology of institutions, see Appendix C.

† These data are not comparable to the undergraduate data on participation in demonstrations. The undergraduate data report participation in *any* demonstration since entering college; faculty data report participation in the *most recent* demonstration.

‡ Percentages include only those institutions which had a protest incident.

Limited emphasis on doctoral programs	Nondoctoral: liberal arts and occupational		Liberal arts colleges		Two-year colleges	Schools of engineering, technology
	Compre-hensive programs	Limited programs	I	II		
36%	26%	41%	36%	26%	22%	36%
20	26	16	22	29	26	18
27	27	18	21	25	30	24
15	19	25	19	19	21	15
2	2	0.2	2	1	1	7
100%	100%	100%	100%	100%	100%	100%

Table 12 *(cont.)*

	All institutions	Doctoral-granting institutions		
		Heavy emphasis on research	*Moderate emphasis on research*	*Moderate emphasis on doctoral programs*
Faculty role in most recent campus protest incident				
Helped plan, organize, lead	0.4%	0.3%	0.1%	0.1%
Joined in protest	1	1	1	1
Openly supported	5	9	6	5
Openly opposed	2	4	2	2
Tried to mediate	4	6	4	3
Was not involved	29	66	49	48
No incident†	60	16	38	42
Total§	101.4%	102.3%	100.1%	101.1%

† These data are not comparable to the undergraduate data on participation in demonstrations. The undergraduate data report participation in *any* demonstration since entering college; faculty data report participation in the *most recent* demonstration.

§ Percentages add to more than 100% because of involvement in more than one role.

SOURCE: Carnegie Commission survey of faculty in 1969–70.

Limited emphasis on doctoral programs	Nondoctoral: liberal arts and occupational		Liberal arts colleges		Two-year colleges	Schools of engineering, technology
	Compre-hensive programs	Limited programs	*I*	*II*		
0.3%	0.2%	1%	1%	0.2%	0.4%	0.0%
0.4	1	1	2	0.4	0.3	0.1
9	5	3	11	5	4	3
2	2	1	2	1	2	0.4
4	4	1	9	6	2	1
48	34	18	35	19	20	5
38	54	76	44	69	72	91
101.7%	100.2%	101%	104%	100.6%	100.7%	100.5%

Table 13: Faculty Attitudes about Student Political Activism, by Carnegie Commission Typology of Institutions* (Percent Agreeing Strongly or Agreeing with Reservations)

		Doctoral-granting institutions		
	All insti- tutions	*Heavy emphasis on research*	*Moderate emphasis on research*	*Moderate emphasis on doctoral programs*
Campus disruptions by militant students are a threat to academic freedom.	85%	83%	84%	82%
Student demonstra- tions have no place on the college campus.	33	20	27	29
Most campus demon- strations are created by far left groups trying to cause trouble.	53	46	52	49
Political activities by students have no place on a college campus.	17	10	15	16
Students who dis- rupt the functioning of a college should be expelled or suspended.	82	75	84	80

* For a description of the Carnegie Commission typology of institutions, see Appendix C.

SOURCE: Carnegie Commission survey of faculty in 1969–70.

Limited emphasis on doctoral programs	Nondoctoral: liberal arts and occupational		Liberal arts colleges		Two-year colleges	Schools of engineering, technology
	Compre-hensive programs	Limited programs	I	II		
79%	85%	87%	82%	81%	87%	87%
25	30	31	24	35	44	41
46	51	59	42	48	62	62
14	14	16	12	17	23	29
75	82	82	77	79	86	85

Appendix C: Carnegie Commission Classification of Institutions of Higher Education, 1968

The classification includes all institutions listed in U.S. Office of Education, *Opening Fall Enrollment in Higher Education: Part B, Institutional Data, 1968.* Whenever a campus of a multicampus institution is listed separately, it is included as a separate institution in our classification. In a few instances, the Office of Education includes all campuses of an institution in a single listing, and in such cases the institution is treated as a single entry in our classification. Our classification includes 2,763 institutions, as compared with the Office of Education total of 2,491 for 1968. The difference is explained by the fact that, for purposes of obtaining the total number of institutions, we have treated each campus as an institution, whereas the Office of Education treats multicampus systems as single institutions for purposes of obtaining the total number of institutions.

Perhaps the most significant problem in this connection arises in connection with medical schools, schools of engineering, schools of business administration, and law schools. These institutions appear separately only if they are listed as separate institutions in *Opening Fall Enrollment.* Most of these professional schools are not listed separately, since their enrollment is included in the enrollment of the parent university or university campus. This is true even in a number of instances in which the professional school is not located on the main campus of the university, but on a separate campus, e.g., Johns Hopkins University School of Medicine.

The classification includes five main groups of institutions and a number of subcategories, or 18 categories in all. They are as follows:

1 *Doctoral-granting institutions*

1.1 *Heavy emphasis on research* The 50 leading institutions in terms of federal financial support of academic science in at least two of the three years, 1965–66, 1966–67, and 1967–68, provided they awarded at least 50 Ph.D.'s (plus M.D.'s if the medical school was on the same campus) in 1967–68.

1.2 *Moderate emphasis on research* These institutions were on the list of 100 leading institutions in terms of federal financial support in at least two out of three of the above three years and awarded at least 50 Ph.D.'s (plus M.D.'s if the medical school was on the same campus) in 1967–68, or they were among the leading 50 institutions in terms of number of Ph.D.'s (plus M.D.'s if on the same campus) awarded in that year. In addition, a few institutions that did not quite meet these criteria, but which have graduate programs of high quality and with impressive promise for future development, have been included in 1.2.

1.3 *Moderate emphasis on doctoral programs* These institutions awarded 40 or more Ph.D.'s in 1967–68 or received at least $4 million in total federal financial support in 1967–68.

1.4 *Limited emphasis on doctoral programs* These institutions awarded at least 10 Ph.D.'s in 1967–68, with the exception of a few new doctoral-granting institutions which may be expected to increase the number of Ph.D.'s awarded within a few years.

2 *Nondoctoral institutions, liberal arts and occupational programs*

2.1 *Comprehensive programs* This group includes institutions that offered a liberal arts program as well as several other programs, such as engineering, business administration, etc. Many of them offered master's degrees, but all lacked a doctoral program or had only an extremely limited doctoral program. Private institutions with less than 1,500 students and public institutions with less than 1,000 students are not included even though they may offer a selection of programs, since they cannot be regarded as comprehensive. Such institutions are classified as liberal arts colleges. The differentiation between private and public institutions is based on the fact that public state colleges are experiencing relatively rapid increases in enrollment and are likely to have at least 1,500 students within a few years even if they did not in 1968. Most of the state colleges with relatively few students were established quite recently.

2.2 *Limited programs* This list includes state colleges and some private colleges that offered a liberal arts program and one or two other programs, such as teacher's education or nursing. Many of the institutions in this group are former teachers' colleges which have recently broadened their programs to include a liberal arts curriculum. Again, except in the case of a few small institutions that are almost exclusively teachers' colleges, private institutions with less than 1,500 students and public institutions with less than 1,000 students are not included.

3 *Liberal Arts Colleges*

3.1 *Liberal Arts Colleges—Selectivity I* These colleges scored 60 or above on Astin's selectivity index (Alexander W. Astin, *Who Goes Where To College?*, Science Research Associates, Chicago, 1965), *or* they were included in the list of 300 leading baccalaureate-granting institutions in terms of numbers of their graduates receiving Ph.D.'s at 40 leading doctoral-granting institutions, 1958–66 (National Academy of Sciences, *Doctorate Recipients from United States Universities, 1958–66*).

3.2 *Liberal Arts Colleges—Selectivity II*

4 *All Two-year Colleges and Institutes*

5 *Professional Schools and Other Specialized Institutions*

5.1 *Theological Seminaries, Bible Colleges, and Other Institutions Offering Degrees in Religion* (not including colleges with religious affiliations offering a liberal arts program as well as degrees in religion).

5.2 *Medical Schools and Medical Centers* As indicated above, this list includes only those that are listed as separate campuses in *Opening Fall Enrollment*. In some instances, the medical center includes other health professional schools, e.g., dentistry, pharmacy, nursing, etc.

5.3 *Other Separate Health Professional Schools*

5.4 *Schools of Engineering and Technology*   Technical institutes are included only if they award a bachelor's degree and if their program is limited exclusively or almost exclusively to technical fields of study.

5.5 *Schools of Business and Management*   Business schools are included only if they award a bachelor's or higher degree and if their program is limited exclusively or almost exclusively to a business curriculum.

5.6 *Schools of Art, Music, Design, etc.*

5.7 *Schools of Law*

5.8 *Schools of Education*   Schools of education are included only if they do not have a liberal arts program.

5.9 *Other Specialized Institutions*   Includes graduate centers, maritime academies, military institutes (lacking a liberal arts program), and miscellaneous.

NOTE: Extension divisions of universities and campuses offering only extension programs are not included.

  In this report, *Dissent and Disruption,* data are not available for subcategories of Professional Schools and Other Specialized Institutions (5.1–5.9), with the exception of Schools of Engineering and Technology (5.4).

Appendix D: *State* *Legislation Enacted in 1969 and 1970 Regarding Campus Unrest, by Type of Legislation*

Twenty-nine of the fifty states enacted legislation in 1969 and 1970 regarding student unrest.

Type of legislation	Number of states which enacted specific legislation*
Legislation regarding campus unrest:	
Concerning campus interference[a]	21
Firearms on campus[b]	4
General anti-disturbance[c]	8
Require or authorize regulations[d]	9
Other legislation[e]	14
Legislation regarding penalties for campus unrest:	
Criminal offense[f]	20
Student financial aid curtailment[g]	10
Student suspension, expulsion, or withholding of funds[h]	7
Faculty/employee discipline or withholding of funds[i]	6

* Any legislation enacted prior to 1969, or in 1971, is not included here. Rules or policies adopted by state coordinating councils or boards of regents are likewise excluded.

[a] *Concerning campus interference:* Legislation providing that it is a criminal offense to interfere with the lawful use of the college or university, for example, barring hallways or doors, seizing control of buildings, disrupting classes, erecting barricades at campus entrances, disturbing the peace, denying lawful freedom of movement, and refusing to leave when requested by proper authority. This category also includes legislation prohibiting damaging property or rioting on campus, although few states had such legislation introduced (probably because existing laws already applied). In most cases, legislation in this category applies to all colleges, both public and private, but in a few states only state colleges and universities are affected.

^b *Firearms on campus:* Legislation specifically prohibiting or restricting the use of firearms on campus; legislation regarding firearms which does not refer to campuses is not included here.

^c *General anti-disturbance:* Legislation against civil disturbances which is not specifically directed against campus unrest, but which may be used in dealing with it (for example, tightening the definitions of rioting and of disorderly conduct, and increasing the penalties for interference with law enforcement officers).

^d *Require or authorize regulations:* Legislation requiring or authorizing colleges and universities to adopt codes of conduct and/or procedures for dealing with demonstrations.

^e *Other legislation:* Any legislation regarding campus unrest which does not fall into any of the above categories.

^f *Criminal offense:* Legislation providing that certain acts in connection with campus unrest are criminal offenses, punishable by fine, imprisonment, or both.

^g *Student financial aid curtailment:* Legislation providing that students committing certain offenses are ineligible for state scholarships, loans, grants, etc. Offenses vary from state to state, as do disciplinary procedures — some states require conviction in a court of law, while others provide for special hearings.

^h *Student suspension, expulsion, or withholding of funds:* Legislation which provides that funds not be appropriated for students who commit certain offenses, or which provides for student suspension or expulsion. As in the case of financial aid curtailment, offenses and procedures vary from state to state.

ⁱ *Faculty/employee discipline or withholding of funds:* Legislation providing that appropriations not be used for payment of faculty or employees who commit certain offenses, or legislation requiring disciplinary action for faculty or employees. As above, offenses and procedures vary from state to state.

SOURCE: Prepared by Carnegie Commission staff from information contained in *Higher Education in the States,* vol. 1, pp. 85–108 (September 1970); additional information was obtained from Alaska and Wyoming.

Appendix E: American Civil Liberties Union — Academic Freedom and Civil Liberties of Students in Colleges and Universities

> *Our Nation is deeply committed to safeguarding academic free-*
> *dom, which is of transcendent value to all of us. . . . That freedom*
> *is therefore a special concern of the First Amendment, which does*
> *not tolerate laws that cast a pall of orthodoxy over the classroom.*
> Keyishian v. Board of Regents, 385 U.S. 589, 603 (1967).

INTRODUC-
TION
The past several years have been marked by great tension. Unrest among college students, involving confrontations and bordering in some cases on rebellion, has swept from one American campus to another. Students have asserted the right to participate in decision-making in matters relating to student life and discipline, to the formulation of academic policies, and the governance of their institutions. Many have also strongly opposed what they consider the distortion or perversion of the university's proper purposes in serving ends established by agencies other than the academic community. They have condemned, *inter alia,* the university's ties to military agencies, secret research, the status on campus of the Reserve Officers Training Corps, recruitment for the military or defense industries, and the failure adequately to enroll and educate black and other disadvantaged Americans. As we enter a new decade there is little reason to think that these concerns will abate.

The American Civil Liberties Union and its Academic Freedom Committee recognize that many of the protesters, who include not only undergraduate and graduate students but some (particularly younger) faculty members, are moved by deep conviction and urgent concern in the attempt to correct what they deem educational inequities and, beyond that, to eliminate or mitigate the social, economic and political injustices of our society. Whatever differences of opinion exist with respect to and on how best to serve these causes, the ACLU is convinced that methods of protest which violate and subvert the basic principles of freedom of expression and academic freedom are abhorrent and must be condemned.

We believe in the right, and are committed to the protection of, all peaceful forms of protest, including mass demonstrations, picketing, rallies and other dramatic forms. But actions which deprive others of the opportunity to speak or be heard, involve takeovers of buildings that disrupt the educational process, incarceration of or assaults on persons, destruction of property and rifling of files, are anti-civil libertarian and incompatible with the nature and functions of educational institutions.

Fundamental to the very nature of a free society is the conviction expressed by Mr. Justice Holmes that "the best truth is the power of the thought to get itself accepted in the competition of the market." When men govern themselves they have a right to decide for themselves which views and proposals are sound and which unsound. This means that all points of view are entitled to be expressed and heard. This is particularly true in universities which render great services to society when they function as centers of free, uncoerced, independent and creative thought and experience. Universities have existed and can exist without bricks and mortar but they cannot function without freedom of inquiry and expression.

For these reasons, the American Civil Liberties Union has from its very inception defended free expression for all groups and all points of view, including the most radical and the most unpopular within the society and the university. To abandon the democratic process in the interest of "good" causes, without a willingness to pay the penalty for civil disobedience, is to risk the destruction of freedom not just for the present but for the future, not just for our social order but for any future social order as well. Freedom, the world has learned to its sorrow, is a fragile plant that must be protected and cultivated.

It should be axiomatic that if the college or university* is to

---

* In this pamphlet [of the ACLU], the words "college" and "university" are used interchangeably to refer to all institutions of higher education.

survive as a free institution without recourse to the law-enforcement authorities, without interposition by the courts or interference from legislators, it must strive to create its own workable, forward-looking, self-governing society. In addition, as Calvin H. Plimpton, President of Amherst College, wrote in a letter addressed to President Nixon, on May 2, 1969, in behalf of the entire Amherst college community, recognition must be given to the fact that part of the turmoil in universities "derives from the distance separating the American dream from the American reality."

It is obvious that our universities and colleges do not have the power to redress the ills of our society. But the more forward-looking are re-examining their structure and policies to preserve and extend the freedom and autonomy of the university community. In this connection, the ACLU has already endorsed measures which would enhance the role of faculty and students in the governing of academic institutions, which set standards for the Reserve Officers Training Corps programs to operate on campus in harmony with principles of academic freedom, and which call for continuing scrutiny of curricula and extracurricula programs. (The ACLU has also taken the position that the present draft system is unconstitutional and violates civil liberties guarantees.)

In this time of challenge and change, the Union trusts that the guidelines set forth in this revised edition of "Academic Freedom and Civil Liberties of Students in Colleges and Universities" will serve as a basis for discussion and decision for all members of the academic community.

I. THE STUDENT AS A MEMBER OF THE ACADEMIC COMMUNITY

The student's freedom to learn is a complement of the faculty member's freedom to teach. An academic community dedicated to its ideals will safeguard the one as vigorously as it does the other.

A. Admission Policies

Admission to college should not be granted or denied on the basis of ethnic origin, race, religion, or political belief or affiliation. In order to achieve genuine equality of educational opportunity, colleges may, in respect to persons previously denied opportunity for equal educational advantage, properly apply standards and methods of evaluating applications different from those used with other applicants, as long as these standards and methods are reasonably designed to increase equality of educational opportunity. Massive compensatory programs for educationally deprived students should be simultaneously instituted.

B.   Freedom in the Classroom
Free and open discussion, speculation and investigation are basic to academic freedom. Students as well as teachers should be free to present their own opinions and findings. Teachers should evaluate student performance with scrupulous adherence to professional standards and without prejudice to the expression of views that may be controversial or unorthodox.

C.   Safeguarding the Privileged Student-Teacher Relationship
The essential safeguard of academic freedom is mutual trust and the realization by both student and teacher that their freedom is reciprocal. Any abrogation of or restriction on the academic freedom of the one will, inevitably, adversely affect the other.

1. *Inquiries by Outside Agencies.*   Because the student-teacher relationship is a privileged one, the student does not expect that the views he expresses, either orally or in writing, and either in or outside the classroom, will be reported by his professors beyond the walls of the college community. If he anticipated that anything he said or wrote might be disclosed, he might not feel free to express his thoughts and ideas and the critical inquiry, probing and investigation essential to a free academy might well be impaired.

The following standards are recommended as general guidelines: when questioned directly by representatives of government agencies or by prospective employers of any kind, public or private, or by investigative agencies or other persons, or indirectly by the institution's administrative officers in behalf of such agencies, a teacher may safely answer questions which he finds clearly concerned with the student's competence and fitness for the job. There is always the chance, however, that even questions of this kind will inadvertently cause the teacher to violate academic privacy. Questions and answers in written form make it easier to avoid pitfalls, but the teacher's alertness is always essential. Ordinarily, questions relating to the student's academic performance as, for example, the ability to write clearly, to solve problems, to reason well, to direct projects—pose no threat to educational privacy. But questions relating to the student's loyalty and patriotism, his political, religious, moral or social beliefs and attitudes, his general outlook, his private life may, if answered, violate the student's academic freedom and jeopardize the student-teacher relationship.

As a safeguard against the danger of placing the student in an unfavorable light with government agencies or employers of any category, teachers may preface each questionnaire with a brief *pro forma* statement that the academic policy to which they subscribe makes it inadvisable to answer certain types of questions about any or all students. Once this academic policy becomes widespread, presumptive inferences about individual students will no longer be made by employers.

Even when the student requests his teacher to disclose information other than relating to his academic performance because he thinks it would be to his advantage, such disclosure should not be made since disclosure in individual cases would raise doubts about students who had made no such request. A satisfactory principle, therefore, would foreclose disclosure in all cases.

Faculty senates or other representative faculty bodies, it is hoped, will take cognizance of the teacher-disclosure problem, recommend action which will leave inviolate the teacher-student relationship, and protect the privacy of the student. (See VII., "Confidentiality of Student Records.")

2. Use of Electronic Recording Devices. Television cameras, tape recorders and similar devices are being used with increasing frequency for educational purposes in colleges and universities. The use of such equipment in classrooms, in an ethical manner and for legitimate educational purposes, is not to be criticized. Caution must be exercised, however, to prevent the misuse of sight and sound recordings where they are likely to inhibit free and open discussion by teacher and student. Students who wish to use tape recorders for the purpose of recording class lectures and/or discussions should do so only with the explicit knowledge and consent of the teacher and participants, and then only for that purpose. A faculty-student committee should establish guidelines for the use of electronic recording devices and for the disposition of records which are made.

D. The Student's Role in the Formulation of Academic Policy
Colleges and universities should take whatever steps are necessary to enable student representatives to participate in an effective

capacity with the faculty and administration in determining at every level, beginning with the departmental, such basic educational policies as course offerings and curriculum; the manner of grading; class size; standards for evaluating the performance of faculty members; and the relative allocation of the institution's resources among its various educational programs. Determination of what constitutes participation in an effective capacity in specific areas of decision-making may be assessed by individual institutions in accordance with reasonable standards. Student participation in some areas may be solely advisory, while in other areas, a voting role would be appropriate.

E. The Ethics of Scholarship
So that students may become fully aware of the ethics of scholarship, the faculty should draw up a clear statement as to what constitutes plagiarism, setting forth principles the students will understand and respect. This should be made available to students. Any student charged with such a violation should be accorded a due process hearing as outlined in Chapter V.

II. EXTRA-CURRICULAR ACTIVITIES — Students receive their college education not only in the classroom but also in out-of-class activities which they themselves organize through their association with fellow students, the student press, student organizations and in other ways. It is vital, therefore, that their freedom as campus citizens be respected and ensured.

A. Student Government
Student government in the past has had as one of its chief functions the regulation of student-sponsored activities, organizations, publications, etc. In exercising this function, no student government should be permitted to allocate resources so as to bar or intimidate any campus organization or publication nor make regulations which violate basic principles of academic freedom and civil liberties.

1. Election Procedures. Delegates to the student government should be elected by democratic process by the student body and should not represent merely clubs or organizations. Designation of officers, committees, and boards should also be by democratic process, should be non-discriminatory, and should not be subject either to administrative or faculty approval. Any enrolled student should be eligible for election to student office. In universities, graduate students should be afforded the opportunity to participate in student government.

2. *Funding.* Operational funds should be supplied by the students themselves or the college administration. No student government, nor its national affiliate, should be covertly subsidized by any governmental agency.

B. Student Clubs and Societies

1. *The Right to Organize.* Students should be free, without restraint by either the college administration or the student government, to organize and join campus clubs or associations for educational, political, social, religious or cultural purposes. No such organization should discriminate on grounds of race, religion, color or national origin. The administration should not discriminate against a student because of membership in any campus organization.

The guidelines in this section apply to student organizations that seek official university recognition, subsidy, or free use of university facilities. They do not necessarily apply to off-campus organizations or those which do not have these privileges. (See Section III. B., Students' Political Freedom Off-Campus.)

2. *Registration and Disclosure.* A procedure for official recognition of student organizations may be established by the student government. The group applying for recognition may be required only to submit the names of its officers and, if considered advisable, an affidavit that the organization is composed of students and stating their number if related to funding. The names of officers should not be disclosed without the consent of the individuals involved. The fact of affiliation with any extramural association should not, in itself, bar a group from recognition, but disclosure of such fact may be required.

3. *Use of Campus Facilities.* Meeting rooms and other campus facilities should be made available to student organizations on a non-discriminatory basis as far as their primary use for educational purposes permits. Bulletin boards should be provided for the use of student organizations; school-wide circulation of all notices and leaflets should be permitted.

4. *Advisers for Organizations.* No student organization should be required to have a faculty adviser, but if it wishes one, it should be free to choose one for itself. An adviser should consult with and counsel the organization but should have no authority or responsibility to regulate or control its activities.

C. *Student-sponsored Forums*
Students should have the right to assemble, to select speakers and guests, and to discuss issues of their choice. It should be clear to the public that an invitation to a speaker does not imply approval of the speaker's views by either the student group or the college administration. Students should enjoy the same right as other citizens to hear different points of view and draw their own conclusions. When a student group wishes to hear a controversial or socially unpopular speaker, the college should not require that a spokesman for an opposing viewpoint be scheduled either simultaneously or on a subsequent occasion.

D. *Student Publications*
All student publications—college newspapers, literary and humor magazines, academic periodicals and yearbooks—should enjoy full freedom of the press, and not be restricted by either the administration or the student government. This should be the practice even though most college publications, except for the relatively few university dailies which are financially autonomous, are dependent on the administration's favor for the use of campus facilities, and are subsidized either directly or indirectly by a tax on student funds. Student initiation of competing publications should not be discouraged.

College newspapers—and so far as appropriate, all student publications—whether or not supported from student fees or other resources of the college, should impartially cover news and should serve as a forum for opposing views on controversial issues as do public newspapers. They may also be expected to deal in news columns and editorials with the political and social issues that are relevant to the concerns of the students as citizens of the larger community. Neither the faculty, administration, board of trustees nor legislature should be immune from criticism.

Wherever possible a student newspaper should be financially and physically separate from the college, existing as a legally independent corporation. The college would then be absolved from legal liability for the publication and bear no direct responsibility to the community for the views expressed. In those cases where college papers do not enjoy financial independence, no representative of the college should exercise veto power in the absence of a specific finding of potential libel as determined by an impartial legal authority. In no case, however, should the decision of the editor or editors be challenged or overruled simply because of pressure from alumni, the board of trustees, the state legislature, the college administration or the student government.

Where there is a college publications board, it should be composed of at least a majority of students selected by the student government or council, or by some other democratic method. Should the board, or in case the paper has no board, an *ad hoc* committee selected by the faculty and student government, maintain that the editor has been guilty of deliberate malice or deliberate distortion, the validity of this charge should be determined through due process.

E. Radio and Television

Campus radio and television stations should enjoy and exercise the same editorial freedom as the college press. Stations whose signals go beyond the campus operate under a license granted by the Federal Communications Commission and, therefore, must conform to the applicable regulations of the Commission.

F. Artistic Presentations

The same freedom from censorship enjoyed by other communications media should be extended to on-campus artistic presentations.

III. STUDENTS' POLITICAL FREEDOM American college students possess the same right to freedom of speech, assembly and association as do other residents of the United States. They are also subject to the same obligations and responsibilities as persons who are not members of the academic communities.

A. On-campus

Students should be free through organized action on campus to register their political views or their disapprobation of university policies, but within peaceful limits. The use of force on a college campus — whether by students, the campus police, or outside police called in by the administration—is always to be regretted. Outside police should not be summoned to a campus to deal with internal problems unless essential and unless all other techniques have clearly failed. (See V.D., Law Enforcement on the Campus.)

Failure of communication among administration, faculty and students has been a recurrent cause of campus crises. Prompt consultation by the administration with faculty and student spokesmen may serve to prevent potentially disastrous confrontations which disrupt the orderly processes of the institution.

1. *Ground Rules.* Picketing, demonstrations, sit-ins, or student strikes, provided they are conducted in an orderly and non-obstructive manner, are a legitimate mode of expression, whether politically motivated or directed against the college administration, and should not be prohibited. Demonstrators, however, have no right to deprive others of the opportunity to speak or be heard; take hostages; physically obstruct the movement of others; or otherwise disrupt the educational or institutional processes in a way that interferes with the safety or freedom of others.

Students should be free, and no special permission be required, to distribute pamphlets or collect names for petitions concerned with campus or off-campus issues.

2. *Tripartite Regulations.* Regulations governing demonstrations should be made by a committee of administrators, representative faculty, and democratically selected students. The regulations should be drawn so as to protect the students' First Amendment rights to the fullest extent possible and, at the same time, ensure against disruption of the academic process as, for example, by the use of high volume loudspeakers or other techniques which curtail the freedom of others.

B. *Off-campus*

Student participation in off-campus activities such as peace marches, civil rights demonstrations, draft protests, picketing, boycotts, political campaigns, public rallies, non-campus publications and acts of civil disobedience is not the legitimate concern of the college or university. (See V.C., "Double Penalties")

Students, like teachers, have the right to identify themselves as members of a particular academic community. But they also have the moral obligation not to misrepresent the views of others in their academic community.

College students should be free to organize their personal lives and determine their private behavior free from institutional interference. In the past many colleges, with the approval of parents and the acquiescence of students, have played the role of surrogate parents. This function is now being strongly challenged. An increasing number of institutions today recognize that students, as part of the maturing process, must be permitted to assume responsibility for their private lives—even if, in some instances, their philosophies or conduct are at variance with traditional standards.

The college community should not regard itself as the arbiter of personal behavior or morals, as long as the conduct does not interfere with the rights of others. Regulation is appropriate only if necessary to protect the health, safety, and academic pursuits of members of the academic community.

Some specific areas of personal behavior:

1. *Student Residences.* Although on-campus living is often regarded as an important part of the total educational experience, it should not be made compulsory.

2. *Personal Appearance.* Dress and grooming are modes of personal expression and taste which should be left to the individual except for reasonable requirements related to health and safety, and except for ceremonial occasions the nature of which requires particular dress or grooming.

3. *Pregnancy.* If a student is pregnant she should be free to decide, in consultation with her physician or with college health authorities, when to take leave of her studies.

4. *Search and Seizure.* A student's locker should not be opened, nor his room searched, without his consent except in conformity with the spirit of the Fourth Amendment which requires that a warrant first be obtained on a showing of probable cause, supported by oath or affirmation, and particularly describing the things to be seized.

Regulations governing student conduct should be in harmony with and essential to the fulfillment of the college's educational objectives. Students should participate fully and effectively in formulating and adjudicating college regulations governing student conduct. Reasonable procedures should be established and followed in enforcing discipline.

A. Enacting and Promulgating Regulations

1. Regulations should be clear and unambiguous. Phrases such as "conduct unbecoming a student," or "actions against the best interests of the college," should be avoided because they allow too much latitude for interpretation.

2. The range of penalties for the violation of regulations should be clearly specified.

3. Regulations should be published and circulated to the entire academic community.

B. Academic Due Process

1. Minor infractions of college regulations, penalized by small fines or reprimands which do not become part of a student's permanent record, may be handled summarily by the appropriate administrative, faculty or student officer. However, the student should have the right to appeal.

2. In the case of infractions of college regulations which may lead to more serious penalties, such as suspension, expulsion, or notation on a student's permanent record, the student is entitled to formal procedures in order to prevent a miscarriage of justice.[1]

These procedures should include a formal hearing by a student-faculty or a student judicial committee. No member of the hearing committee who is involved in the particular case should sit in judgment.

Prior to the hearing the student should be:

a. advised in writing of the charges against him, including a summary of the evidence upon which the charges are based.

---

[1] A student may be suspended only in exceptional circumstances involving danger to health, safety or disruption of the educational process. Within twenty-four hours of suspension, or whenever possible prior to such action, the student should be given a written statement explaining why the suspension could not await a hearing.

b. advised that he is entitled to be represented and advised at all times during the course of the proceedings by a person of his own choosing, including outside counsel.

c. advised of the procedures to be followed at the hearing.

At the hearing, the student (or his representative) and the member of the academic community bringing charges (or his representative) should each have the right to testify, although the student should not be compelled to do so, and each should have the right to examine and cross-examine witnesses and to present documentary and other evidence in support of respective contentions. The college administration should make available to the student such authority as it may possess to require the presence of witnesses and the production of documents at the hearing. A full record should be taken at the hearing and it should be made available in identical form to the hearing panel, the administration and the student. After the hearing is closed, the panel should adjudicate the matter before it with reasonable promptness and submit its finding and conclusions in writing. Copies thereof should be made available in identical form, and at the same time, to the administration and the student. The cost should be met by the institution.

3. After completion of summary or formal proceedings, the right of appeal should be permitted only to the student. On appeal, the decision of the hearing Board should be affirmed, modified or reversed but the penalty, if any, not increased.

C. Double Penalties

Respect for the presumption of innocence requires that a college not impose academic sanctions for the sole reason that a student is or has been involved in criminal proceedings.

A student charged with or convicted of a crime should not be subject to academic sanctions by the college for the same conduct unless the offense is of such a nature that the institution needs to impose its own sanction upon the student for the protection of other students or to safeguard the academic process. Where there is a possibility that testimony and other evidence at a college hearing would be subject to disclosure by way of subpoena in a subsequent court proceeding, college disciplinary hearings should be postponed to safeguard the student's right to a fair determination in the criminal proceeding.

Colleges should be especially scrupulous to avoid further sanctions attendant upon criminal convictions:

a. for conduct that should have been entitled to the protection of the First Amendment even if the student's First Amendment claim was not recognized by the Court which convicted him: for example, draft card burning.

b. for conduct which, while validly punishable, was a peaceable act of social, political or religious protest that did not threaten the academic process: for example, a trespass or breach of the peace.

c. for refusal to accept military service. (Students who have chosen imprisonment as an alternative to military service should be eligible on release for readmission to a college or university without prejudice to opportunities for financial aid.)

D. Law Enforcement on the Campus
Police presence on the campus is detrimental to the educational mission of the university and should be avoided if at all possible. In those last-resort situations, where all efforts to resolve campus disorders internally have failed, the institution may have to invite police to the campus to maintain or restore public order.

Guidelines and procedures for summoning off-campus law enforcement authorities should be established by a committee representing the administration, faculty and students. This committee should also determine the duties and prerogatives of campus security officers.

The proper function of law officers in crime detection cannot be impeded. Members of the academic community, however, should not function surreptitiously on campus as agents for law enforcement authorities. Such action is harmful to the climate of free association essential to a college community.

VI. STUDENTS AND THE MILITARY Colleges have an educational function to perform and should not become an adjunct of the military. Such a development would constitute a threat to their survival as centers of critical inquiry.

A. Extent of Cooperation with the Selective Service System
Information concerning the student's enrollment and standing

should be submitted to Selective Service by the college only at the request of the student.[2]

B. *Unconstitutional Reclassification*

Draft boards should be considered to have violated the First Amendment when they cancel the deferment of students because they have participated in anti-war demonstrations.[3]

C. *Recruitment on Campus*

Unless a college bars all occupational recruitment of students, the Army, Navy and Air Force should be allowed the same campus facilities as other government agencies and private corporations.[4]

D. *ROTC*[5]

On campuses where Reserve Officer Training Corps programs exist, student enrollment should be on a voluntary basis. Academic credit should be granted only for those ROTC courses which are acceptable to and under the control of the regular faculty. ROTC

[2] In a letter to the ACLU, dated December 2, 1968, Deputy Director of Selective Service, Daniel O. Omer, stated: "The responsibility for keeping a selective service board informed regarding the current student status of a registrant is upon the registrant himself and not upon the college."

[3] The ACLU has protested as unconstitutional the recommendation to draft boards from Selective Service Director General Lewis B. Hershey, on October 26, 1967, that any student adjudged to have interfered "illegally" with draft processes or military recruitment be deprived of his deferment and reclassified on the ground that his action was not "in the national interest." In a case brought by the ACLU *(Gutknecht v. U.S.,* 38 U.S. L.W. 4075 Jan., 1969), the Supreme Court ruled that draft boards do not have legal power to accelerate the induction of young men because they turn in their draft cards or otherwise violate the Selective Service Act.

[4] Since on-campus recruitment is essentially a service to students and not central to the educational purposes of the university, colleges may prohibit all recruitment as a matter of institutional policy. But if outside recruitment is allowed, the ACLU believes it should be on a non-discriminatory basis and in accordance with established policies and procedures. Selective exclusions, arising primarily from a political controversy, that deny students access to particular recruiters are discriminatory in their applications and suggest a possible infringement of the spirit of the equal protection clause of the Constitution.

[5] Without taking a position on the question of whether ROTC programs should exist on college campuses, the ACLU has concluded that such programs should comply with the standards stated above. Programs that fail to meet these standards threaten to undermine the value of free inquiry and academic autonomy which are at the heart of academic freedom and should, therefore, be eliminated in institutions of higher learning.

instructors should not hold academic rank unless they are members of an academic department subject to the regular procedures of appointment and removal. All ROTC programs should fully observe ACLU policies regarding the maintenance of records which relate or refer to social, religious, or political views or associations of the student, as set forth in this pamphlet. (See VII. Confidentiality of Student Records.)

1. No record, including that of conviction in a court of law, should be noted in a student's file unless there is a demonstrable need for it which is reasonably related to the basic purposes and necessities of the university.[7] Relevant records, such as academic, disciplinary, medical and psychiatric, should be maintained in separate files.

2. No mention should be made in any university record of a student's religious or political beliefs or association.

3. Access to student records should be confined to authorized university personnel who require access in connection with the performance of their duties. All persons having access to student records should be instructed that the information contained therein must be kept confidential, and should be required to sign and date their adherence to this procedure.

4. Particular safeguards should be established with respect to medical (including psychiatric) records. Such records should be subject to the same rules of confidentiality as apply for non-students and should not be construed to be 'student records' for purposes of this section.

5. Persons outside the university could not have access to student academic records without the student's written permission, or to

---

[6] The guidelines recommended for teachers in responding to inquiries by outside agencies are also applicable to this section. (See Section I.-C.,1.)

[7] In October, 1966, the United States Civil Service Commission dropped all inquiries concerning arrest from its federal employment application forms, stating that such queries "infringed the spirit of due process and was particularly hurtful to those citizens who were arrested not for committing ordinary crimes, but as reprisal for exercising First Amendment rights of speech and association in civil right demonstrations."

any other records, except in response to a constitutionally valid subpoena.[8]

6. The rules regarding the keeping and release of records should be made known and available to the university community.

---

[8] The term "constitutionally valid subpoena" is used to exclude subpoenas based on political investigation or other situations which, in the opinion of the Union, are unconstitutional.

For example, in August 1966, the then U.S. House Committee on Un-American activities subpoenaed from the University of Michigan, the University of California at Berkeley, and Stanford University, copies of certification or statements of membership filed with the university by campus political organizations known to be critical of America's involvement in the war in Vietnam. The ACLU sent a letter to over 1,000 university and college presidents protesting this action by HUAC as one of the most serious breaches of academic freedom in recent decades and called upon institutions to resist, in every possible legal manner, such subpoenas if extended to other universities and colleges.

In a statement released July, 1967, the American Council on Education, referring to the HUAC subpoenas, said: "It is . . . in the interests of the entire academic community to protect vigilantly its traditions of free debate and investigation by safeguarding students and their records from pressure that may curtail their liberties . . . Colleges and universities should discontinue the maintenance of membership lists of student organizations, especially those related to matters of political belief or action. If rosters of this kind do not exist, they cannot be subpoenaed, and the institution is therefore freed of some major elements of conflict and from the risks of contempt proceedings or a suit."

This issue is of continuing concern in light of the subpoenas issued in May, 1969, by the Senate Permanent Subcommittee on Investigations to several institutions (including Harvard, Columbia, Cornell, Stanford and Boston Universities; the University of California at Berkeley, Brooklyn College, and City College of the City University of New York) for information on persons and groups allegedly involved in campus disorders.

SOURCE: *Academic Freedom and Civil Liberties of Students in Colleges and Universities,* American Civil Liberties Union, April 1970.

Appendix F: Cuyahoga Community College — Rights and Responsibilities of the College Community

Herein, our purpose is to set forth the individual rights and responsibilities of all associated with Cuyahoga Community College. It is believed that these elements are inseparable—that one does not exist without the other, for the protection of an individual's rights is the responsibility of those with whom he associates. One's rights are fully coextensive with, but do not exceed, the area in which he regards it as his responsibility to insure the rights of others. If we are to maintain the right to teach and to learn, to express our opinions freely and to move freely, we in turn assume the responsibility of protecting these rights for all others.

It is the desire of the Board that the promulgation of this policy and the precedents established to date during the short history of the College (which have fostered mutual respect and individual growth) will further develop a campus environment conducive to the intellectual and social growth of all at Cuyahoga Community College.

The policy contained in this publication was prepared by a committee consisting of Board members, administrators, faculty and students during the latter half of 1968. It was adopted by the Board of Trustees on December 19, 1968.

INDIVIDUAL RIGHTS & RESPONSIBILITIES

Section 1. Policy and Standards. The Board of Cuyahoga Community College affirms that the freedom to teach and freedom to learn are inseparable facets of academic freedom; that the freedom to learn depends upon providing appropriate opportunities and conditions, particularly those fostered and observed on the College campuses; and that each member of the College community shares the responsibility to secure these general conditions conducive to the freedom to learn. The Board further affirms that these conditions have been established and shall be fostered and observed to encourage open discussion by all members of the College community and that it is the responsibility of each member of the College community to use this opportunity for exchange of ideas, in a manner conducive with such conditions, and to endeavor to exercise their freedom with maturity and judgment.

The Board confirms the policy of the College that channels of communication between and among the constituent parts of the College community shall be kept open and unimpeded to assist in the understanding of points of view, objectives, desires, suggestions and grievances, and to that end the administration and faculty, at all times and to the fullest extent practical, shall continue to provide full opportunity to students and others of the College community for the orderly presentation of their views, objectives, desires, suggestions and grievances.

The Board declares that all members of the College community shall be free to support their convictions by means which do not violate individual rights and freedoms nor disrupt the regular operation of the College or of College activities.

The foregoing freedoms of all members of the College community will be successfully preserved by the exercise of considerateness, reason and restraint by each member of the College community, and it is the responsibility of each to assist in the protection of the freedoms of all and to assist in fostering conditions under which the essential teaching and learning processes of the College may be conducted in order and dignity and with fairness to all.

The foregoing are the basic policies and standards for the support and promotion of which the rules and regulations hereinafter are set forth, and such rules and regulations shall be interpreted, administered and applied consistent with such policies and standards, giving full meaning to the clear import of such rules and regulations.

Section 2. Definitions. In addition to the words and terms elsewhere defined herein, the following words and terms as used in this Resolution shall have the following meanings unless the context or use indicates another or different meaning or intent:

"College activities" means any and all functions and activities of the College conducted under the jurisdiction of the Board or the President, or activities or use of College facilities authorized under the College rules and regulations.

"College community" means the College's students, faculty (which includes faculty, administrators, counselors, librarians, and all other professional personnel), staff, and employees, together with their respective organizations recognized by the College.

"College rules and regulations" means all rules, regulations, standards of conduct, policies, conditions, procedures and requirements established by the Board or by the District President or by such officer or other official or authorized body as the Board or District President may designate for such purpose, and shall include, without limitation thereto, those set forth in the policies of the Board, the policy and procedures of the College, the student handbooks, and under authority thereof, and including those provided in this Resolution.

"College facilities" means any of the campuses of the College, including any lands, buildings, equipment and sites owned or leased by the College and used in the operation of the Cuyahoga Community College.

"Conduct Committee" or *"Committee"* means the committee for each campus of the College provided for in Section 11 of this Resolution.

"Conduct Advisor" or *"Advisor"* means each Campus President or his designee.

"Designee" means such one or more administrative or faculty personnel as shall have been designated by the official named to perform the particular function.

"Established procedures" means those applicable procedures established under the College rules and regulations.

"Person" means any member of the College community and any person who is a guest or visitor of the College or any person who is on College facilities.

"Student" means all persons who are registered as students of the College under any classification as to course, subject matter, or as full or part-time, day or evening, as well as other persons who may not be registered, but who attend courses or other educational programs at the campus as a part of the curriculum of the College or as a part of the community services program of the College.

"Admonition" means an oral or written warning issued to a student pursuant to Section 8 of this Resolution, but which does not become a part of his academic record.

"Probation" means that the student is precluded from representing the College in any official capacity, including, without limitation, intercollegiate activities and athletics or student offices and office in any student organization, and may include suspension of other specific privileges, other than class attendance and the taking of examinations, as determined in the imposition of such probation, all for a period of time of not less than one week nor more than one College academic year.

"Suspension" means that the student is fully separated from the College and foreclosed from participation in all College activities, excepting those as may, but need not be, excepted in the imposition of suspension, for a specified period of time of not less than one week nor more than one College academic year, after which he shall be eligible to return to enrollment at the College. Suspended students may be denied access to all College facilities upon a determination by the Campus President that such denial is necessary to avoid a substantial risk of disrupting the orderly conduct of lawful activities of the College. Suspended students are not entitled to a fee refund and shall be assigned the grades which would be appropriate if they were withdrawing voluntarily, except in the case of academic dishonesty, in which instance a failing grade may be made a part of the disciplinary action.

"Dismissal" means the involuntary and indefinite total separation of a student from the College. Dismissed students may be denied access to all College facilities upon a determination by the Campus President that such denial is necessary to avoid a substantial risk of disrupting the orderly conduct of lawful activities of the College. Dismissed students are not entitled to a fee refund and shall be assigned the grades which would be appropriate if they were withdrawing voluntarily, except in the case of academic dishonesty, in which instance a failing grade may be part of the disciplinary action. Dismissed students may be reinstated only upon receipt of a petition for reinstatement together with a favorable action on that petition by the campus admissions board.

"Sanction" means admonition, probation, suspension, or any combination thereof, or dismissal.

Any reference to an officer herein, shall include his successor in office and, in case of change in the title of the office, shall mean the person performing most of the functions of that office as presently described in the College rules and regulations.

Section 3. Use of College Facilities.   (a) The authorization to use College facilities by members of the College community and community groups for meetings and other activities shall be subject to the established procedures, and such procedures shall be complied with before such meetings or other activities are announced, or if not announced then before the same are convened or commenced.

(b) College facilities shall be made available for use during the regularly scheduled instructional day if the proposed meeting or the proposed activity is consonant with the broad educational functions of the College, and if the use of the College facility for such meeting or activity does not conflict with other previously scheduled use and is requested by one of the following:

(i) a member of the College faculty or staff,

(ii) an authorized officer of a recognized College related activity, e.g., the Faculty Wives and Alumni Association, for its use,

(iii) an authorized officer of a recognized student organization, for its use,

(iv) one or more students for purposes permitted under established procedures.

(c) Members of the College community and their respective organizations may invite and hear any person of their own choosing in or on College facilities made available for such purposes under this section. Such events shall be conducted in a manner consistent with educational objectives and standards of the College and the College rules and regulations. Sponsorship of guest speakers shall not necessarily imply approval or endorsement by the sponsoring individual or group of the views expressed.

(d) The authorized use of College facilities by members of the College community and guest speakers, and the freedom accorded to members of the College community to express their views and espouse causes, in no way implies endorsement by the College, and it is the responsibility of such persons to exercise care to avoid such implication.

Section 4. Prescribed Conduct.   No person shall on or in College facilities or in connection with College activities violate or act contrary to the College rules and regulations. Without limiting the foregoing prohibition, the following conduct shall be deemed to violate College rules and regulations:

(a) Threatening, attempting, or committing physical violence against any person.

(b) Preventing or attempting to prevent any student from attending class or any other College activities.

(c) Preventing or attempting to prevent any person or any visitor to or guest of the College, on or off College facilities, from lawfully entering, leaving, or using any College facility.

(d) Preventing or attempting to prevent any member of the College community from carrying out his duties or any person from carrying on any lawful business or purpose he may have while on College facilities.

(e) Blocking pedestrian or vehicular traffic.

(f) Preventing, impeding or disrupting, or attempting to prevent, impede or disrupt, any College activity.

(g) Violating on-campus traffic rules and regulations.

(h) Endangering personal health, safety and welfare of himself or any other person.

(i) Damaging or destroying College facilities.

(j) Violating, while on College facilities, any municipal, county, state, or federal law, statute or ordinance.

(k) Using language that is degrading or abusive to any person.

(l) Preventing or attempting to prevent any guest speaker from being heard or causing such speaker to suspend or interrupt his presentation.

(m) Violating any suspension or probation or the conditions thereof.

(n) Entering upon College facilities other than for the purpose of carrying on in good faith proper functions as a member of the College community, an authorized guest speaker, or a visitor of the College.

(o) Forging, altering, or using College documents, records, or instruments with intent to defraud or furnishing false information to the College.

Section 5. Violation by Any Person.   Any person who violates or acts contrary to the College rules and regulations shall be subject to physical ejection from College facilities, and any other sanctions provided under College rules and regulations.

Section 6. Violation by Students.   A student who violates or acts contrary to the College rules and regulations shall be subject to the sanctions of admonition, probation, suspension, or any combination thereof, or dismissal; provided that this Section does not negate any penalty provided therefor under any other College rules and regulations. A student who is determined to have violated or acted contrary to College rules and regulations while on probation must receive the sanction of suspension for a minimum of the remainder of the quarter in which the violation occurs.

Section 7. Initiation of Disciplinary Proceedings. Any member of the College community may report instances of alleged misconduct to the Conduct Advisor.

Section 8. Student Conference. When it comes to the attention of a Conduct Advisor that a student has violated or acted contrary to the College rules or regulations, such Advisor shall first give such student an opportunity to confer with him concerning such conduct prior to instituting proceedings before the Conduct Committee by notice as hereinafter provided. At such conference, the student shall have the opportunity to explain his conduct.

(a) If the Advisor determines that the conduct warrants a sanction of admonition or probation for not more than three months of the academic schedule, he may proceed to impose such sanction.

(b) If probation for longer than three months, suspension or dismissal is deemed appropriate by the Advisor, the student shall have the option of (1) accepting the sanction proposed by the Advisor or (2) requesting adjudication of the case in a hearing before the Conduct Committee, as hereafter provided.

(1) If the student chooses option (1), accepting the sanction deemed appropriate by the Advisor, the nature of the sanction thus agreed upon shall be set forth in writing, signed by each, and a copy thereof given to the student, whereupon the sanction shall be imposed in accordance with its terms. Such writing shall identify the claimed conduct, and the student may not thereafter be subject to further proceedings under section 8, 9, and 10 hereof on account of said conduct. The acceptance of the sanction and signing of such writing by the student shall not for any purpose constitute or be deemed to constitute an admission that the student engaged in such conduct, but the sanction shall be final.

(2) If the student chooses option (2), requesting adjudication of the case in a hearing before the Conduct Committee, or if the student fails to attend a conference with the Advisor at the time designated by him, or if the student and Advisor fail to agree in the manner aforesaid on the appropriate sanction to be applied, in cases where the Advisor in his sole judgment determines that there is reasonable cause to believe that the claimed misconduct did occur and that the appropriate sanction for such misconduct, if it did occur, should be more severe than admonition or probation for three months of the academic year, the Advisor shall give written notice of the claimed misconduct to the student and cause a copy thereof to be filed with the Conduct Committee.

(c) At any time prior to the final disposition of a claimed violation of the College rules and regulations by a student, the Conduct Advisor or the President may order suspension of the student until such final disposition, if the Advisor or the Campus President determines in his discretion that such temporary suspension is advisable for reasons relating to the physical or emotional safety and well being of the student, or for reasons related to the safety of members of the College community or of College facilities. Written notice of such temporary suspension and the reasons for it shall be given to the student and, in case it has not yet heard the matter, then also to the Conduct Committee. The Advisor or the Campus President, whichever has imposed such temporary suspension, may at any time terminate such temporary suspension.

Section 9. Conduct Committee Hearing.   Upon receipt of copy of notice by the Conduct Advisor of claimed misconduct of a student, pursuant to Section 9 hereof, the Conduct Committee, or its appropriate representative for such purpose, shall promptly set a hearing at an early date, giving priority to cases where temporary suspension has been imposed, and notify the student and the Advisor in writing of the time and place of such hearing. Such hearing shall be set for a time no later than twenty calendar days after receipt of such notice by the Committee unless under the rules of the campus a continuance is granted at the request of the student. At such hearing the Conduct Committee shall hear information forming the basis for the notice and the student shall be given fair opportunity to present his position and information and explanations germane to the claimed misconduct forming the basis of the notice and affecting the question of whether he has acted contrary to or in violation of College rules and regulations and the question of sanctions, if any, which are appropriate. The student may have the assistance of any advisor of his own choice at such hearing. Failure of the student to appear at the hearing shall not require suspension of the hearing nor prevent the Committee from deciding the case. The Committee may consider prior instances of imposition of sanctions against such student in determining the appropriate sanction for the misconduct at issue, but not for the purpose of determining whether the misconduct at issue took place unless it be an element of the claimed violation of the College rules and regulations at issue, and may receive information of such prior sanctions in the notice given under Section 8 or any time in the hearing. The Conduct Committee may establish further rules pertaining to the conduct of fair and impartial hearings, including rules relating to notices to be given and the orderly submission of information and arguments, and, in general, the conduct of the hearing and of parties and persons presenting information to the Committee.

On the basis of information presented, the Conduct Committee shall determine whether or not the student violated or acted contrary to College rules and regulations and if they find that he did, the Committee shall determine the sanction or sanctions to be imposed, provided that for good cause shown, the Committee may suspend or modify the sanction.

The hearing shall be attended by at least a majority of the Conduct Committee. No adjourned hearing shall be reconvened except in the presence of at least six members of the Committee who were in attendance throughout the prior sessions of the hearing. If fewer than six members of the Committee are in attendance, such hearing shall be adjourned and reconvened at another time. The Committee's decision shall be that which is concurred with by at least a majority of the Committee in attendance throughout the hearing and only those members who have been in attendance throughout the meetings may vote thereon.

Section 10. Appeal. The Campus President, or his designee, shall have general supervision over all matters of student discipline. Rules of the Conduct Committee shall be subject to his prior approval.

Determinations of the Conduct Committee in particular cases

shall be final, provided that the student have the right to appeal to the Campus President by filing with him a written notice of appeal not more than ten calendar days after announcement of the decision of the Conduct Committee. Upon such appeal, the Campus President or his designee may make such investigation as he deems appropriate and he may return the case to the Committee for a new hearing and determination, or he may reduce or withdraw the sanction, or if he determines that the sanction that was imposed by the Committee was not sufficiently severe, he shall return the matter to the Committee with his recommendation, whereupon at least a majority of the same members of the Committee who were in attendance throughout the hearing shall reconsider the sanction and make a final determination, imposing a sanction not greater than that recommended by the Campus President nor less than that previously determined by the Committee, for which there shall be no further appeal.

The Campus President, or his designee may, on his own initiative, within ten calendar days after the announcement of the determination of the Conduct Committee in any case, give written notice to the student and to the Conduct Committee of his intention to review the determination of the Committee. He may, upon such review, conduct such investigation as he deems appropriate, and he may return the case to the Committee for a new hearing and determination, or he may reduce or withdraw the sanction, or if he determines that the sanction is not sufficiently severe he may return the case to the Conduct Committee with his recommendation, whereupon at least a majority of the same members of the Committee who were in attendance throughout the hearing shall reconsider the sanction and make a final determination, imposing a sanction not greater than that recommended by the Campus President nor less than that previously determined by the Committee, from which there shall be no further appeal. Upon such review, the Campus President, or his designee, also may reverse the determination of the Committee and may impose or increase the sanction, provided that he shall not reverse a determination by the Committee that the student did not violate or act contrary to the College rules and regulations and shall not increase the sanction determined by the Committee unless he shall have first provided the student with a fair opportunity to be heard by him as to all matters relating to the claimed misconduct and to the sanction. Upon any such appeal to or review by the Campus

President or his designee, he and the student may agree upon an appropriate sanction in the same manner and with the same effect as the agreed sanction under Section 8(b) (1) hereof. Except as otherwise indicated, the determination of the Campus President or his designee shall be final. In cases in which the Campus President witnesses the alleged misconduct, the District President shall be substituted for the Campus President in all appeal procedures outlined in this section.

Section 11. Conduct Committee. On each campus of the College there shall be a Conduct Committee. Each Conduct Committee shall be comprised of eleven members and the membership of each Conduct Committee shall include six students of such campus, three instructional faculty of such campus, and two administrators of such campus. The method of selecting members of the Conduct Committee, their terms of offices, method of replacement, and other matters pertaining to the composition of the Conduct Committee shall be determined by the Campus Presidents. The Campus President may appoint student, faculty and administrative alternates to serve in the event of absences. He shall endeavor to assure that the Conduct Committee is broadly representative of the College community on the campus. The Conduct Committee shall have jurisdiction in cases of student conduct on its campus as provided in Sections 8 and 9 hereof. A member of the Conduct Committee who presents evidence as a witness in a hearing shall be disqualified from participating in Committee determinations for that hearing.

Section 12. Abatement of Danger. If in the conduct of any meeting or assembly on or in College facilities, conduct or incidents occur which cause or threaten to cause or present the risk of causing injury or damage to persons or property, or if such meeting or assembly is being conducted contrary to the College rules and regulations, the District President or the Campus Presidents, or designee of either, may order the termination of such meeting or assembly and the evacuation by all persons of the area, or of a prescribed area, or of all College facilities. No person shall fail to obey such order promptly.

Section 13. General Protection of College Facilities. The District President and the Vice-President for Finance and Business Affairs of the College are hereby directed and authorized to take all steps necessary, consistent with the College rules and regulations, to insure the safeguarding and protection of all College facilities. The District President, Executive Vice-President, Campus Presidents, Vice-President for Finance and Business Affairs, or in their absence, the individual then acting in such capacity, are hereby authorized to request assistance from municipal, county, state, or federal law enforcement agencies when, in their discretion, the College security officers and other members of the College community are unable to adequately protect College facilities or deal with incidents of violation of College rules and regulations.

Appendix G:
Harvard University —
Universitywide Statement
on Rights and Responsibilities

(This Statement, and the interpretation that follows it, were adopted on an interim basis by the Governing Boards on September 20, 1970.)

The central functions of an academic community are learning, teaching, research and scholarship. By accepting membership in the University, an individual joins a community ideally characterized by free expression, free inquiry, intellectual honesty, respect for the dignity of others, and openness to constructive change. The rights and responsibilities exercised within the community must be compatible with these qualities.

The rights of members of the University are not fundamentally different from those of other members of society. The University, however, has a special autonomy and reasoned dissent plays a particularly vital part in its existence. All members of the University have the right to press for action on matters of concern by any appropriate means. The University must affirm, assure and protect the rights of its members to organize and join political associations, convene and conduct public meetings, publicly demonstrate and picket in orderly fashion, advocate and publicize opinion by print, sign, and voice.

The University places special emphasis, as well, upon certain values which are essential to its nature as an academic community. Among these are freedom of speech and academic freedom, freedom from personal force and violence, and freedom of movement. Interference with any of these freedoms must be regarded as a serious violation of the personal rights upon which the community is based. Furthermore, although the administrative process and activities of the University cannot be ends in themselves, such functions are vital to the orderly pursuit of the work of all members of the University. Therefore, interference with members of the University in performance of their normal duties and activities must be regarded as unacceptable obstruction of the essential processes of the University. Theft or willful destruction of the property of the University or its members must also be considered an unacceptable violation of the rights of individuals or of the community as a whole.

Moreover, it is the responsibility of all members of the academic community to maintain an atmosphere in which violations of rights are unlikely to occur and to develop processes by which these rights are fully assured. In particular, it is the responsibility of officers of administration and instruction to be alert to the needs of the University community; to give full and fair hearing to reasoned expressions of grievances; and to respond promptly and in good faith to such expressions and to widely-expressed needs for change. In making decisions which concern the community as a whole or any part of the community, officers are expected to consult with those affected by the decisions. Failures to meet these responsibilities may be profoundly damaging to the life of the University. Therefore, the University community has the right to establish orderly procedures consistent with imperatives of academic freedom to assess the policies and assure the responsibility of those whose decisions affect the life of the University.

No violation of the rights of members of the University, nor any failure to meet responsibilities, should be interpreted as justifying any violation of the rights of members of the University. All members of the community — students and officers alike — should uphold the rights and responsibilities expressed in this Statement if the University is to be characterized by mutual respect and trust.

Interpretation
It is implicit in the language of the Statement on Rights and Responsibilities that intense personal harassment of such a character as to amount to grave disrespect for the dignity of others be regarded as an unacceptable violation of the personal rights on which the University is based.

Appendix H:
The University of North Carolina — Policies, Procedures, and Disciplinary Actions in Cases of Disruption of Educational Process

A thorough and conscientious effort, which involved University trustees, administrative officers, faculty members, and student representatives, has been made to improve and clarify the University's policies and procedures for dealing with disruptive conduct. Basic to this endeavor has been the goal of preserving the right of all individuals to engage in peaceful dissent while proscribing conduct intended to obstruct or disrupt the normal operations of the University. It is sincerely believed and earnestly hoped that the results will prove to be fair and equitable to all concerned.

POLICIES RELATING TO DISRUPTIVE CONDUCT The University of North Carolina has long honored the right of free discussion and expression, peaceful picketing and demonstrations, the right to petition and peaceably to assemble. That these rights are a part of the fabric of this institution is not questioned. They must remain secure. It is equally clear, however, that in a community of learning willful disruption of the educational process, destruction of property, and interference with the rights of other members of the community cannot be tolerated. Accordingly, it shall be the policy of the University to deal with any such disruption, destruction or interference promptly and effectively, but also fairly and impartially without regard to race, religion, sex or political beliefs.

Definition of Disruptive Conduct

(a) Any faculty member (the term "faculty member", wherever used in this Chapter V, shall include regular faculty members, full-time instructors, lecturers, and all other persons exempt from the North Carolina State Personnel System [Chapter 126 of the General Statutes as amended] who receive compensation for teaching, or other instructional functions, or research at the University), any graduate student engaged in the instructional program, or any student who, with the intent to obstruct or disrupt any normal operation or function of the University or any of its component institutions, engages, or incites others to engage, in individual or collective conduct which destroys or significantly damages any University property, or which impairs or threatens impairment of the physical well-being of any member of the University community, or which, because of its violent, forceful, threatening or intimidating nature or because it restrains freedom of lawful movement, otherwise prevents any member of the University community from conducting his normal activities within the University, shall be subject to prompt and appropriate disciplinary action, which may include suspension, expulsion, discharge or dismissal from the University.

The following, while not intended to be exclusive, illustrate the offenses encompassed herein, when done for the purpose of obstructing or disrupting any normal operation or function of the University or any of its component institutions: (1) occupation of any University building or part thereof with intent to deprive others of its normal use; (2) blocking the entrance or exit of any University building or corridor or room therein with intent to deprive others of lawful access to or from, or use of, said building or corridor or room; (3) setting fire to or by any other means destroying or substantially damaging any University building or property, or the property of others on University premises; (4) any possession or display of, or attempt or threat to use, for any unlawful purpose, any weapon, dangerous instrument, explosive, or inflammable material in any University building or on any University campus; (5) prevention of, or attempt to prevent by physical act, the attending, convening, continuation or orderly conduct of any University class or activity or of any lawful meeting or assembly in any University building or on any University campus; and (6) blocking normal pedestrian or vehicular traffic on or into any University campus.

(b) Any person engaged in the instructional program who fails or refuses to carry out validly assigned duties, with the intent to obstruct or disrupt any normal operation or function of the University or any of its component institutions, shall be subject to prompt and appropriate disciplinary action under this Chapter V if (but only if) his status is such that he is not subject to the provisions of Section 4-3 of Chapter IV.

RESPON-
SIBILITIES
OF CHAN-
CELLORS

(a) When any Chancellor has cause to believe that any of the provisions of this Chapter V have been violated, he shall forthwith investigate or cause to be investigated the occurrence, and upon identification of the parties involved shall promptly determine whether any charge is to be made with respect thereto.

(b) If he decides that a charge is to be made, he shall, within thirty (30) days after he has information as to the identity of the alleged perpetrator of the offense but in no event more than twelve (12) months after the occurrence of the alleged offense, (i) refer the case to the appropriate existing University judicial body, or (ii) refer the matter to a Hearing Committee drawn from a previously selected Hearings Panel which, under this option, is required to implement action for violation of Section 5-2 (a) or (b) of this Chapter. If the case is referred to an existing University judicial body under (i) above, the procedural rules of that body shall be followed, and subsections (c) through (f) below shall not be applicable. If the matter is referred to a Hearing Committee under (ii) above, the procedural rules prescribed in subsections (c) through (f) below shall be followed.

(c) The accused shall be given written notice by personal service or registered mail, return receipt requested, stating:

(1) The specific violations of this Chapter V with which the accused is charged.

(2) The designated time and place of the hearing on the charge by the Hearing Committee, which time shall be not earlier than seven (7) nor later than ten (10) days following receipt of the notice.

(3) That the accused shall be entitled to the presumption of innocence until found guilty, the right to retain counsel, the right to present the testimony of witnesses and other evidence, the right to cross-examine all witnesses against him, the right to examine all documents and demonstrative evidence adverse to him, and the right to a transcript of the proceedings of the hearing.

(d) The Hearing Committee shall determine the guilt or innocence of the accused. If the person charged is found guilty, the Hearing Committee shall recommend to the Chancellor such discipline as said body determines to be appropriate. After considering such recommendation the Chancellor shall prescribe such discipline as he deems proper. In any event, whether the person is found guilty or not guilty, a written report shall be made by the Chancellor to the President within ten (10) days.

(e) Any person found guilty shall have ten (10) days after notice of such finding in which to appeal to the President of the University. Such an appeal if taken shall be upon the grounds set forth in Section 5-5.

(f) Any accused person who, without good cause, shall fail to appear at the time and place fixed for the hearing of his case by the Hearing Committee shall be suspended indefinitely or discharged from University employment.

(g) A Chancellor, unless so ordered or otherwise prevented by court, shall not be precluded from carrying out his duties under this Chapter V by reason of any pending action in any State or Federal court. Should a delay occur in prosecuting the charge against the accused because the accused or witnesses that may be necessary to a determination of the charge are involved in State or Federal court actions, the time limitations set forth above in this Section 5-3 shall not apply.

(h) Conviction in any State or Federal court shall not preclude the University or any of its officers from exercising disciplinary action in any offense referred to in this Chapter V.

(i) Nothing contained in this Chapter V shall preclude the President or any Chancellor from taking any other steps, including injunctive relief or other legal action, which he may deem advisable to protect the best interests of the University.

(a)   The Chancellor of each of the component institutions of the University shall appoint an Emergency Consultative Panel which shall be composed of not less than three (3) nor more than five (5) faculty members and not less than three (3) nor more than five (5) students who shall be available to advise with the Chancellor in any emergency. No member of such Panel shall serve for more than one (1) year unless he be reappointed by the Chancellor. The Chancellor may make appointments, either temporary or for a full year, to fill any vacancies which may exist on the Panel.

(b)   If, in the judgment of the Chancellor, there is clear and convincing evidence that a person has committed any of the acts prohibited under this Chapter V which, because of the aggravated character or probable repetition of such act or acts, necessitates immediate action to protect the University from substantial interference with any of its orderly operations or functions, or to prevent threats to or acts which endanger life or property, the Chancellor, with the concurrence as hereinafter provided of the Emergency Consultative Panel established pursuant to (a) above, may forthwith suspend such person from the University and bar him from the University campus; provided, however, that in the event of such suspension the person suspended shall be given written notice of the reason for his suspension, either personally or by registered mail addressed to his last known addresses, and shall be afforded a prompt hearing, which, if requested, shall be commenced within ten (10) days of the suspension. Except for purposes of attending personally any hearings conducted under this Chapter V, the bar against the appearance of the accused on the University campus shall remain in effect until final judgment has been rendered in his case and all appellant proceedings have been concluded, unless such restriction is earlier lifted by written notice from the Chancellor.

(c)   A quorum of the Emergency Consultative Panel provided for in (a) above shall consist of not less than four (4) of its members, and the required concurrence shall have been obtained if a majority of such quorum shall indicate their concurrence. The Chancellor shall meet personally with members of such Panel at the time he seeks concurrence, if it is feasible to do so. However, if the circumstances are such that the Chancellor deems it not to be feasible to personally assemble such members, then he may communicate with them or the required number of them individually by telephone or by such other means as he may choose to employ, in which event he may proceed as provided in (b) above after the required majority of such members have communicated their concurrence to him.

(d) In the Chancellor's absence or inability to act, the President may exercise the powers of the Chancellor specified in this Section 5-4 in the same manner and to the same extent as could the Chancellor but for such absence or inability to act.

RIGHT OF APPEAL

Any person found guilty of violating the provisions of this Chapter V by the Hearing Committee referred to in Section 5-3 shall have the right to appeal the finding and the discipline imposed upon him to the President of the University. Any such appeal shall be in writing, shall be based solely upon the record, and shall be limited to one or more of the following grounds:

(1) That the finding is not supported by substantial evidence;

(2) That a fair hearing was not accorded the accused; or

(3) That the discipline imposed was excessive or inappropriate.

It shall be the responsibility of the President to make prompt disposition of all such appeals, and his decision shall be rendered within thirty (30) days after receipt of the complete record on appeal.

NO AMNESTY

No administrative official, faculty member, or student of the University shall have authority to grant amnesty or to make any promise as to prosecution or non-prosecution in any court, State or Federal, or before any student, faculty, administrative, or Trustee committee to any person charged with or suspected of violating Section 5-2 (a) or (b) of these Bylaws.

PUBLICATION

The provisions of this Chapter V shall be given wide dissemination in such manner as the President or Chancellors may deem advisable, and shall be printed in the official catalogues which may be issued by each component institution of the University.

University of Washington —
Rules of Conduct on Campus

(Adopted by the Board of Regents, University of Washington, September 1970)

At its meeting of September 18, the Board of Regents adopted a consolidated set of rules on conduct designed to protect freedom of expression and, at the same time, to assure the rights of all members of the University community and the maintenance of a peaceful atmosphere on the campus.

The conduct rules were proposed last spring in the wake of a series of disruptive events on the campus and were the subject of an open hearing on a preliminary draft before a subcommittee of the Board of Regents on June 1. As finally adopted, the rules incorporate a number of changes suggested in written or oral comments by students, faculty, and staff as well as most of the suggestions made by the new Student-Faculty Joint Council on Student Conduct and Activities.

In large part, the prohibitions contained in the rules have been implicit in earlier University regulations, particularly the Regents' policy statement of November 22, 1968, the Student Code approved in June 1969, the Faculty Disciplinary Regulations approved by faculty vote last spring, and a number of other policy statements issued in connection with disruptive incidents over the last several years.

The revised rules of conduct also codify and more carefully define the authority granted in 1968 to the President of the University and his designated representatives to impose interim suspension on students and members of the faculty and staff pending formal disciplinary hearings whenever there is reasonable cause to believe that such persons have committed and may reasonably be expected to thereafter commit any of the prohibited acts.

Commenting on the conduct rules, President Odegaard said: "In the light of recent experiences here and elsewhere, it is increasingly apparent that colleges and universities must be very specific about the kinds of conduct that will and will not be tolerated. It is obvious that the vast majority of students and others on the campus do not need the guidance of such rules and hence can hardly be said to be directly affected by them. However, it should be clear to others who may be inclined to engage in such activities that there are sanctions, both in the University's disciplinary regulations and in the criminal law, that can and will be applied to this kind of conduct."

RULES OF CONDUCT ON CAMPUS

It is the policy of the University of Washington to support and promote each individual's right to express his views and opinions for or against actions or ideas in which he has an interest, to associate freely with others, and to assemble peacefully.

The above rights exist in equal measure for each member of the University community. They exist regardless of the professional stature or rank of the individual and regardless of the degree of acceptability among others of the views or opinions advocated.

In order to safeguard the right of every citizen to criticize and to seek meaningful change, each individual has an obligation to respect the rights of all members of the University community.

In order to assure those rights to all members of the University community and to maintain a peaceful atmosphere in which the University may continue to make its special contribution to society, the following types of conduct are hereby prohibited on or in property either owned, controlled or operated by the University which is used or set aside for University purposes, hereinafter referred to as the University Campus:

1 Conduct which intentionally and substantially obstructs or disrupts teaching or freedom of movement or other lawful activities on the University Campus;

2 Physical abuse of any person or conduct which is intended unlawfully to threaten imminent bodily harm or to endanger the health or safety of any person on the University Campus;

3   Malicious damage to or malicious misuse of University property, or the property of any person where such property is located on the University Campus;

4   Refusal to comply with any lawful order to leave the University Campus or any portion thereof;

5   Possession or use of firearms, explosives, dangerous chemicals or other dangerous weapons or instrumentalities on the University Campus, except for authorized University purposes, unless prior written approval has been obtained from the Vice President for Student Affairs, or any other person designated by the President of the University;

6   Intentionally inciting others to engage immediately in any of the conduct prohibited herein, which incitement leads directly to such conduct. (Inciting is that advocacy which prepares the group addressed for imminent action and steels it to the conduct prohibited herein.)

Any person while on the University Campus who wilfully refuses the request of a uniformed Campus police officer to desist from conduct prohibited by these rules may be required by such officer to leave such premises.

Disciplinary action which may result in dismissal from the University will be initiated against faculty, staff or students who violate these rules, in accordance with the applicable disciplinary codes or other appropriate due process procedures.

Sanctions which may be imposed against faculty are set forth in the Faculty Code under sections 2551 and 2574.

Sanctions which may be imposed against students are set forth in Section 3 of the Student Code (Faculty Handbook, Vol. 2, Ch. V, Part D., pp. 48–51b [1969]).

Sanctions which may be imposed against the classified staff are set forth in the Rules for the Classified Staff, WAC-251-12-010.

Violation of any of the above regulations may also constitute violation of the criminal laws or ordinances of the City of Seattle, the State of Washington or the United States and may subject a violator to criminal sanctions in addition to any sanctions imposed by the University.

The President or, in his absence, any officer of the University designated by him for this purpose, may impose on any student, faculty member or staff member an interim suspension whenever there is reasonable cause to believe that such person has committed, and may reasonably be expected thereafter to commit, any of the acts prohibited herein. The notice of such suspension shall state the nature, terms and conditions of such suspension and shall include such restrictions on use of Campus facilities as the President or his designee deems in the best interest of the University.

Any person so placed on interim suspension shall be given prompt notice of charges and shall be given the opportunity to show cause at a preliminary hearing why such interim suspension should not continue until a formal hearing is held. To obtain such preliminary hearing, the person shall submit a written request therefor within seven days from the date interim suspension was imposed. Such written request shall state the address to which notice of hearing is to be sent. The President or, in his absence, any officer of the University designated by him, shall grant such a preliminary hearing before a person or persons designated by him not later than four days from the date of receipt of such request and shall immediately mail a written notice of the time, place and date of such hearing to such person. The preliminary hearing shall consider only whether there is reasonable cause to believe that such person committed, and may reasonably be expected thereafter to commit, any of the acts prohibited herein.

Interim suspension may be removed by the President or, in his absence, by any officer of the University designated by him, whenever he has reason to believe that the person on whom interim suspension was imposed will not constitute a substantial and material threat to the orderly operation of the University Campus or endanger the health and safety of any person thereon.

These rules are additional to any others duly promulgated by the University.

If any provision or clause of these rules or any application thereof to any person or circumstances is held invalid, such invalidity shall not affect other provisions or application of these rules which can be given effect without the invalid provision or application, and to this end the provisions of these rules are declared to be severable.

Joint Statement on Rights and Freedoms of Students

*In June 1967, a joint committee, composed of representatives from
the American Association of University Professors, United States
National Student Association, Association of American Colleges,
National Association of Student Personnel Administrators, and
National Association of Women Deans and Counselors, met in
Washington, D.C., and drafted the* Joint Statement on Rights and
Freedoms of Students *published below.*

*Since its formulation, the Joint Statement has been endorsed by
each of its five national sponsors, as well as by a number of other
professional bodies.*

PREAMBLE   Academic institutions exist for the transmission of knowledge,
the pursuit of truth, the development of students, and the general
well-being of society. Free inquiry and free expression are indispensable to the attainment of these goals. As members of the academic community, students should be encouraged to develop the
capacity for critical judgment and to engage in a sustained and
independent search for truth. Institutional procedures for achieving these purposes may vary from campus to campus, but the minimal standards of academic freedom of students outlined below are
essential to any community of scholars.

Freedom to teach and freedom to learn are inseparable facets
of academic freedom. The freedom to learn depends upon appropriate opportunities and conditions in the classroom, on the campus, and in the larger community. Students should exercise their
freedom with responsibility.

The responsibility to secure and to respect general conditions
conducive to the freedom to learn is shared by all members of the
academic community. Each college and university has a duty to

develop policies and procedures which provide and safeguard this freedom. Such policies and procedures should be developed at each institution within the framework of general standards and with the broadest possible participation of the members of the academic community. The purpose of this statement is to enumerate the essential provisions for student freedom to learn.

I. FREEDOM OF ACCESS TO HIGHER EDUCATION

The admissions policies of each college and university are a matter of institutional choice provided that each college and university makes clear the characteristics and expectations of students which it considers relevant to success in the institution's program. While church-related institutions may give admission preference to students of their own persuasion, such a preference should be clearly and publicly stated. Under no circumstances should a student be barred from admission to a particular institution on the basis of race. Thus, within the limits of its facilities, each college and university should be open to all students who are qualified according to its admission standards. The facilities and services of a college should be open to all of its enrolled students, and institutions should use their influence to secure equal access for all students to public facilities in the local community.

II. IN THE CLASSROOM

The professor in the classroom and in conference should encourage free discussion, inquiry, and expression. Student performance should be evaluated solely on an academic basis, not on opinions or conduct in matters unrelated to academic standards.

A. Protection of freedom of expression
Students should be free to take reasoned exception to the data or views offered in any course of study and to reserve judgment about matters of opinion, but they are responsible for learning the content of any course of study for which they are enrolled.

B. Protection against improper academic evaluation
Students should have protection through orderly procedures against prejudiced or capricious academic evaluation. At the same time, they are responsible for maintaining standards of academic performance established for each course in which they are enrolled.

C. *Protection against improper disclosure*

Information about student views, beliefs, and political associations which professors acquire in the course of their work as instructors, advisers, and counselors should be considered confidential. Protection against improper disclosure is a serious professional obligation. Judgments of ability and character may be provided under appropriate circumstances, normally with the knowledge or consent of the student.

III. STUDENT RECORDS

Institutions should have a carefully considered policy as to the information which should be part of a student's permanent educational record and as to the conditions of its disclosure. To minimize the risk of improper disclosure, academic and disciplinary records should be separate, and the conditions of access to each should be set forth in an explicit policy statement. Transcripts of academic records should contain only information about academic status. Information from disciplinary or counseling files should not be available to unauthorized persons on campus, or to any person off campus without the express consent of the student involved except under legal compulsion or in cases where the safety of persons or property is involved. No records should be kept which reflect the political activities or beliefs of students. Provisions should also be made for periodic routine destruction of noncurrent disciplinary records. Administrative staff and faculty members should respect confidential information about students which they acquire in the course of their work.

IV. STUDENT AFFAIRS

In student affairs, certain standards must be maintained if the freedom of students is to be preserved.

A. *Freedom of association*

Students bring to the campus a variety of interests previously acquired and develop many new interests as members of the academic community. They should be free to organize and join associations to promote their common interests.

1 The membership, policies, and actions of a student organization usually will be determined by vote of only those persons who hold bona fide membership in the college or university community.

2 Affiliation with an extramural organization should not of itself disqualify a student organization from institutional recognition.

3 If campus advisers are required, each organization should be free to choose its own adviser, and institutional recognition should not be withheld or withdrawn solely because of the inability of a student organization to secure an adviser. Campus advisers may advise organizations in the exercise of responsibility, but they should not have the authority to control the policy of such organizations.

4 Student organizations may be required to submit a statement of purpose, criteria for membership, rules of procedures, and a current list of officers. They should not be required to submit a membership list as a condition of institutional recognition.

5 Campus organizations, including those affiliated with an extramural organization, should be open to all students without respect to race, creed, or national origin, except for religious qualifications which may be required by organizations whose aims are primarily sectarian.

B. Freedom of inquiry and expression

1 Students and student organizations should be free to examine and discuss all questions of interest to them, and to express opinions publicly and privately. They should always be free to support causes by orderly means which do not disrupt the regular and essential operation of the institution. At the same time, it should be made clear to the academic and the larger community that in their public expressions or demonstrations students or student organizations speak only for themselves.

2 Students should be allowed to invite and hear any person of their own choosing. Those routine procedures required by an institution before a guest speaker is invited to appear on campus should be designed only to insure that there is orderly scheduling of facilities and adequate preparation for the event, and that the occasion is conducted in a manner appropriate to an academic community. The institutional control of campus facilities should not be used as a device of censorship. It should be made clear to the academic and large community that sponsorship of guest speakers does not necessarily imply approval or endorsement of the views expressed, either by the sponsoring group or the institution.

C. Student participation in institutional government

As constituents of the academic community, students should be free, individually and collectively, to express their views on issues of institutional policy and on matters of general interest to the student body. The student body should have clearly defined means to participate in the formulation and application of institutional policy affecting academic and student affairs. The role of the student government and both its general and specific responsibilities should be made explicit, and the actions of the student government within the areas of its jurisdiction should be reviewed only through orderly and prescribed procedures.

D. Student publications

Student publications and the student press are a valuable aid in establishing and maintaining an atmosphere of free and responsible discussion and of intellectual exploration on the campus. They are a means of bringing student concerns to the attention of the faculty and the institutional authorities and of formulating student opinion on various issues on the campus and in the world at large.

Whenever possible the student newspaper should be an independent corporation financially and legally separate from the university. Where financial and legal autonomy is not possible, the institution, as the publisher of student publications, may have to bear the legal responsibility for the contents of the publications. In the delegation of editorial responsibility to students the institution must provide sufficient editorial freedom and financial autonomy for the student publications to maintain their integrity of purpose as vehicles for free inquiry and free expression in an academic community.

Institutional authorities, in consultation with students and faculty, have a responsibility to provide written clarification of the role of the student publications, the standards to be used in their evaluation, and the limitations on external control of their operation. At the same time, the editorial freedom of student editors and managers entails corollary responsibilities to be governed by the canons of responsible journalism, such as the avoidance of libel, indecency, undocumented allegations, attacks on personal integrity, and the techniques of harassment and innuendo. As safeguards for the editorial freedom of student publications the following provisions are necessary.

1 The student press should be free of censorship and advance approval of copy, and its editors and managers should be free to develop their own editorial policies and news coverage.

2 Editors and managers of student publications should be protected from arbitrary suspension and removal because of student, faculty, administrative, or public disapproval of editoral policy or content. Only for proper and stated causes should editors and managers be subject to removal and then by orderly and prescribed procedures. The agency responsible for the appointment of editors and managers should be the agency responsible for their removal.

3 All university published and financed student publications should explicitly state on the editoral page that the opinions there expressed are not necessarily those of the college, university, or student body.

V. OFF-CAMPUS FREEDOM OF STUDENTS

A. Exercise of rights of citizenship

College and university students are both citizens and members of the academic community. As citizens, students should enjoy the same freedom of speech, peaceful assembly, and right of petition that other citizens enjoy and, as members of the academic community, they are subject to the obligations which accrue to them by virtue of this membership. Faculty members and administrative officials should insure that institutional powers are not employed to inhibit such intellectual and personal development of students as is often promoted by their exercise of the rights of citizenship both on and off campus.

B. Institutional authority and civil penalties

Activities of students may upon occasion result in violation of law. In such cases, institutional officials should be prepared to apprise students of sources of legal counsel and may offer other assistance. Students who violate the law may incur penalties prescribed by civil authorities, but institutional authority should never be used merely to duplicate the function of general laws. Only where the institution's interests as an academic community are distinct and clearly involved should the special authority of the institution be asserted. The student who incidentally violates institutional regulations in the course of his off-campus activity, such as those relating to class attendance, should be subject to no greater penalty than would normally be imposed. Institutional action should be independent of community pressure.

In developing responsible student conduct, disciplinary proceedings play a role substantially secondary to example, counseling, guidance, and admonition. At the same time, educational institutions have a duty and the corollary disciplinary powers to protect their educational purpose through the setting of standards of scholarship and conduct for the students who attend them and through the regulation of the use of institutional facilities. In the exceptional circumstances when the preferred means fail to resolve problems of student conduct, proper procedural safeguards should be observed to protect the student from the unfair imposition of serious penalties.

The administration of discipline should guarantee procedural fairness to an accused student. Practices in disciplinary cases may vary in formality with the gravity of the offense and the sanctions which may be applied. They should also take into account the presence or absence of an honor code, and the degree to which the institutional officials have direct acquaintance with student life in general and with the involved student and the circumstances of the case in particular. The jurisdictions of faculty or student judicial bodies, the disciplinary responsibilities of institutional officials and the regular disciplinary procedures, including the student's right to appeal a decision, should be clearly formulated and communicated in advance. Minor penalties may be assessed informally under prescribed procedures.

In all situations, procedural fair play requires that the student be informed of the nature of the charges against him, that he be given a fair opportunity to refute them, that the institution not be arbitrary in its actions, and that there be provision for appeal of a decision. The following are recommended as proper safeguards on such proceedings when there are no honor codes offering comparable guarantees.

A.   Standards of conduct expected of students
The institution has an obligation to clarify those standards of behavior which it considers essential to its educational mission and its community life. These general behavioral expectations and the resultant specific regulations should represent a reason-

able regulation of student conduct, but the student should be as free as possible from imposed limitations that have no direct relevance to his education. Offenses should be as clearly defined as possible and interpreted in a manner consistent with the afore-mentioned principles of relevancy and reasonableness. Disciplinary proceedings should be instituted only for violations of standards of conduct formulated with significant student participation and published in advance through such means as a student handbook or a generally available body of institutional regulations.

B.   Investigation of student conduct

1   Except under extreme emergency circumstances, premises occupied by students and the personal possessions of students should not be searched unless appropriate authorization has been obtained. For premises such as residence halls controlled by the institution, an appropriate and responsible authority should be designated to whom application should be made before a search is conducted. The application should specify the reasons for the search and the objects or information sought. The student should be present, if possible, during the search. For premises not controlled by the institution, the ordinary requirements for lawful search should be followed.

2   Students detected or arrested in the course of serious violations of institutional regulations, or infractions of ordinary law, should be informed of their rights. No form of harassment should be used by institutional representatives to coerce admissions of guilt or information about conduct of other suspected persons.

C.   Status of student pending final action

Pending action on the charges, the status of a student should not be altered, or his right to be present on the campus and to attend classes suspended, except for reasons relating to his physical or emotional safety and well-being, or for reasons relating to the safety and well-being of students, faculty, or university property.

D.   Hearing committee procedures

When the misconduct may result in serious penalties and if the student questions the fairness of disciplinary action taken against him, he should be granted, on request, the privilege of a hearing before a regularly constituted hearing committee. The following suggested hearing committee procedures satisfy the requirements of procedural due process in situations requiring a high degree of formality.

1 The hearing committee should include faculty members or students, or, if regularly included or requested by the accused, both faculty and student members. No member of the hearing committee who is otherwise interested in the particular case should sit in judgment during the proceeding.

2 The student should be informed, in writing, of the reasons for the proposed disciplinary action with sufficient particularity, and in sufficient time, to insure opportunity to prepare for the hearing.

3 The student appearing before the hearing committee should have the right to be assisted in his defense by an adviser of his choice.

4 The burden of proof should rest upon the officials bringing the charge.

5 The student should be given an opportunity to testify and to present evidence and witnesses. He should have an opportunity to hear and question adverse witnesses. In no case should the committee consider statements against him unless he has been advised of their content and of the names of those who made them, and unless he has been given an opportunity to rebut unfavorable inferences which might otherwise be drawn.

6 All matters upon which the decision may be based must be introduced into evidence at the proceeding before the hearing committee. The decision should be based solely upon such matters. Improperly acquired evidence should not be admitted.

7 In the absence of a transcript, there should be both a digest and a verbatim record, such as a tape recording, of the hearing.

8 The decision of the hearing committee should be final, subject only to the student's right of appeal to the president or ultimately to the governing board of the institution.

SOURCE: AAUP *Bulletin,* vol. 54, pp. 258–261 (summer 1968).

Appendix K: American Bar Association Law Student Division Committee on Student Rights & Responsibilities — Model Code for Student Rights, Responsibilities & Conduct

§ 1. These rules shall be known as the _____
_____ [insert name of institution] Code of Conduct.

§ 2. The following enumeration of rights shall not be construed to deny or disparage others retained by students in their capacity as members of the student body or as citizens of the community at large;

A. Free inquiry, expression and assembly are guaranteed to all students.

B. Students are free to pursue their educational goals; appropriate opportunities for learning in the classroom and on the campus shall be provided by the institution.

C. The right of students to be secure in their persons, living quarters, papers and effects against unreasonable searches and seizures is guaranteed.

D. No disciplinary sanctions may be imposed upon any student without notice to the accused of the nature and cause of the charges, and a fair hearing which shall include confrontation of witnesses against him and the assistance of a person of his own choosing.

219

E. A student accused of violating institutional regulations is entitled, upon request, to a hearing before a judicial body composed solely of students.

DEFINITIONS § 3. When used in this Code—

(1) The term "institution" means _____
_____ [insert name of college or university] and, collectively, those responsible for its control and operation.

(2) The term "student" includes all persons taking courses at the institution both full-time and part-time pursuing undergraduate, graduate or extension studies.

(3) The term "instructor" means any person hired by the institution to conduct classroom activities. In certain situations a person may be both "student" and "instructor." Determination of his status in a particular situation shall be determined by the surrounding facts.

(4) The term "legal compulsion" means a judicial or legislative order which requires some action by the person to whom it is directed.

(5) The term "organization" means a number of persons who have complied with the formal requirements of institution recognition as provided in § 11.

(6) The term "group" means a number of persons who have not yet complied with the formal requirements for becoming an organization.

(7) The term "student press" means either an organization whose primary purpose is to publish and distribute any publication on campus or a regular publication of an organization.

(8) The term "shall" is used in the imperative sense.

(9) The term "may" is used in the permissive sense.

(10) All other terms have their natural meaning unless the context dictates otherwise.

ACCESS TO HIGHER EDUCATION § 4. Within the limits of its facilities, the institution shall be open to all applicants who are qualified according to its admission requirements.

A. The institution shall make clear the characteristics and expectations of students which it considers relevant to its programs.

B. Under no circumstances may an applicant be denied admission because of race or ethnic background.

C. (Optional) Religious preference for applicants shall be clearly and publicly stated.

§ 5. Discussion and expression of all views relevant to the subject matter is permitted in the classroom subject only to the responsibility of the instructor to maintain order.

A. Students are responsible for learning the content of any course for which they are enrolled.

B. Requirements of participation in classroom discussion and submission of written exercises are not inconsistent with this Section.

§ 6. Academic Evaluation of student performance shall be neither prejudicial nor capricious.

§ 7. Information about student views, beliefs, and political associations acquired by professors in the course of their work as instructors, advisors, and counselors, is confidential and is not to be disclosed to others unless under legal compulsion.

A. Questions relating to intellectual or skills capacity are not subject to this section except that disclosure must be accompanied by notice to the student.

§ 8. Discussion and expression of all views is permitted within the institution subject only to requirements for the maintenance of order.

A. Support of any cause by orderly means which do not disrupt the operation of the institution is permitted.

§ 9. Students, groups, and campus organizations may invite and hear any persons of their own choosing subject only to the requirements for use of institutional facilities (§ 14, *infra*)

§ 10. Organizations and groups may be established within the institution for any legal purpose. Affiliation with an extramural organization shall not, in itself, disqualify the institution branch or chapter from institution privileges.

§ 11.

A. A group shall become an organization when formally recognized by the institution. All groups that meet the following requirements shall be recognized:

1. Submission of a list of officers and copies of the constitution and by-laws to the appropriate institution official or body. All changes and amendments shall be submitted within one week after they become effective.

2. Where there is affiliation with an extramural organization, that organization's constitution and by-laws shall be filed with the appropriate institution official or body. All amendments shall be submitted within a reasonable time after they become effective.

3. All sources of outside funds shall be disclosed.

B. Upon recognition of an organization, the institution shall make clear that said recognition infers neither approval or disapproval of the aims, objectives and policies of the organization.

C. Groups of a continuing nature must institute proceedings for formal recognition if they are to continue receiving the benefits of § 14, 16, and 17.

D. Any organization which engages in illegal activities, on or off campus, may have sanctions imposed against it, including withdrawal of institution recognition for a period not exceeding one year.

E. Any group which engages in illegal activities on campus may have sanctions imposed against it including the denial of all privileges afforded groups for a period not exceeding one year.

§ 12. Membership in all institution-related organizations, within the limits of their facilities, shall be open to any member of the institution community who is willing to subscribe to the stated aims and meet the stated obligations of the organization.

§ 13. Membership lists are confidential and solely for the use of the organization except that names and addresses of officers may be required as a condition of access to institution funds.

§ 14. Institution facilities shall be asigned to organizations, groups, and individuals within the institution community for regular business meetings, for social programs, and for programs open to the public.

A. Reasonable conditions may be imposed to regulate the timeliness of requests, to determine the appropriateness of the space assigned, to regulate time and use, and insure proper maintenance.

B. Preference may be given to programs designed for audiences consisting primarily of members of the institutional community.

C. Allocation of space shall be made based on priority of requests and the demonstrated needs of the organization, group, or individual.

D. The institution may delegate the assignment function to an administrative official.

D. (Alternate Provision) The institution may delegate the assignment function to a student committee on organizations.

E. Charges may be imposed for any unusual costs for use of facilities.

F. Physical abuse of assigned facilities shall result in reasonable limitations on future allocation of space to offending parties and restitution for damages.

G. The individual, group, or organization requesting space must inform the institution of the general purpose of any meeting open to persons other than members and the names of outside speakers.

§ 15. The authority to allocate institutional funds derived from student fees for use by organizations shall be delegated to a body in which student participation in the decisional process is assured.

A. Approval of requests for funds is conditioned upon submission of budgets to, and approval by this body.

B. Financial accountability is required for all allocated funds, including statement of income and expenses on a regular basis. Otherwise, organizations shall have independent control over the expenditure of allocated funds.

C. (Optional) Any organization seeking access to institutional funds shall choose a faculty member to be a consultant on institution relations. Such a person may not have a veto power.

§ 16. No individual, group, or organization may use the institution without the express authorization of the institution except to identify the institutional affiliation. Institution approval or disapproval of any policy may not be stated or implied by any individual, group, or organization.

PUBLICA-
TIONS
§ 17. A student, group, or organization may distribute written material on campus without prior approval providing such distribution does not disrupt the operations of the institution.

§ 18. The student press is to be free of censorship. The editors and managers shall not be arbitrarily suspended because of student, faculty, administration, alumni, or community disapproval of editorial policy or content. Similar freedom is assured oral statements of views on an institution controlled and student operated radio or television station.

A. This editorial freedom entails a corollary obligation under the canons of responsible journalism and applicable regulations of the Federal Communications Commission.

§ 19. All student communications shall explicitly state on the editorial page or in broadcast that the opinions expressed are not necessarily those of the institution or its student body.

INSTITU-
TIONAL
GOVERNMENT
§ 20. All constituents of the institutional community are free, individually and collectively, to express their views on issues of institutional policy and on matters of interest to the student body. Clearly defined means shall be provided for student expression on all institutional policies affecting academic and student affairs.

§ 21. The role of student government and its responsibilities shall be made explicit. There should be no review of student government actions except where review procedures are agreed upon in advance.

§ 22. Where the institution owns and operates residence halls, the students shall have final authority to make all decisions affecting their personal lives including the imposition of sanctions for violations of stated norms of conduct, except that the institution may impose minimal standards to insure compliance with all federal, state, and local laws.

§ 23. On questions of educational policy, students are entitled to a participatory function.

A. Faculty-student committees shall be created to consider questions of policy affecting student life.

B. Students shall be designated as members of standing and special committees concerned with institutional policy affecting academic and student affairs, including those concerned with curriculum, discipline, admissions, and allocation of student funds.

C. (Optional) There shall be an ombudsman who shall hear and investigate complaints and recommend appropriate remedial action.

§ 24. The right of peaceful protest is granted within the institutional community. The institution retains the right to assure the safety of individuals, the protection of property, and the continuity of the educational process.

§ 25. Orderly picketing and other forms of peaceful protest are permitted on institution premises.

A. Interference with ingress to and egress from institution facilities, interruption of classes, or damage to property exceeds permissible limits.

B. Even though remedies are available through local enforcement bodies, the institution may choose to impose its own disciplinary sanctions.

§ 26. Orderly picketing and orderly demonstrations are permitted in public areas within institution buildings subject to the requirements of non-interference in § 25A.

§ 27. Every student has the right to be interviewed on campus by any legal organization desiring to recruit at the institution.

A. Any student, group, or organization may protest against any such organization provided that protest does not interfere with any other student's right to have such an interview.

VIOLATION OF LAW AND UNIVERSITY DISCIPLINE § 28. If a student is charged with, or convicted of, an off-campus violation of law, the matter is of no disciplinary concern to institution unless the student is incarcerated and unable to comply with academic requirements, except,

A. The institution may impose sanctions for grave misconduct demonstrating flagrant disregard for the rights of others. In such cases, expulsion is not permitted until the student has been adjudged guilty in a court of law, and;

B. Once a student is adjudged guilty in a court of law the institution may impose sanctions if it considers the misconduct to be so grave as to demonstrate flagrant disregard for the rights of others.

§ 29. Under § 28A, the institution shall reinstate the student if he is acquitted or the charges are withdrawn.

§ 30. The institution may institute its own proceedings against a student who violates a law on campus which is also a violation of a published institution regulation.

PRIVACY
§ 31. Students have the same rights of privacy as any other citizen and surrender none of those rights by becoming members of the academic community. These rights of privacy extend to residence hall living. Nothing in the institutional relationship or residence hall contract may expressly or impliedly give the institution or residence hall officials authority to consent to a search of a student's room by police or other government officials.

§ 32. The institution is neither arbiter or enforcer of student morals. No inquiry is permitted into the activities of students away from the campus where their behavior is subject to regulation and control by public authorities. Social morality on campus, not in violation of law, is of no disciplinary concern to the institution.

§ 33. When the institution seeks access to a student room in a residence hall to determine compliance with provisions of applicable multiple dwelling unit laws or for improvement or repairs, the occupant shall be notified of such action not less than twenty-four hours in advance. There may be entry without notice in emergencies where imminent danger to life, safety, health, or property is reasonably feared.

§ 34. The institution may conduct a search of a student room in a residence hall to determine compliance with federal, state and local criminal law where there is probable cause to believe that a violation has occurred or is taking place. "Probable cause" exists where the facts and circumstances within the knowledge of the institution and of which it has reasonably trustworthy information are sufficient in themselves to warrant a man of reasonable caution in the belief that an offense has been or is being committed.

§ 35. The privacy and confidentiality of all student records shall be preserved. Official student academic records, supporting documents, and other student files shall be maintained only by full-time members of the institution staff employed for that purpose. Separate files shall be maintained of the following; academic records, supporting documents, and general educational records; records of discipline proceedings; medical and psychiatric records; financial aid records.

§ 36. No entry may be made on a student's academic record and no document may be placed in his file without actual notice to the student. Publication of grades and announcement of honors constitute notice.

§ 37. Access to his records and files is guaranteed every student subject only to reasonable regulation as to time, place, and supervision.

A. A student may challenge the accuracy of any entry or the presence of any item by bringing the equivalent of an equitable action against the appropriate person before the judicial body to which the student would be responsible under § 52.

§ 38. No record may be made in relation to any of the following matters except upon the express written request of the student;

A. Race;

B. Religion; (omit if § 4C is enacted)

C. Political or social views; and

D. Membership in any organization other than honorary and professional organizations directly related to the educational process.

§ 39. No information in any student file may be released to anyone except with the prior written consent of the student concerned or as stated below;

A. Members of the faculty with administrative assignments may have access for internal educational purposes as well as routinely necessary administrative and statistical purposes.

B. The following data may be given any inquirer; school or division of enrollment, periods of enrollment, and degrees awarded, honors, major field, and date.

C. If an inquiry is made in person or by mail, the following information may be given in addition to that in Subsection B; address and telephone number, date of birth, and confirmation of signature.

D. Properly identified officials from federal, state and local government agencies may be given the following information upon express request in addition to that in Subsections B and C; name and address of parent or guardian if student is a minor, and any information required under legal compulsion.

E. Unless under legal compulsion, personal access to a student's file shall be denied to any person making an inquiry.

§ **40.** Upon graduation or withdrawal from the institution, the records and files of former students shall continue to be subject to the provisions of this Code of Conduct.

SANCTIONS § **41.** The following sanctions may be imposed upon students;

A. *Admonition:* An oral statement to a student that he is violating or has violated institution rules.

B. *Warning:* Notice, orally or in writing, that continuation or repetition of conduct found wrongful, within a period of time stated in the warning, may be cause for more severe disciplinary action.

C. *Censure:* A written reprimand for violation of specified regulations, including the possibility of more severe disciplinary sanctions in the event of the finding of a violation of any institution regulation within a stated period of time.

D. *Disciplinary probation:* Exclusion from participation in privileged or extracurricular institution activities as set forth in the notice for a period of time not exceeding one school year.

E. *Restitution:* Reimbursement for damage to or misappropriation of property. This may take the form of appropriate service or other compensation.

F. *Suspension:* Exclusion from classes and other privileges or activities as set forth in the notice for a definite period of time not to exceed two years.

G. *Expulsion:* Termination of student status for an indefinite period. The conditions of readmission, if any, shall be stated in the order of expulsion.

§ **42.** No sanctions may be imposed for violations of rules and regulations for which there is not actual or constructive notice.

§ 43. Generally, institutional discipline shall be limited to conduct which adversely affects the institutional community's pursuit of its educational objectives. The following misconduct is subject to disciplinary action:

A. All forms of dishonesty including cheating, plagiarism, knowingly furnishing false information to the institution, and forgery, alteration or use of institution documents or instruments of identification with intent to defraud.

B. Intentional disruption or obstruction of teaching, research, administration, disciplinary proceedings or other institution activities.

C. Physical abuse of any person on institution premises or at institution sponsored or supervised functions.

D. Theft from or damage to institution premises or damage to property of a member of the institutional community on institution premises.

E. Failure to comply with directions of institution officials acting in performance of their duties.

F. Violation of published institutional regulations including those relating to entry and use of institutional facilities, the rules in this Code of Conduct, and any other regulations which may be enacted.

G. Violation of published rules governing residence halls.

H. Violation of law on institutional premises or residence halls in a way that affects the institutional community's pursuit of its proper educational purposes.

§ 44. Any academic or administrative official, faculty member or student may file charges against any student for misconduct. In extraordinary circumstances the student may be suspended pending consideration of the case. Such suspension shall not exceed a reasonable time.

§ 45. The institution may make a preliminary investigation to determine if the charges can be disposed of informally by mutual consent without the initiation of disciplinary proceedings.

§ 45. (Alternate) The institution may make a preliminary investigation to determine if the charges can be disposed of informally by mutual consent without the initiation of disciplinary proceedings. Such disposal will be final and there shall be no subsequent proceedings or appeals.

§ 46. All charges shall be presented to the accused student in written form and he shall respond within seven school days. The time may be extended for such response. A time shall be set for a hearing which shall not be less than seven or more than fifteen school days after the student's response.

§ 47. A calendar of the hearings in a disciplinary proceeding shall be fixed after consultation with the parties. The institution shall have discretion to alter the calendar for good cause.

§ 48. Hearings shall be conducted in such manner as to do substantial justice.

A. Hearings shall be private if requested by the accused student. In hearings involving more than one student, severance shall be allowed upon request.

B. An accused student has the right to be represented by counsel or an adviser who may come from within or without the institution.

C. Any party to the proceedings may request the privilege of presenting witnesses subject to the right of cross-examination by the other parties.

D. Production of records and other exhibits may be required.

§ 49. In the absence of a transcript, there shall be both a digest and a verbatim record, such as a tape recording, of the hearing in cases that may result in the imposition of the sanctions of restitution, as suspension, and expulsion as defined in § 41.

§ 50. No recommendation for the imposition of sanctions may be based solely upon the failure of the accused student to answer the charges or appear at the hearing. In such a case, the evidence in support of the charges shall be presented and considered.

§ 51. An appeal from a decision by the initial hearing board may be made by any party to the appropriate appeal board within ten days of the decision.

A. An appeal shall be limited to a review of the full report of the hearing board for the purpose of determining whether it acted fairly in light of the charges and evidence presented.

B. An appeal may not result in a more severe sanction for the accused student.

C. An appeal by the institution, in which the decision is reversed, shall be remanded to the initial hearing board for a determination of the appropriate sanction.

JUDICIAL
AUTHORITY

§ 52. Appropriate judicial bodies shall be formed to handle all questions of student discipline. The initial hearing board shall be composed solely of students and any appeal board shall have voting student representation.

§ 53. The judicial bodies may formulate procedural rules which are not inconsistent with the provision of this Code.

§ 54. The judicial bodies may give advisory opinions, at their sole discretion, on issues not before any judicial body and where no violation of institutional regulations has taken place. Such opinions shall not be binding on the party making the request nor may it be used as precedent in future proceedings.

§ 55. A judicial body may be designated as arbiter of disputes within the institutional community. All parties must agree to arbitration and agree to be bound by the decision with no right of appeal.

Appendix L:
Cleveland State University — Policy on Maintenance of the Educational Environment and Student Bill of Rights and Responsibilities

POLICY
PROVISION The Cleveland State University stands for freedom of speech, freedom of inquiry, freedom to dissent, freedom to assemble, and freedom to demonstrate in peaceful fashion. The University also stands for the right of all faculty and students to pursue their legitimate educational goals without interference. The University, therefore, cannot tolerate any attempt by any individual, group, or organization to disrupt the regularly scheduled activities of the University.

Accordingly, the University encourages and expects its students, faculty, staff and visitors to conduct themselves, at all times and on every occasion, in accordance with the regulations and rules of the University, and in accordance with all applicable laws of the city, state, and federal government. All regulations and rules of the University now in existence as well as those enacted in the future shall be published in such a manner as to come to the attention of the faculty, students, staff and visitors of the University. No regulation or rule shall be applied in such a manner as to restrict the freedom of speech or the right of persons to assemble peacefully.

ENFORCE-
MENT The Department of Security Operations of Cleveland State University pursuant to and in accordance with the authority speci-

fied in Section 3345.04 of the *Ohio Revised Code* shall be responsible for the enforcement of the University regulations and rules relating to the maintenance of law and order. Should the Department of Security Operations be unable to maintain law and order, the President of the University or a representative designated by him is hereby authorized to call upon city, county, state, or federal law enforcement agencies for assistance.

DISPOSITION OF VIOLATIONS Students responsible for violations of these regulations and rules shall be dealt with in accordance with the procedures specified in the Cleveland State University *Student Bill of Rights and Responsibilities.*

Visitors and guests responsible for violations of these regulations and rules are subject to ejection from University property as well as arrest and prosecution under applicable law.

Employees of the University responsible for violations of these regulations and rules may be subject to disciplinary action or to arrest and prosecution under applicable law. Disciplinary action in addition to court action may be taken only if such violations are in direct conflict with the educational interests of the University. Specifically, disciplinary action against classified personnel shall be dealt with through procedures specified in *Ohio Revised Code* Section 143.27. Disciplinary action against an administrative officer or nonacademic, nonclassified employee shall follow procedural due process similar to that provided students and faculty. Disciplinary action against a faculty member shall be taken in accordance with the *Faculty Personnel Policies and Bylaws of the Faculty Organization.*

POLICY ON DEMONSTRATIONS AND PROTESTS ON UNIVERSITY PROPERTY A. It is recognized that free speech is essential in a democratic society. Members of the University community (faculty, students, and staff) as individuals or as members of groups are permitted to demonstrate and protest on University property[1] in opposition to University, City, State, or National

*As adopted by the Board of Trustees of The Cleveland State University by Resolution 69-8, January 9, 1969.

[1] "University property" as used herein is defined as "all real or personal property owned, or leased to, and operated exclusively by the University and any property when it is used by the University for such official functions as registration, classroom or laboratory instruction, lectures, concerts, assemblies, intramurals, or intercollegiate athletic events."

policy provided that they do not violate any applicable local, state, or federal law, and no acts are performed which:

1. Cause damage to property (personal or University).
2. Cause physical injury to any individual.
3. Prevent any student from attending class, entering or leaving any University facility, or attending any special program on University property.
4. Prevent administrative officers, faculty, student, employees or invited guests of the University from performing duties they are authorized to perform.
5. Block the normal business of the University, particularly classroom or laboratory instruction.
6. Block pedestrian or vehicle traffic.

B. Persons who are not members of the University community shall conduct themselves while on University property in such a way that the normal and regular business of the University, including properly authorized and scheduled events, may go forward without interruption or disturbance.

C. Any student or group of students desiring to set up tables or booths on University property as part of a protest or demonstration must schedule such activity through the Office of Student Affairs.

PREAMBLE   It is assumed that the student who attends Cleveland State University intends to gain maximum educational benefits. These benefits include classroom, laboratory, field, and other formal academic experiences. Also included among these benefits are those which accrue from participation in the structured and unstructured political, social, recreational, cultural, and aesthetic experiences related to the nonacademic life of the University community.

The *Student Bill of Rights and Responsibilities* is an effort to insure a University environment in which the student has every opportunity to attain these benefits. Further, it is an attempt to establish the role of the student as a participating mem-

*Adopted by the Board of Trustees, October 17, 1968.

ber of the University community—a community committed to the honoring of responsibilities, the protection of rights, and the goal of equality of treatment for all without regard to race, creed, or national origin.

I. *Rights*

A. The student shall have the right to pursue educational, recreational, social, cultural, and residential activities.

B. The student shall have the right to a campus environment characterized by safety and order.

C. The student shall have the right to organize and join associations to promote interests he has in common with other students.

D. The student shall have the right to the services of the faculty, administrative offices, and counseling agencies of the University.

E. The student shall have the right to fair and impartial academic evaluation.

F. The student shall have the right to have the University keep accurate records of his academic performance and the academic performance of his fellow students with whom he is compared for grading and graduation purposes.

G. The student shall have the right to have the University maintain and protect the confidential status of his records of academic and conduct performance. Information released to agencies outside the University in terms of academic, counseling, and conduct records shall be restricted to name, address, dates of attendance, and degree received except under legal compulsion or in cases where the safety of persons or property is involved. Written permission from the student shall be necessary to release any other information from these records. No records shall be kept reflecting political activities or beliefs of the student. Judgments of ability and character of the student may be provided to outside agencies under appropriate circumstances normally with the knowledge or consent of the student.

H. The student shall have the right to participate through his representatives in the formulation of regulations affecting student affairs.

I. The student shall have the right to dissent, to protest, or to demonstrate on University property[1] in opposition to University, city, state,

---

[1] The term University property, or campus, as used in this document is defined as "all real and personal property owned or leased to, and operated exclusively by the University, and any property when it is used by the University for such official functions as registration, classroom or laboratory instruction, lectures, concerts, assemblies, intramurals, or intercollegiate athletic events."

or national policy providing that his behavior does not infringe on the rights of others, as already established through the Board of Trustees Student Demonstrations and Protests policy, approved May 10, 1968.

II. *Responsibilities*

A. The student shall have the responsibility for maintaining standards of academic performance as established by his instructors.

B. The student shall be responsible for acting in such a manner as to insure to other students the rights declared in Section I.

C. The student shall be responsible for his actions with respect to University rules and regulations.

D. The student shall be responsible for his actions with respect to provisions of local, state, and federal law.

E. The student shall be responsible for conducting himself in a manner which helps to create and maintain a learning atmosphere in which the rights, dignity, and worth of every individual in the University community are respected.

III. *Participation in university government*

A. The primary role of the student in University government shall lie in the various student councils.

B. Students elected by student councils shall serve jointly with faculty and administrative personnel on certain governing committees such as the Student Affairs Committee, Assembly Committee, and other committees such as are determined in the future.

C. Representatives of the student councils shall be authorized to attend meetings of the Faculty Council.

D. Students may also serve on various administrative committees of the University where appropriate.

IV. *Student discipline*

A. Premises

Student discipline shall be based on the following premises:

1. The student shall be considered a citizen with all rights and responsibilities prescribed under local, state, and federal law. When the student commits, either on or off University property, an act contrary to the law he shall be subject to prosecution by civil authorities. Enforcement of law and prosecution of offenders

shall be considered the task of agencies and courts established by the general society for those purposes. On the campus the Department of Security Operations shall represent law enforcement of the general society and refer law violations to civil authorities for prosecution.

2. The University shall not duplicate the function of general law through disciplinary measures taken in addition to court action with the exception of certain offenses which involve the unique and distinct interests of the academic community.

3. The role assumed by the University shall be that of a counselor rather than a disciplinarian in cases of law violation by the student when offenses do not involve the unique and distinct interests of the University.

4. The University shall have a specialized set of rules necessary to provide the student with an opportunity to take optimum advantage of educational experiences available on the campus. Disciplinary action in terms of violation of these rules shall be the responsibility of the University since these rules are not covered under general law.

B. Disciplinary Review Bodies

1. The *Residence Halls Court,* established by the Residence Halls Council, shall hear violations of Residence Halls rules.

2. The *Student Judiciary* shall consist of five students elected by the student body and a nonvoting faculty or administrative adviser elected by the student members of the Judiciary. It shall hear cases of individual and student group violations of University rules and regulations with the exception of (1) academic cheating and plagiarism and (2) infractions committed by publications which are financed out of student activity funds. (The former shall be dealt with through procedures specified by the Admissions and Standards Committee of the Faculty Council, and the latter shall be referred to the Student Publications Board.)

The Student Judiciary shall rule on complaints of unconstitutionality of student council actions and hear appeals of decisions made by the Residence Halls Court.

Disputes between student organizations or between individual students and organizations shall be dealt with by the Student Judiciary.

3. The *Student Conduct Committee* shall consist of three teaching faculty members elected by the Faculty Council and three student members elected by the Student Affairs Committee. One of the faculty members shall serve as chairman. Legal counsel shall be provided for the Student Conduct Committee.

The Student Conduct Committee shall determine disposition of law violation cases as specified in Section IV.E.3.

The Student Conduct Committee shall also periodically review rules pertaining to student conduct and make recommendations to the Student Affairs Committee for revisions and additions to this document.

C. Disciplinary Action

Action taken by Student Judiciary may include:

1. *Official Reprimand.* The student or student group shall be informed that any subsequent violation of University rules during the same or the next two quarters will result in more serious disciplinary action.

2. *Disciplinary Probation.* The student shall be informed that any subsequent violation of University rules during a specified probationary period will result in suspension or expulsion from the University. Restrictions on privileges such as participation in activities on campus may also be conditions of probation. This action may also be taken with respect to student organizations.

3. *Disciplinary Suspension.* The student shall be informed that he must leave the University for a specified period of time after which he is eligible to petition for readmission. This action in terms of a student organization shall mean suspension of operations through loss of recognition.

4. *Disciplinary Expulsion.* The student shall be informed that he is separated from the University on a permanent basis.

5. *Reparation for Damages.* In addition to the above action a student group can be required to pay for any damage to University property for which that student or student group is responsible.

D. Procedural Due Process

A hearing conducted by the Student Judiciary or the Student Conduct Committee shall be open or closed at the option of the accused student or organization. The following rights of the accused shall be recognized:

1. The right to have, at least forty-eight hours prior to the hearing, a written statement concerning the alleged misconduct and the the University regulation violated.

2. The right to remain silent or to cease answering questions at any time he believes he may be incriminating himself or that his personal or constitutional rights are being infringed upon.

3. The right to confront witnesses against him.

4. The right to be assisted in his defense by an adviser of his choice.

5. The right to present witnesses and a defense in his behalf.

6. The right to a written transcript of the hearing if he so requests.

7. The right to appeal the decision of the Student Judiciary to the Student Conduct Committee, or a decision of the Student Conduct Committee to the President of the University or his delegated agent. (All appeals must be in writing and submitted within seven days of the announcement of the decision.)

E. Student Misconduct and Disposition of Cases

All law violations occurring off the campus of the University shall be considered the responsibility of the law enforcement agencies and courts of the general society.

1. The following conduct in violation of law is a danger to life, safety, and property interests in any community of the State of Ohio regardless of any distinct objectives that community might have. Therefore, law violation on campus in the following general classifications shall be referred by the Department of Security Operations to civil authorities for prosecution:

    a. Threatening, attempting, or committing physical violence against any student, faculty member, administrative officer, employee, or invited guest of the University.

    b. Destruction, damage, or theft of personal or University property, including incidents of arson, vandalism, larceny, burglary, breaking and entering, or robbery.

    c. Unlawful possession or use of firearms, air guns, explosive devices or materials of any description, or deadly weapons.

    d. Unlawful possession, use, or distribution of narcotics, hallucinogens, barbiturates, or amphetamines.

    e. Unlawful possession, use, or distribution of beer, wine, or intoxicating liquor. (It is lawful and permissible for a student who is 21 years of age or older to possess and consume beer and intoxicating liquor in the Fenn Tower dormitories. It is also lawful for a student who is 18 years of age or older to purchase and consume 3.2 beer in Fat Glenn's, the rathskeller in University Hall.)[2]

    f. Any law violation considered a felony under the provisions of the Ohio Revised Code.

2. The following conduct on campus has special significance in the University community. It is prohibited and cases involving violations shall be referred to the Student Judiciary:

    a. Tampering with or misuse of fire-fighting equipment.

    b. Unauthorized possession or use of firearms or fireworks.

    c. Turning in a false fire alarm.

    d. Throwing or intentionally dropping an object from a window or roof of any University building.

    e. Forgery, alteration, or misuse of University documents, records, or identification cards.

    f. Furnishing false information to the University with intent to deceive.

    g. Possession or use of intoxicating liquor on University property.

    h. Failure to comply with directions of University officials acting in the performance of their duties.

3. The following examples of student behavior on campus can be both violation of general law and in conflict with the distinct interests of the University community. When a violation has occurred it shall be referred to the Student Conduct Committee for a decision as to whether it is to be considered by the Student Judiciary and/or referred to civil authorities for prosecution:

    a. Hazing.

    b. Gambling.

---

[2] As adopted by the Board of Trustees, 70-10, February 12, 1970 and 70-14, March 12, 1970.

c. Lewd and lascivious behavior or indecent exposure.

d. Disorderly conduct.

e. Action taken by one or more persons during a demonstration or protest when this action:

1) Causes injury to an individual.
2) Causes damage to personal or University property.
3) Prevents any student, against his will, from attending class, entering, leaving, or using any University facility, or attending any special authorized program on University property.
4) Prevents any faculty member, administrative officer, student, employee, or invited guest of the University from performing authorized duties.
5) Blocks the normal business of the University, particularly classroom or laboratory instruction.
6) Blocks pedestrian or vehicle traffic.

Appendix M: The National Union of Students and The National Council for Civil Liberties (Great Britain) — Academic Freedom and the Law, 1970

The issues raised by the notion of academic freedom are concerned with the protection and extension of freedom for the community as a whole as well as members of institutions of higher education.

These rights include:

(i)   the right to study and to have access to facilities for study

(ii) the right of freedom of thought and interpretation

(iii) the right of those who teach within or service an institution to withdraw their labour for 'industrial' reasons.

Many of the disputes now arising in colleges can only be resolved by a form of college government.

Internal disciplinary proceedings need not be taken against students in every instance of a breach of the substantive rules. College authorities should not institute such proceedings where to do so is likely to result in an extension of the disorder or conflict and to contribute to worsening relations within the college. In particular, disciplinary proceedings should never be taken in the event of

(i) a boycott of classes, or
(ii) an occupation

where these actions do not involve any conflict with the rights of others to study and to have access to facilities for study. (ch. 2 passim)

No information should be gathered or recorded relating to the lawful activities of a student within or without a college for the purpose of a possible subsequent discrimination against a student, and that no other information should be noted in a student's file unless there is demonstrable need for it which is reasonably related to the basic purpose and necessities of the university or college. Relevant records such as academic, disciplinary, medical and psychiatric should be maintained in separate files.

The Commission further recommends that:

(i) no mention should be made in any university or college record of a student's religious or political beliefs or activities;

(ii) access to student records should be confined to authorised staff who require access in connection with the performance of their duties. All persons having access to student records should be instructed that the information contained therein must be kept confidential and should be required to sign and date their adherence to this procedure;

(iii) medical records, whether held by an official college or university student health service or not, should be subject to the same rules of confidentiality as apply generally and outside colleges to medical records; and should not be included within the embrace of the term 'student records';

(iv) persons outside the university or college should not have access to a student's records except with the student's written permission, and except where the information (for instance, in the case of degree examination results) is public in any event;

(v) references of a confidential nature should not be written except at the explicit request of the student concerned, and should in no circumstances include reference to the student's political or religious beliefs or activities;

(vi) students should be allowed to inspect those parts of their own records which contain information not confidential from them; they should be informed of the broad contents of those parts of the records which are confidential from them, and should be permitted to invoke the prescribed 'safeguard-mechanism' where they desire to ensure that the record rules have not been breached. Such safeguard mechanism should include inspection by an independent third party such as a lawyer or other person acceptable to both sides; (the precise arrangement must be a matter for agreement within each college). Special additional arrangements for safeguards should be made in respect of data banks. In this respect readers are referred to Appendix 5:

(vii) the rules regarding the keeping and release of records should be made known and available to all within the college community.

STUDENT
TENURE

All colleges should as soon as is practicable adopt the practice of setting out in a single document the terms of the contract between the college and the students and that a copy of the contract should be given to the student prior to registration.

STUDENT
DISCIPLINE

The term 'academic offence' should be restricted to a failure to fulfil the requirements of an academic course, and that these requirements should be seen only in terms of the formal system of academic assessment.

College regulations should prescribe the following offences, and no others:—

'It shall be an offence for any student:

(i) to engage in conduct which actively disrupts the teaching or study or research of the college;

(ii) to damage or deface any property of the college.'

In no circumstances should a college discipline a student for conduct which has already been the subject of criminal proceedings.

A college should never make any attempt to make an arrangement with prosecuting authorities whereby a criminal prosecution is waived in return for internal disciplinary proceedings being taken against a student.

A student ought not to be given any immunity from genuine police enquiry which follows the commission of a criminal offence even when this requires the police to enter the college campus.

FIRST
DEGREE AND
OTHER
EQUIVALENT
AWARDS

An award should be terminated only when the student has been finally dismissed after due process.

In all cases involving suspension or termination of awards the initiative should lie with the university or college authority and in no case should an award be terminated unless both the LEA and the university or college authority are in aggreement that this is necessary. . . .

THE HIGHER
EDUCATION
ADVISORY
BOARD

A Higher Education Advisory Board should be established, to be responsible in general for the preservation and advancement of the rights contained in the concept of academic freedom. In particular:

a) the constitution of the Board should be laid down by Act of Parliament;

b) the Board should keep the charters and statutes of universities and the articles of government of colleges under review, and should be empowered to suggest amendments;

c) the Board should provide help and advice to colleges on disciplinary provisions, and should be empowered to approve the disciplinary provisions made by a particular college;

d) the Board should appoint a Judicial Committee to hear appeals from the final disciplinary tribunal in every college;

e) the Board should further appoint an Academic Committee to hear appeals against the final decision of a college to expel a student or to refuse readmission on academic grounds.

SOURCE: The National Union of Students and The National Council for Civil Liberties, *Academic Freedom and the Law,* London, 1970. The recommendations in the above excerpt have not been approved as policy by the National Conference of the Union.

Appendix N: University of Oregon — Student Conduct Program

A. General Policies

1. The University is dedicated not only to learning and the advancement of knowledge but also to the development of ethically sensitive and responsible persons. It seeks to achieve these goals through a sound educational program and policies governing student contact that encourage independence and maturity.

2. The University distinguishes its responsibility for student conduct from the control functions of the wider community. When a student has been apprehended for the violation of a law of the community, the state, or the nation, the University will not request or agree to special consideration for the student because of his status as a student. The University will cooperate fully, however, with law enforcement agencies, and with other agencies in any program for the rehabilitation of the student.

3. The University may apply sanctions or take other appropriate action only when student conduct directly and significantly interferes with the University's (a) primary educational responsibility of ensuring the opportunity of all members of the University community to attain their educational objectives, or (b) subsidiary responsibilities of protecting the health and safety of persons in the University community, maintaining and protecting property, keeping records, providing living accommodations and other services, and sponsoring non-classroom activities such as lectures, concerts, athletic events, and social functions.

4. Procedural fairness is basic to the proper enforcement of all University rules. In particular, no disciplinary sanction as serious

as expulsion, suspension, disciplinary probation, or entry of an adverse notation on any permanent record available to persons outside the University shall be imposed unless the student has been notified in writing of the charges against him and has had an opportunity (a) to appear alone or with any other persons to advise and assist him before an appropriate committee, court, or official, (b) to know the nature and source of the evidence against him and to present evidence in his own behalf, and (c) to have his case reviewed by the University Appeals Board (*March 4, 1970*).

5. Students shall have an opportunity to participate fully in the formulation of all policies and rules pertaining to student conduct and in the enforcement of all such rules.

6. Rules and sanctions affecting the conduct of men and women shall be based on general principles of equal treatment, including like penalties for like violations.

B. Violations

1. No sanction or other disciplinary action shall be imposed on a student by or in the name of the University except in accordance with this Code.

2. Expulsion or suspension from the University or any lesser sanction may result from the commission of any of the following offenses:

a. Academic cheating or plagiarism

b. Furnishing false information to the University with intent to deceive

c. Forgery, alteration, or misuse of University documents, records, or identification cards

d. Physical abuse of another person in the University community

e. Malicious destruction, damage, or misuse of University property, including library materials, or of private property on the campus

f. Theft or conversion of another's property occurring under the conditions of paragraph A-3 (*June 6, 1968*)

g. Vandalism or kidnapping committed on other campuses

h. Participation in hazing

i. Lewd or indecent conduct occurring under the conditions of paragraph A-3

j. Conduct which intentionally obstructs or disrupts the University functions stated in paragraph A-3 of the Code of Student Conduct

k. Two or more (or the repetition of) offenses listed in paragraph 3 below.

3. Disciplinary probation or any lesser sanction may result from the commission of any of the following offenses:

a. Possession, consumption, or furnishing of alcoholic beverages on University owned or controlled property (except in living quarters of married students), in University related housing for single students, or at University sponsored or supervised functions

b. Disorderly conduct, including disorderly conduct resulting from drunkenness, occurring under the conditions of paragraph A-3 *(June 12, 1964)*

c. Failure to disperse, to leave a University building, room or other premise, or to cease the use of loudspeakers, amplifiers, or other forms of noise after being given notice to do so by a person properly designated and identified as having authority from the president of the University to give such notice.

d. Raiding of University related living units

e. Violation of closing hour restrictions

f. Violation of visiting hour rules

g. Violation of any University rule approved by the Student Conduct Committee for the infraction of which sanctions may be imposed under this Code.

4. All rules approved by the Student Conduct Committee pursuant to paragraph 3 (g) shall be in writing and shall be published, distributed, or posted in such a manner as to furnish adequate notice of their contents to students affected by such rules. The University's failure to comply with this requirement shall be a complete defense to any charge of violation of a rule of which the student has no actual knowledge.

C. Sanctions

1. Sanctions which may be imposed for the commission of University offenses shall include the following:

a. Expulsion from the University

b. Suspension from the University for a definite or indefinite period of time

c. Disciplinary probation with or without loss of designated privileges for a definite period of time. The violation of the terms of disciplinary probation or the infraction of any University rule during the period of disciplinary probation may be grounds for suspension or expulsion from the University. The parents of any student under 21 years of age who is placed on disciplinary probation, suspended, or expelled shall be so notified.

d. Loss of privileges:
   1. Restriction to campus living quarters
   2. Denial of use of an automobile for a designated time
   3. Removal from dormitory or other University housing
   4. Loss of such other privileges as may be consistent with the offense committed and the rehabilitation of the student

e. Admonition and warning

f. Such other sanctions as may be approved by the Student Conduct Committee.

2. The sanctions of expulsion or suspension shall not be imposed except upon proper determination by the Student Court or the University Appeals Board (March 4, 1970).

3. The General Policies, Violations, and Sanctions shall be printed and made readily available to all students. The campus newspaper shall be requested by the Student Conduct Committee to publish the same at the beginning of each school year.

D. Group Offenses

(Adopted by the Student Conduct Committee December 20, 1963 in Part II of the Code of Student Conduct, pursuant to Part I, E4 of the Code. Adopted as a part of Part I of this Code by the Faculty on February 5, 1964)

1. Living organizations, societies, clubs and similar organized groups are responsible for compliance with University regulations. Upon satisfactory proof that the group has encouraged, or did not take reasonable steps, as a group, to prevent violations of University regulations, the group may be subjected to permanent or temporary suspension of charter, social probation, denial of use of University facilities, or other like sanctions (*March 2, 1966*).

2. All living organizations are responsible for compliance with University regulations on discrimination. Upon satisfactory proof that the group has encouraged, or did not take reasonable steps as a group to prevent violations of University regulations, the group may be subjected to permanent or temporary suspension

of charter, social probation, denial of use of University facilities or other like sanctions (*December 6, 1967*).

3. The determination that a group is liable to sanction under the foregoing Sections 1 and 2, and of the sanction to be imposed, shall be made by the University Appeals Board at a hearing held for that purpose. The president or principal officer of the group must be given a reasonable notice of the time and place of said hearing and of the nature of the charges. He or any other member of the group is entitled to attend and be heard at the hearing *(March 4, 1970)*.

4. Nothing herein authorizes the imposition of individual sanctions on any person other than in accordance with the Code of Student Conduct.

E. The Student Conduct Committee

1. The Student Conduct Committee, by faculty legislation and by delegation of the President of the University, is designated as the agency within the University which has primary responsibility for the student-conduct program. The Committee shall be responsible to the faculty and the President of the University for recommending policies relating to student conduct, for formulating or approving rules and enforcement procedures within the framework of existing policies, and for recommending to the President of the University changes in the administration of any aspect of the student-conduct program *(March 4, 1970)*.

2. The Committee shall consist of four faculty members and three student members, each appointed by the President of the University. Each student member shall serve for a period of one year with one member retiring at the end of each academic term (Fall, Winter, Spring). Members of the Committee may be reappointed. The President may appoint temporary members of the Committee to serve during a summer session or such other times as are necessary to assure full membership of the Committee.

3. The President of the University shall designate a Coordinator of Student Conduct who shall serve as Secretary of the Committee and assist the Committee in the discharge of its responsibilities. He shall coordinate the activities of all officials, committees, student groups, and tribunals responsible for student conduct.

4. All regulations or rules relating to student conduct that are established by any University official, committee or student group, and for which sanctions may be imposed in the name of the University, must be submitted to the Committee for approval. Fraternity, sorority, or cooperative "housekeeping" rules adopted by members for the internal management of the living unit are not considered University rules for the purpose of this Code.

5. The Committee may delegate jurisdiction to handle infractions of University rules to the Student Court and such other tribunals as may be established. With the consent of the President of the University, the Committee also may delegate such jurisdiction to appropriate University officials. In all instances such jurisdiction shall be defined by the Committee, ordinarily in terms of specified offenses, maximum sanctions, or designated living units. The Committee may, at its discretion, withdraw delegation of jurisdiction in any case and dispose of such case itself.

6. The Committee shall require from University officials and tribunals periodic written reports of the disposition of all student-conduct cases handled under their jurisdiction. The gathering of such reports and their submission to the Committee shall be the responsibility of the Coordinator of Student Conduct. The Committee shall examine such reports for consistency with existing policies and, where necessary, review the reports with the appropriate officials or tribunals.

7. The Committee shall submit to the faculty and the President of the University each Spring term a written report covering the entire student conduct program, including an evaluation of existing rules, policies, and enforcement procedures. It shall recommend changes in policy to the faculty and the President and changes in the administration of the program to the President.

F. University Appeals Board (March 4, 1970)
1. The University Appeals Board, by faculty legislation and by delegation of the President of the University, is the final appeals body under the Student Conduct Code.

2. The Board shall consist of three student members recommended by the President of the ASUO, and three faculty members, each a member of the University community in good standing, and shall

be appointed by the President of the University. A quorum shall consist of two students and two faculty members. Terms of membership shall be one year from the time of appointment. Members may be reappointed, but no member may serve more than two consecutive terms. The President of the University may appoint temporary members to the Board to serve during such times as are necessary to assure full membership of the Board. The Board shall elect its own chairman.

3. In any case the Student Conduct Committee may appoint one of its members to serve as an additional non-voting member of the University Appeals Board. The presence of this member will not affect the Board's quorum.

4. The Board shall establish rules of procedure for itself; however, an affirmative vote of four members of the Board shall be necessary to overrule a decision of a lower court or to find that a violation has occurred in cases in which no lower court has made a decision. Inability of the Board to make an affirmative decision to overrule or find that a violation has occurred shall be deemed a decision to affirm or find no violation.

G. Student Tribunals

1. The President of the University shall appoint five members to a Senior Court Panel, no more than two of them from the faculty and the rest from the Student Body. The student members shall be recommended by the President of the Associated Students. The appointments will be for one year, but members may be reappointed, and the President is urged to preserve continuity of membership from year to year. Senior Court Panel members shall be selected for their knowledge of the Student Conduct program in general, and for their understanding of the operation of the Student Court in particular.

The Senior Court panel will select an impartial system for choosing a court for each case and will be responsible for formulating rules of practice and procedure in hearings under this Code. Such rules are subject to review and revision by the University Appeals Board.

2. The President of the University shall appoint a Panel of Associates. The size of this panel shall be determined by the Student

Conduct Committee, but no more than one-third of its members shall be from the faculty. The student members shall be recommended by the President of the Associated Students.

3. A Student Court shall consist of three members, at least two of whom shall be students. One member of each student court shall be chosen from the Senior Court Panel, and this member will be the Chairman of the Student Court. The remaining members of the Student Court may be chosen from either the Senior Court Panel or the Panel of Associates. The jurisdiction of the Student Court shall be determined by the Student Conduct Committee, and the procedural rules will be established by the Senior Court Panel under the supervision of the University Appeals Board.

4. A Student Court shall decide on all matters of fact, on the ultimate question of whether the Code has been violated, and on the sanction to be imposed, by majority vote. Decisions on procedural matters (e.g. on the admissibility of evidence) will be made by the Chairman of the Court. The Chairman will also decide which are matters of substance and which are matters of procedure, though on such decisions he may well seek the opinion of the other members of the court before ruling. A decision of the Chairman of the Court under this section can be reviewed only by appeal to the University Appeals Board.

5. The Student Conduct Committee, with the assistance of the Coordinator of Student Conduct, may establish minor tribunals composed of students. When appropriate, University officials or faculty members may serve as advisers. No minor tribunal shall have jurisdiction to impose the sanction of expulsion or suspension.

6. No tribunal shall have any function except the enforcement of University rules or the performance of other duties which may be delegated to it by the Student Conduct Committee.

H. Records

1. The Coordinator of Student Conduct shall be responsible to the Student Conduct Committee for the maintenance of adequate records pertaining to the student-conduct program.

2. These records shall include a report on the disposition of each disciplinary case. Such reports shall be submitted to the Coordina-

tor of Student Conduct by every official, tribunal, court, or committee authorized to impose sanctions under this Code.

3. In order to accomplish these record-keeping responsibilities, the Student Conduct Committee and the Coordinator of Student Conduct may prescribe reporting procedures to be followed by those authorized to impose sanctions under this Code.

I. Amendments

1. The above Code may be amended only by action of the general faculty of the University of Oregon.

II. THE ADMINISTRATION OF THE CODE

A. The Student Court

1. The Court shall maintain, with the assistance of the Coordinator of Student Conduct, an adequate record of the history and disposition of each case to come before it. The record shall include a summary of the evidence upon which the Court based its decision.

2. The jurisdiction of the Court shall extend to all violations of the Code.

3. The Court may impose any authorized sanction which is warranted by the circumstances of the case. Pursuant to the authority vested in the Student Conduct Committee by Sections I.C.1.f. and I.E.5., the Student Court is hereby authorized by said Committee to impose sanctions involving the rendition of labor or services. Such sanctions should be employed only in cases where principles of restitution or rehabilitation render such type sanctions peculiarly appropriate. This sanction may be in addition to other authorized sanctions. *(November 24, 1964)*

4. Any student whose case is referred to the Court shall be notified of such referral in writing by the Coordinator of Student Conduct at least three days before the hearing and shall be apprised in the notice of the charges against him. During the hearing the student shall have the opportunity (a) to appear in person or through counsel, (b) to know the evidence against him, and (c) to present evidence and argument in his own behalf. A request by a student for a hearing closed to the public will be given due consideration.

In the resolution of factual disputes, the Court will hear the testimony of witnesses and otherwise seek the best evidence obtainable.

5. The Coordinator of Student Conduct shall appoint, upon recommendation of a Committee comprised of one member of the University Appeals Board, one member of the Law School Faculty, the President of the ASUO, and the Coordinator of Student Conduct, one or more law students to serve as prosecutors for the Student Court and University Appeals Board. The Prosecutors shall prepare and present all cases which are to be heard in the Student Court and University Appeals Board. The Coordinator of Student Conduct shall, following a preliminary investigation of his own, turn over to the Student Prosecutors all cases which are to be heard by the Student Court or University Appeals Board. The Prosecutors shall then prepare the case for hearing and may either present it to the Student Court or University Appeals Board or recommend to the Conduct Committee that it be dropped without a hearing *(August 4, 1970)*.

6. The defendant and/or the prosecutor may call witnesses to appear in their behalf before Student Court or University Appeals Board *(March 4, 1970)*.

a. The party wishing to call the witness or the party's agent shall serve on the witness at least one full day before the trial a form procured from the Office of Student Conduct notifying the witness of the reason, time, date and place that he is to appear.

b. Any witness who has been duly served notice in accordance with IIA9a and who willfully fails to appear before the hearing body as instructed, without an excuse acceptable to the Court, shall be sanctionable pursuant to I.B.3.g. by the Student Court *(May 15, 1968)*.

7. The Coordinator of Student Conduct shall execute the decisions of the Court.

8. *Rules of Procedure (November 4, 1963)*

    a. Notice

        1. A student who is charged with an offense under the Student Conduct Code shall receive written notice at least three days before his case is to be considered by the Court. The Notice shall be in the form approved by the Student Conduct Committee as shown in Form A (Appendix I.) *A student may, in writing, waive the three day notice of hearing (January 9, 1968)*.

b. Outline of Proceedings

1. *Student does not appear.* A student may elect not to appear for a hearing. If, in writing, he agrees not to contest the case and, also in writing, waives a hearing, the Court will dispose of the case as provided for in Part II.F.5.e. of the Student Conduct Program. If he does not so agree in writing or does not waive a hearing in writing, but still does not appear personally or through his representative at the hearing, the Court will dispose of the case in the manner it believes is just.

2. *Student not reasonably able to appear.* If the case is disposed of under paragraph 11 b.1. of Section II.A., and it is subsequently determined by the Court that the student was not reasonably able to appear and not reasonably able to give notice of this prior to or at the time of the hearing, the Court may set aside its disposition and set the case for rehearing. Notice of any re-scheduled hearing will be given the student in writing three days in advance of the hearing.

3. *Student appears personally or through representative.* If a student appears at a hearing, the charge against him shall be read in his or his representative's presence. The student then shall state whether the charge is accurate and, if so, whether he has an excuse. If the student admits the facts as charged and offers no adequate excuse, the Court will proceed to determine the sanction. If the student does not admit the facts as charged or assert an adequate excuse, the hearing will proceed as follows: the Coordinator of Student Conduct, or his representative, will present the evidence he has obtained; the student will present his evidence; the Coordinator of Student Conduct (or his representative), the student (or his representative), or the Court may ask questions. After it has been determined whether the student committed the offense as charged, the Court will proceed to dismiss the case or to impose sanction, whichever is appropriate. Before imposing sanction, the Court will listen to any statement on behalf of the student. In addition the Court may conduct any investigation it believes is necessary to a fair disposition of the case.

4. *Variations in order of procedure.* The order of procedure set forth in this rule is not rigid. The Court may vary it whenever it believes a variation would be wise.

c. Evidence.

1. *Hearsay evidence.* All statements that are proposed to be used against the student shall be reduced to writing, and the student shall be given the opportunity to examine them. If he objects to their

use within the time set in the Notice of Hearing that he receives, the statement will not be used. If he does not object within that time, he will be understood to have waived his objection. If any other hearsay evidence is used at his hearing, the student may enter an objection based on the lack of opportunity to cross-examine at any time within the period established for appeals from decisions of the Court.

2. *Other evidence.* Except as provided in the case of hearsay evidence any evidence that the court believes is relevant is admissible.

d. Objections and motions.

1. The Court may rule on objections and motions at the time they are made. However, the Court may reserve decision on an objection or motion, require that it be reduced to writing, and order that the proceedings continue.

e. Decisions of the Court.

1. *Vote required.* A decision that a student has committed an offense requires an affirmative vote of two-thirds of the members of the Court deciding the case. Sanctions of suspension or expulsion may likewise be imposed only by two-thirds of the members voting on the question. Sanctions of lesser severity than suspension or expulsion may be imposed by a majority of the members who vote. The Chairman of the Court may rule on all other questions that come before the Court. If no member of the Court objects to a ruling of the Chairman before the case has been disposed of, it stands as the ruling of the Court. If any member of the Court does object to a ruling of the Chairman before the case has been disposed of, a majority of the members voting will determine its effect.

2. *Student's copy.* A written copy of the decision shall be given to the student. If a sanction of expulsion, suspension, or probation is imposed, the decision shall advise the student of his right to appeal.

f. Standard of Proof.

1. No member of the Court shall vote that the student has committed the offense as charged unless the evidence is clear and convincing to him.

g. Appeal.

1. A student may appeal from any decision by delivering to the Coordinator of Student Conduct within five days of receiving written notice of his right to appeal, a signed statement containing: (1) a statement that he appeals from a designated decision; and (2) a brief statement of the respects in which he considers the decision is wrong.

h. Amendment.

1. The Court may, by a vote of five or more members, amend the rules by adding or changing them. The vote to amend shall be subject to approval by the Student Conduct Committee.

9. *Student Defender.* The Student Defender shall be a second or third year law student appointed by the ASUO President on recommendation from the previous Student Defender, a representative of the Student Conduct Committee, and a member of the Law School faculty. The appointment shall be subject to the approval of the President of the University. His function shall be to obtain counsel for all students charged with violations of the Student Conduct Code who request him to do so. *(January 23, 1968)*

B. Minor Courts
(Adopted by the Student Conduct Committee October 25, 1963)

1. There will be a system of minor courts of such numbers as may from time to time be found necessary. Such courts have jurisdiction to determine cases involving alleged violation of Section I.B.3.a. through I.B.3.g. of the Code of Student Conduct. *(January 15, 1969)* Such courts shall have jurisdiction to impose only those sanctions referred to in subparagraphs 1.c., 1.d., 1.e., and 1.f. of Section I.C. Pursuant to the authority vested in the Student Conduct Committee by Section I.C.1.f. and I.E.5., each minor court is hereby specifically authorized by said committee to impose sanctions involving the rendition of labor or services. Such sanctions should be employed only in cases where principles of restitution or rehabilitation render such type sanctions peculiarly appropriate. This sanction may be in addition to other authorized sanctions. *(November 24, 1964)*

2. Each court shall have five members, with three being a quorum. Members shall be recommended by the President of the ASUO and appointed by the President of the University. *(March 2, 1970)*

3. No court member may hear a case involving a member of his own unit *(October 13, 1964)*.

4. Cases shall be referred to the courts through the office of the Coordinator of Student Conduct who shall appoint an assistant, subject to the approval of the Student Conduct Committee, to act as an adviser to the minor courts. His duties shall be to:

a. assist the President of the Associated Students to recruit and nominate to the President of the University candidates for membership on the courts.

b. organize the courts.

c. receive all cases from the Coordinator of Student Conduct, interview those charged, assign the cases to the courts in rotation, and serve the necessary papers.

d. attend court hearings and to serve as adviser to the court.

e. report results of hearings in accordance with I.G.2 of the Student Conduct Code. *(January 26, 1966)*

5. Each head counselor shall submit a weekly report to the Coordinator of Student Conduct, listing all cases of infractions within his unit. The report will include the name of the hall, name of the counselor, date of report, a brief description of each offense and its disposition. *(October 13, 1964)*

6. Students may appeal to the Student Court from a decision of a Minor Court imposing any sanction and may appeal to the Minor Court from the sanction of a counselor. *(January 23, 1968)*

7. Rules of Procedure *(November 1, 1963)*

a. *Notice.* A student charged with an offense under the Student Conduct Code shall be given written notice at least three days before his case is to be heard. Notice shall be given by handing to the student Form B (Appendix II) filled out except for the blanks provided for "Finding," "Sanction," "Chairman of Court" and "Date of Hearing." A student may, in writing, waive the three day notice of hearing. The notice may be filed and signed by the Coordinator of Student Conduct or by a counselor, in which case the Notice must be initialed by the Coordinator of Student Conduct. The original notice is to be given to the student charged and two copies are to be given to the court *(January 24, 1968).*

b. *Hearing.* The Chairman of the court shall read the charge and ask the parties if they are ready to proceed. If anyone requests a postponement of the hearing, the court will decide summarily on such request. If no such request is made, or it is denied, the hearing will proceed as follows: (1) The Coordinator of Student Conduct, or his representatives shall state the case against the student; (2) The student, or his representative, may answer; (3) If any facts are in dispute the parties, in turn, may introduce any relevant evidence and may cross-examine each other's witnesses; (4) The parties may each make a closing statement commenting on any evidence that has been introduced and making proposals in respect to the possible sanction.

If the student charged fails to appear without adequate excuse, the court shall ask for proof that he was duly notified and, if satisfied that he was, shall dispose of the case on the basis of the written charge and any statement that the Coordinator of Student Conduct, or his representative wishes to make.

c. *Decision.* When the testimony and statements of parties are concluded, the courts shall retire to decide as to the facts and what sanction, if any, should be imposed. Decision shall be by majority vote and must be based on matter brought out during the hearing. When a decision is reached, the Chairman shall complete all three copies of Form B by filling in the case number, the findings and sanction, his signature and the date. The finding should be limited to "guilty" or "not guilty" plus a *very brief* indication of any mitigating or aggravating factors. The sanction must be stated sufficiently specifically to enable it to be executed by one not otherwise acquainted with the court's thinking.

d. *Announcement of Decision.* As soon as a decision is reached, court shall be reconvened and the Findings and Sanction shall be read in the presence of the parties. The Chairman of the court shall hand the completed original Form B to the student charged and shall advise him orally that he may appeal within five days. *(January 24, 1968)*

e. *Appeal.* A student may initiate an appeal from a sanction by handling to the Coordinator of Student Conduct within five days of the date thereof the original copy of Form B bearing his signed statement: "I appeal from this decision." *(January 24, 1968)*

C. Fraternity & Sorority Tribunals

1. Pursuant to Section I.E.4., the Conduct Committee hereby delegates to Panhellenic and Inter-Fraternity Council the authority to establish rules regarding the conduct of their respective member groups and individuals off campus, these rules being subject to the approval of the Conduct Committee.

a. Pursuant to Section I.E.5., the Committee further delegates jurisdiction to handle infractions of such rules to Panhellenic Judiciary Board and Inter-Fraternity Council Tribunal, respectively. Sanctions shall be imposed in accordance with Section I.C. Groups or individuals may appeal to the University Appeals Board decisions made under this delegation of jurisdiction. *(March 4, 1970)*

b. Pursuant to Section I.E.6., Panhellenic Judiciary Board and Inter-Fraternity Council Tribunal shall submit to the Coordinator of Student Conduct periodic written reports of the disposition of all cases handled under their jurisdiction *(January 30, 1968).*

D. Dormitory Judiciary (February 16, 1970)

1. Each residence hall unit shall have a student judiciary. Alleged violations of the Student Conduct Code occurring within a dormitory unit shall be handled in that unit by the unit's judiciary if the alleged violation directly affects the living conditions of the dormitory unit unless the unit judiciary by a majority vote refers the case to the defendant's unit judiciary, the IFC or Panhellenic tribunal, or the Minor Court or Student Court, whichever is appropriate. Dormitory judiciaries shall have the authority equal to that of the Minor Courts and shall be empowered to impose sanctions in accordance with the provisions for Minor Courts found in Code section II.B.1.

2. Each judiciary shall have five members with three members being a quorum. No restrictions for membership shall exist by class. Each unit shall have the option exercised through its hall government for choosing the manner in which members of the judiciaries shall be selected. Alternatives for membership selection shall include:

a. A floor representative system with at least one student per floor elected by the residents of the floor.

b. Membership on the judiciary on an organized rotating membership basis.

Other methods as may be recommended by the hall government are subject to review by the Student Conduct Committee.

3. Cases may be referred to the judiciary by any resident of the local unit. Referral shall be through the chairman of the judiciary on a form provided for that purpose. The counselor shall serve as advisor to the judiciary with no vote. It shall be the duty of the court chairman to inform the student of the fact of referral and arrange a time and date for the hearing.

4. Any member of the unit judiciary may disqualify himself from the hearing of a particular case. In the event that three or more persons disqualify themselves on any case, the case shall be referred to a Minor Court.

5. A record of the unit judiciary hearing and the action taken shall be made by the court chairman, one copy of which shall be submitted to the Coordinator of Student Conduct. The report will include the name of the residence hall, date of report, a brief description of each offense and its disposition.

6. In the interest of consistency, the Coordinator of Student Conduct or his representative, together with the Housing Office, shall be responsible for orientation and advising of the various judiciary boards and the members. The Student Conduct Committee shall make periodic review of the action of the unit judiciary boards in order to insure this same consistency.

7. Rules of Procedure:

a. *Notice:* A student charged with an offense under the Student Conduct Code and referred to the unit judiciary shall be given written notice at least 24 hours before his case is to be heard. Notice shall be given by handing to the student a form provided which shall include a notice as to the code violation and a brief description of the circumstances.

b. *Hearing:* The chairman of the court shall read the charge and ask the person making the referral to the judiciary board to explain the circumstances of the violation. The person charged shall then be asked to respond. Any witnesses to the violation may be questioned by the chairman of the court or other members of the court. The student may speak on his own behalf or may invite any other person to speak on his behalf. Each party may comment on the testimony of the other, or ask questions of the other. Hearings shall be open to any and only residents of that unit unless the chairman, on request, rules to close the hearing to all persons not directly related to the case.

c. *Deliberation:* The judiciary shall deliberate on the decision in a closed session.

d. *Decision:* A decision of the judiciary shall be by a majority vote and must be based solely on matter brought out during the hearing. The readings of the decision shall take place in the presence of all concerned. The student shall be advised orally that he may appeal within five days.

e. *Appeal:* A student may appeal any sanction imposed by filing notice of appeal with the Coordinator of Student Conduct within five office days.

f. *Additional Rules of Procedure:* Judiciary rules of procedure shall be proposed by judiciary members and adopted by a ⅔ vote of the members of the living organization. Such rules of procedure are subject to the restriction that any rules must include adequate safe-guards against infringement upon student rights and must have the approval of the Student Conduct Committee.

8. *Special Procedure Regarding Sanction of Eviction.* If a student is to be evicted from a dormitory as a sanction for violation of the Student Conduct Code, (as distinguished from eviction in an incident of the landlord-tenant relationship between student and the University) the following procedure must be followed.

a. A student tribunal upon finding that a student has violated the Code and concluding that eviction is an appropriate sanction must consult with the pertinent complex director and the Director of Housing and obtain the agreement of these persons before imposing such sanction.

b. A complex director may initiate action to evict a student if a student tribunal has found that he has committed one or more violations of the Code relevant to the dormitory living situation and the sanctions imposed by the tribunal have not protected the interests of the University or other dormitory residents. In such cases the complex director shall inform the appropriate tribunal of his decision and give the tribunal a chance to react or propose an alternative. If the tribunal wishes to assume no further role and the complex director still feels that eviction is the only alternative, he will ask for a recommendation by a special standing committee composed of two Associate Deans (Student Services) or their representatives and three members of the Interdormitory Council appointed by the IDC president before he makes a final decision. This committee will conduct a hearing, giving the student reasonable notice and an opportunity to be heard, and make a recommendation as to whether the student shall be evicted. Thereupon the Director of Housing will make the final decision in the case.

c. As an aid to construction and administration of this section II.D.8 reference is made to a letter dated August 20, 1970, and entitled *Recommendations Regarding Eviction of Students from Dormitories Due to Misconduct,* a copy of which is incorporated in the minutes of the meeting of August 28, 1970.

The Student Conduct Committee may delegate administrative authority to the University Housing Office beyond that delineated in Clause 6 as the Committee sees fit.

E. Student Traffic Court

1. The Student Traffic Court shall consist of five students recommended by the President of the Associated Students and appointed by the President of the University. The Coordinator of Student Conduct or his representative shall serve as secretary and advisor to the court *(January 9, 1968).*

2. The Court shall recommend to the Building and Ground Committee policies and regulations to govern the use and parking of student cars on University grounds.

3. Students who receive citations for the violation of Campus Traffic and Parking Regulations may present their cases to the Student Traffic Court which may, upon a finding of innocence, dismiss the charges. *(May 25, 1970)*

4. Students who are cited for the violation of Campus Traffic and Parking Regulations and admit violating the Regulations, or are found guilty of the violation by the Student Traffic Court, may authorize the University to remove the amount of the fine imposed from their breakage fee. *(May 25, 1970)*

5. Any student who is found guilty in Student Traffic Court of committing five (5) violations of Campus Parking Regulations during fall quarter or three violations of Campus Traffic and Parking Regulations during winter and spring quarter, may be cited to the Student Traffic Court as an habitual violator. *(May 25, 1970)*

6. Any student who is found guilty in Student Traffic Court of violating Campus Traffic and Parking Regulations is also subject to the following sanctions which may be imposed by the Student Traffic Court. *(May 25, 1970)*

a. Revocation of his parking permit.

b. Imposition of the sanctions permitted by I.B.3.g. of the Student Conduct Code.

c. Imposition of sanctions involving rendition of labor or services. Such sanctions may be imposed only in cases where principles of restitution or rehabilitation render such sanction peculiarly appropriate.

d. Referral of the case to Student Court. *(April 3, 1968)*

7. Decision of the Traffic Court may be appealed to the Student Court within five office days. *(April 3, 1968)*

8. Campus Traffic and Parking Regulations referred to herein above are those regulations appearing in the pamphlet entitled "Campus Parking Information and Regulations." *(April 3, 1968)*

F. General Procedures

1. All serious violations of the law and the Code will be immediately reported to the Coordinator of Student Conduct by any person who has knowledge of the commission of any such violation. The reporting practices of those in a position of responsibility for student conduct may be delineated by the Coordinator of Student Conduct.

2. The Coordinator of Student Conduct shall insure that the best interests of any offending student are served, regardless of whether disciplinary action is taken, by making full use of appropriate medical counseling and other professional services.

3. In those cases of violation of the Code involving psychological abnormality, mental illness, or other unusual circumstances, the Coordinator of Student Conduct may seek professional assistance and advice, consult with the student's parents or guardian, or take other measures to assure a fair disposition of the case, provided that no sanction under I.C. shall be imposed without the consent of the Conduct Committee *(January 23, 1968)*.

4. Where the evidence establishes to the satisfaction of the Coordinator of Student Conduct that a referral to a student court is justified and the case has not been disposed of under paragraphs 3 or 4 above, the following procedure will govern: *(January 23, 1968)*

a. The Coordinator of Student Conduct shall advise the student of the charges and the evidence against him.

b. The Coordinator of Student Conduct shall afford the student an opportunity to state informally or present evidence in support of his side of the case, including mitigating circumstances.

c. The Coordinator of Student Conduct shall refer the case to the Student Court for action.

d. The conduct of the hearing before the Student Court shall be governed by the established rules of procedure of the Court.

e. A student who pleads guilty may elect not to appear for a hearing. The plea and waiver of hearing shall be in writing. In such instances the Coordinator of Student Conduct shall present the written plea and the facts of the case to the Student Court for disposition. (See II.A.11.b.1.) *(January 23, 1968)*

f. In extraordinary cases where the interests of the student or the University can best be served, the Coordinator of Student Conduct may refer the case directly to the University Appeals Board. *(March 4, 1970)*

5. The Coordinator of Student Conduct will keep a record of the nature and disposition of all cases brought before the courts. This record will not contain names of students. A second file will be kept, listing students brought before courts alphabetically with a cross-reference to the record of cases. Entries in this last file will be removed when the student graduates or five years after he leaves school. *(June 2, 1964)*

6. In all instances involving a reported alleged violation of the Code where the Coordinator of Student Conduct does not refer the case to the Student Court or an appropriate minor judicial

tribunal for action, the Coordinator of Student Conduct shall make a full report of the basic facts and the reasons for the non-referral for judicial proceedings to the Student Conduct Committee. *(January 26, 1971)*

7. The Coordinator of Student Conduct shall have the full rights of membership on the Student Conduct Committee except; (1) he shall not vote and (2) he shall not be present during closed deliberative sessions on judicial matters. *(November 27, 1967)*

8. The notice of hearing shall be reduced to 24 hours during the last ten calendar days of each term. Any cases that cannot be handled under this provision will be considered holdover cases and will be brought before the courts at the earliest possible time following. *(October 14, 1970)*

9. Anyone who is enrolled for one or more hours, or in a special program approved by the University, is subject to the Code. *(January 16, 1968)*

10. *Hearings on New Rules, Regulations, and Policies.*

a. Upon receipt of a request for the approval of policies, rules and regulations pursuant to Section I.A.5. and I.E.4., the Student Conduct Committee shall give notice of such request to the Oregon Daily Emerald and prescribe the procedures for notice and hearing on the proposed rules. The Committee shall set a time not later than 14 days after receipt of such request for members of the University community to be heard, either orally or in writing on the desirability of adopting the proposed rules and shall prescribe the manner in which such proposed rules shall be publicly posted prior to the time of the hearing.

b. The Committee, at any time after such rules have been approved may upon giving notice and an opportunity for interested persons to be heard, as provided in II.E.11.a., modify, amend, or disapprove any approved rules or regulations. *(April 4, 1967)*

c. Recommendations to the faculty for amendments to Section I of the Code of Student Conduct shall be made only after holding a public hearing. *(January 15, 1969)*

G. *Appeal Procedures*

1. The student shall have the right to appeal from any decision of any court that imposes any sanction and from any decision of a counselor that imposes a sanction. See further II.G.2. *(April 2, 1968)*

2. The Student Court shall serve as the appellate tribunal to hear appeals from minor judicial tribunals. The appellate decision of the Student Court shall be final except in the case where disciplinary probation has been imposed as a sanction. Appeals from any decision of a counselor shall be heard de novo by a Minor Court. *(February 22, 1966)*

3. The University Appeals Board shall serve as the appellate tribunal to hear appeals from the Student Conduct Court. *(March 4, 1970)*

4. The tribunal or court which initially imposes a sanction of expulsion, suspension, or probation shall advise the student in writing of his right to appeal. The student shall have five days from receipt of such advice to notify the Office of the Coordinator of Student Conduct of his intention to appeal. *(January 23, 1968)*

5.

a. The appellate tribunal shall meet as soon as practicable to consider an appeal. Ordinarily on appeals from the Student Court, consideration shall be limited to a review of the evidence as established in the initial hearing. However, the (appellate tribunal) University Appeals Board, at its discretion, may consider further evidence and call witnesses. The student may appear before the appellate tribunal in person or through counsel. *(March 4, 1970)*

b. Appeals from Minor Court in which a plea of "not guilty" was entered shall be tried de novo in the Student Court, but only as to issues of fact. In cases where the defendant has pleaded guilty in Minor Court but is able to show by a preponderance of the evidence in Student Court that his plea was mistakenly entered, and that he was unaware, at the time, of his legal rights, the Student Court shall remand the case to a Minor Court with instruction that the defendant be allowed to withdraw his plea.

c. In all cases where the plea of guilty in the Minor Court stands, the only grounds for appeal shall be (1) harshness of sanction or (2) lack of jurisdiction in the Minor Court to hear the case. In all appeals other than those from issues of fact, the burden shall be on the defendant.

d. In the case of an appeal heard de novo by the Student Court, if the defendant is found guilty, the sentence of the Minor Court shall be affirmed unless the defendant shows that the sentence was manifestly unreasonable. This provision shall also apply to cases involving only the appeal of a sanction. *(February 26, 1969)*

6. The (appellate tribunal) University Appeals Board shall affirm the initial decision of the Student Court unless, in its opinion, such decision is unreasonable or arbitrary or not supported by substantial evidence. In cases where the decision is not to affirm, the (appellate tribunal) University Appeals Board may (a) dismiss the charges, (b) reduce or modify but not increase the severity of the sanction, or (c) return the case to the (lower tribunal) Student Court for further consideration consistent with the directions of the (appellate tribunal) Appeals Board. *(March 4, 1970)*

7. The Student Conduct Committee may review on its own motion a decision of any judicial tribunal or counselor in any case regardless of the sanction imposed. The procedure outlined immediately above shall govern the conduct of such a review.

8. The prosecution shall have the right to appeal from any decision of the Student Court made on a matter of law. This section shall not be construed to allow an appeal on an issue concerning only the facts of a case. *(October 12, 1970)*

H. Closing Hours for Living Organizations
University Dormitories

1. The University operates two kinds of student dormitory units:

a. Dormitory units for which no closing hours are established.

b. Dormitory units for which closing hours are established.

2. Any student shall have the opportunity of choosing to live in either a dormitory unit where there are no closing hours or a dormitory unit where there are closing hours.

3. The general opening and closing hours for students living in Dormitory Units with closing hours shall be:

a. Sunday through Thursday—6:00 a.m. to 12:00 midnight.

b. Friday and Saturday—6:00 a.m. to 2:00 a.m. (the following day).

4. Special closing hours for students living in Dormitory Units with closing hours shall be:

a. 2:00 a.m. the night before a legal holiday observed by the University.

b. Twenty minutes after the termination of any activity recognized as a University function which continues past normal closing hours.

Cooperatives, Fraternities, and Sororities

1. A cooperative, fraternity, or sorority may establish closing hour rules for its own residents or for residents living in housing within its jurisdiction.

2. Closing hour rules established by any cooperative, fraternity, or sorority shall be considered "housekeeping" rules within the meaning of Section I.E.4.

I. Definitions

1. "Malicious" as used in this Code shall be deemed only to mean "willfully and knowingly." *(February 26, 1969)*

J. Amendments

1. Part II above, the Administration of the Code, and Part III below, Rules and Regulations, may be amended only by the action of the Student Conduct Committee. Amendments affecting the duties of administrative personnel shall be made with the approval of the President of the University.

III. RULES AND REGULATIONS

Pursuant to Section I.B.3.g., I.B.4., I.E.1. and I.E.4. of the Student Conduct Code . . . *(January 15, 1969)* the following rules and regulations are adopted by the Student Conduct Committee as rules for the violation of which sanctions may be imposed. *(The sections in this part were consolidated by the Student Conduct Committee as a new Part III on April 29, 1964.)*

A. Dormitory Rules
(October 21, 1963)

1. Students may be held responsible for damage to University-owned property.

a. Any student who causes damage beyond reasonable wear and tear to any room, facility, equipment, or furnishing owned by the University and located in or on University-owned housing shall be held financially responsible for such damage.

b. The Assistant Director of Dormitories or his duly authorized representatives are hereby authorized to levy against any student who violates

Section III.A.1.a., a charge sufficient in amount to compensate the University for any loss caused by such student.

c. Nothing in Section III.A.1.b. shall preclude any authorized court from imposing any other sanction included in Section I.C.1., provided that such sanction shall not be imposed except in cases of malicious destruction.

d. Any student aggrieved by a decision made pursuant to Section III.A.1.b. may within five days appeal that decision to Minor Court. *(June 7, 1968)*

2. Sanctions may be imposed for failure to comply with the following rules, which pertain specifically to the room renting situation:

a. Locked doors and fire doors must not be propped open.

b. Fire alarms and equipment must not be tampered with.

c. Dormitory equipment and furnishings must not be removed.

d. Electrical appliances must be used only in their proper places. No ironing or cooking in rooms.

e. Laundry facilities are restricted to residents of the building only.

f. Residents must stay off roofs and sides of dormitory buildings.

g. No pets are permitted.

h. House guests must be registered with counselor or head resident.

i. Actions that may create a hazard to the health or safety of residents, or cause damage to property are not permitted in the dormitories; e.g., water fights, water balloon dropping, shaving cream fights, fire crackers, intentionally set fires, conspicuously unsanitary conditions, etc.

j. All residents must vacate the buildings at the time of fire alarms and fire drills. *(November 4, 1965)*

k. Gambling is prohibited. *(May 18, 1966)*

3. Sanctions may be imposed for infraction of rules pursuant to the following:

a. Each unit shall operate with established quiet hours.

b. Each unit, building, or complex may, upon the initiation of a majority thereof, establish housekeeping rules for internal management.

All such rules must be approved pursuant to I.E.4. above. *(January 14, 1966)*

B. Visiting Rules

1. In order to respect the privacy of those in residence, members of the opposite sex are allowed in living areas of the buildings

housing the respective living organizations only during the designated visiting hours and only when accompanied by a resident of that living organization. Administration of designated visiting hours shall be the responsibility of the respective living organizations, subject only to the restrictions that all such rules be adopted by a secret ballot vote passed by two-thirds of the total population of the living organization concerned and approved by the Student Conduct Committee. *(January 15, 1969)*

2. Dating in University controlled or related housing after closing hours shall be considered a violation of closing hours. *(April 9, 1964)*

C. Social Activity Eligibility
(April 20, 1965)
1. Any student who has been expelled or suspended from the University as a result of disciplinary action shall be denied the privileges of the institution and of the organizations in any way connected with it during the period of such expulsion or suspension. Such students shall not be permitted to participate in any University recognized function, or invited or allowed to reside in any fraternity, sorority, co-operative or dormitory.

2. Any individual who is invited or allowed to reside in any fraternity, sorority, or co-operative and who is not otherwise subject as an individual to the University of Oregon Code of Student Conduct, may subject such fraternity, sorority, or co-operative to sanctions for Group Offenses set forth in I.D. of this Code, by conduct that would constitute a violation of this Code if such individual were a student subject to the jurisdiction of this Code.

D. Compliance with Request to Cease Violation
Failure to comply with a request to discontinue conduct which constitutes a violation under this Code shall be considered to be an aggravation of that offense. *(March 2, 1970)*

E. Compliance with Sanction
A student duly sanctioned under this Code shall comply with all provisions of such sanctions. *(November 20, 1967)*

F. Discrimination
Living Organizations Shall Not Discriminate In Pledgeship or Membership Choice On The Basis of Race, Color, Or Religion.

When a hearing is held on an alleged violation of this rule, the existence of any of the following conditions shall be sufficient evidence of guilt unless there is clear and convincing evidence to the contrary:

1. An alumnus or national officer of the organization has the power to veto the pledgeship or membership bid.

2. A letter of recommendation for an alumnus is required for pledgeship or membership.

3. A system of voting on pledgeship or membership exists such that one or a small minority of members can veto a pledgeship or membership bid.

4. The organization consistently refuses to admit members of minority groups to pledgeship or membership in the organization. *(April 17, 1968)*

G. Firearms
Firearms, including antique guns, ammunition, air guns and pellet guns, fireworks or explosives may not be brought into any University building or carried on campus. The only exceptions will be equipment owned, used and maintained by a University School or Department. *(July 18, 1968)*

H. EMU Checks
All students, within 10 days of official notification, shall reimburse the Erb Memorial Union and pay a service charge for a check returned by a bank for Non-Sufficient Funds. *(July 18, 1968)*

I. Contempt
1. Contempt of Adjudicative Proceedings. When any person, in the presence of any tribunal created under this Code, and while sitting as an adjudicative body, exhibits conduct tending to impair or to interrupt the due course of a trial or other adjudicative proceedings, such person may be held in contempt and sanctioned therefor. *(October 30, 1969)*

2. Sanction Imposed. Any sanction which may be imposed for the violation of a rule promulgated pursuant to I.B.3.g. may be imposed for the commission of a contempt.

3. Adjudication of Contempt and Imposition of Sanction. The adjudication of contempt shall be made by the then presiding officer, alone and summarily. Thereupon the proceedings shall be recessed and the entire tribunal shall decide whether the presiding

officer's adjudication shall be upheld and, if so, what sanction shall be imposed. Such decision shall be made as in any other case. Upon the adjudication and sanction, if any, the presiding officer shall certify to the Coordinator of Student Conduct the facts constituting the contempt and the sanction imposed therefor. Persons so adjudicated in contempt shall have the same right to appeal as are afforded in any other case adjudicated in that tribunal. *(May 27, 1969)*

Appendix O:
University of California — Interim Report of the Statewide Academic Council

The rights and responsibilities of faculty members as teachers, scholars, colleagues and citizens are here set forth in general terms.

Responsibilities Rights cannot be claimed unless responsibilities are met. Faculty members meet their professorial responsibilities primarily through conscientious self-discipline and adherence to standards developed by the faculty. This statement is designed to articulate these standards. It is neither a complete list of acceptable acts nor of acts that necessarily warrant discipline. Herein, the general principle of discipline is that it should be imposed only for conduct that impairs the University's integrity.

I. Teaching

Teachers and students have the right to expect that conditions favorable to the educational process will be maintained. Teaching at the University requires free presentation and critical examination of available knowledge and conflicting viewpoints. Discussion of many subjects cannot occur without revealing personal opinions; thus it is proper for a student or a teacher to express his views on a subject under consideration in class. To maintain such conditions a faculty member should not, for example,

1. structure his presentations to exclude opinions other than his own;

2. introduce material that has little or no relation to the subject matter;

275

3. depart materially from the subject matter of the course as approved by the faculty;

4. refuse to enroll or teach students on the grounds of their beliefs or the possible uses to which they may put the knowledge to be gained in a course;

5. evaluate and grade students with prejudice, favoritism, or caprice;

6. deny recognition to students for their contributions to his research and writing;

7. fail to meet his classes as scheduled and keep his office hours, except for legitimate reasons;

8. condone or abet disruption, interference or intimidation in the classroom.

II. The University

In the affairs of the academic community, the faculty should neither incite to the use of force nor tolerate the threat of force or coercion from any source. They should make every effort to protect orderly dissent. For example, a faculty member should not

1. obstruct or disrupt activities sponsored or authorized by the University;

2. forcibly detain or intimidate students, faculty and officers of the University;

3. use University facilities or resources for commercial, religious or partisan political purposes, except as authorized by or under published University rules.

The faculty member has an obligation to the University, as it has to him. The faculty should give highest priority to their academic responsibilities and scholarly impartiality: For example,

1. the employment of a faculty member by public or private agencies, even when it enhances his competence and his value to the University, should not interfere with the performance of his University duties;

2. a faculty member should not withhold his services from the University for partisan political or other non-academic reasons.

III. Scholarship

The faculty have the responsibility and right, restricted only by compatibility with the character and purpose of the University, to engage in research and creative activity. The faculty have a primary obligation to integrity of scholarship. Thus, for example, a faculty member should not

1. interpret or use the writings, research and findings of others without proper acknowledgment;

2. engage in activities that conflict or interfere with meeting his responsibilities of scholarship.

IV. Colleagues

A faculty is a community of scholars. A faculty member should

1. respect the rights and dignity of his colleagues;

2. encourage and support the free expression of his colleagues' professional viewpoints;

3. assist in the maintenance of standards of professional conduct;

4. protect his colleagues' rights to due process.

V. The Community

Faculty members have the same rights and obligations as all citizens and are free as other citizens to express their views and to participate in the political processes of the community. When they speak or act as private persons, faculty members should avoid creating the impression that they represent the University.

Rights The authority to discipline faculty members in appropriate cases derives from the mutual recognition by the faculty and the administration of the University's obligations as an institution of higher learning. This includes a responsibility of the administration to protect and encourage the faculty in contributing to teaching, learning, research and public service and implies that the function of discipline is to preserve conditions hospitable to these pursuits. Such conditions, as they relate to the faculty, include, for example:

1. free inquiry and exchange of ideas;

2. the right to present controversial material relevant to a course of instruction;

3. enjoyment of constitutionally protected political or religious expression;

4. participation in the governance of the University, including

(a) approval of course content and manner of instruction,

(b) establishment of requirements for matriculation and for degrees,

(c) appointment and promotion of faculty,

(d) selection of chairmen of departments and certain academic administrators,

(e) discipline, including dismissal, of members of the faculty, and the formulation of rules and procedures for discipline of students,

(f) establishment of norms for teaching responsibilities and for evaluation of both faculty and student achievement, and

(g) determination of the forms of departmental governance;

5. the right to be judged, by one's colleagues and in accordance with fair procedures, in matters of promotion, tenure and discipline, on the basis of the faculty member's professional qualifications and professional conduct, and excluding any other test of fitness. In the administration of discipline, as in the general governance of the University, the University must seek to protect and foster these conditions.

Enforcement and Sanctions

Enforcement

Each Division of the Senate should develop its own procedures for initial investigation of allegations of faculty misconduct and to recommend the appropriate sanctions to be imposed. These procedures shall be submitted to and approved by the University Committee on Rules and Jurisdiction and, to insure equitable standards, the University Committee on Privilege and Tenure.

Divisional procedures for initial investigation should meet the following standards:

1. all aspects of the deliberations associated with the investigation of allegations and the recommendation of sanctions shall be confidential;

2. reports shall be delivered only to the administrative officer and to the faculty member against whom allegations have been made;

3. Senate members responsible for the initial investigation of an allegation of faculty misconduct shall not participate in any way in any personnel proceedings that may follow from that investigation.

A complaint against a faculty member may be lodged by any faculty member, University administrator, student or other member of the campus community. Such a complaint normally should be made to the faculty member's department chairman or to his academic dean. This official is obligated to give it proper consideration; if he does not, the complainant may take the matter to a higher level. The official who receives the complaint will inform the faculty member of it. The faculty member will be given opportunity to refute allegations of misconduct and to appeal decisions rendered against him.

The purpose of the initial investigation undertaken on the basis of a complaint against a faculty member shall not be to decide whether the alleged misconduct in fact occurred, but to advise the Chancellor or his designated representative whether the allegations of misconduct establish probable cause for initiating disciplinary procedures. Reasonable efforts shall be made to dispose of complaints informally before formal proceedings are initiated.

While charges are pending, full or partial interim suspension with pay, including suspension from teaching duties, is authorized only if, in the Chancellor's judgment, there is a high probability that the faculty member's continued assignment to his duties would endanger the University community. In such event, a prompt hearing shall be afforded the affected faculty member.

Faculty members against whom allegations are made or charges filed are entitled to all privileges and protections specified in the Standing Orders of the Regents and in provisions of the Manual of the Academic Senate that implement them; specifically, opportunity for a prior hearing by the Divisional Committee on Privilege and Tenure should be afforded before any sanction for misconduct is imposed.

Sanctions

Disciplinary sanction for misconduct may include only the following: written censure; docking of pay; deferral of an impending promotion or merit increase; suspension (other than interim suspension with pay); demotion (in rank or in salary step); dismissal from the employ of the University.

The nature and circumstances of the offense should determine the severity and type of discipline. Provision should also be made for possible removal of sanctions or censure after an appropriate period.

Appendix P:
University of Illinois at Urbana - Champaign — Faculty Senate Statement on Faculty Responsibility and Academic Freedom

In recognition of the climate of social change in a society of which the University is an integral part, in view of current major issues concerning faculty and institutional responsibility, and in consideration of the importance of retaining educational policy matters within the academic community, be it therefore resolved that:

1. Academic freedom is essential to the teaching, research, and public service functions of this University in its contribution to the common good of society.

2. The faculty member has rights and responsibilities common to all citizens, free from institutional censorship, but in such pursuits the services of the University should not be used, and any indication of University affiliation should be accompanied by a statement that it is for identification purposes only.

3. The faculty member has rights consistent with the principles of academic freedom in carrying out his teaching functions and has the responsibility to respect the students' freedom to learn.

4. The faculty member has the responsibility to instruct assigned courses in a manner consistent with scheduled time, course content, and course credit approved by appropriate faculty bodies.

5. The faculty member has the responsibility to meet classes as scheduled, or alternate instruction should be arranged by him or the department.

6 The faculty member has the responsibility to provide the University with an individual evaluation of the work of each student in his classes.

7 All members of the faculty share the responsibility for maintaining a professional atmosphere in which violations of academic freedom and responsibility are unlikely to occur.

8 Faculty members have a right to seek changes of University policies by appropriate means, but means deemed inappropriate include committing or inciting acts of physical violence against individuals, acts which interfere with academic freedom, and acts of destruction of property.

9 Evaluations of faculty performance with regard to academic freedom and responsibility should be made by administrative officers and appropriate academic bodies according to established principles of due process.

10 The attached Statement Reflecting the Sense of the Urbana-Champaign Senate of the University of Illinois on Academic Freedom and Faculty Responsibility represents the sense of this Senate and does not alter existing University statutes.

Explanatory Statement   *Introduction:* This statement is offered by the Urbana-Champaign Senate as a guideline to the faculty for its academic performance. It has been formulated because we are now faced with major issues concerning faculty and institutional responsibility. It does not alter existing University statutes.

The social and academic environment of our University is an integral part of society and in the current climate of change existing patterns of conduct are being challenged. This statement seeks to express the rights and responsibilities of faculty members in dealing with contemporary issues within a University already committed to the basic principles of academic freedom. It speaks to some of these issues, in particular to issues surrounding the rights and responsibilities of a faculty member as a professional individual and as a citizen.

I. The unique role of the university in society

Universities exist to serve the common good and not primarily to further the interests of either individuals or institutions. The basic functions of this University are teaching, research, and public service. By accepting an appointment in this University, an individual assumes a responsibility to pursue scholarly activities. Such pursuits necessitate free inquiry, free expression, intellectual honesty, respect for the dignity and rights of others, and openness to change. The rights and responsibilities exercised within the academic community must be compatible with these characteristics.

II. The importance of academic freedom

Academic freedom is essential to the functioning of a university. It applies to its teaching, research, and public service and involves both faculty and students. The principle of academic freedom is designed to protect the faculty member's freedom to teach and to conduct research. It also protects the student's freedom to learn. The faculty member is responsible for providing the student with the same kind of freedom which he claims for himself, namely, the freedom to consider conflicting views and to make his own evaluation of data, evidence, and doctrines. Furthermore, the faculty member has a responsibility to maintain an atmosphere conducive to intellectual inquiry and rational discussion.

III. An expression of faculty responsibility

A. Responsibilities of a Faculty Member as a Citizen. The faculty member is a citizen as well as a member of a learned profession and an educational institution. When he speaks or writes as a citizen, he should be free from institutional censorship or discipline. As a citizen he has the rights common to all citizens to organize and join political or other associations, convene and conduct public meetings, peacefully demonstrate, picket, and publicize his opinion on political or social issues. In exercising these rights, he should not use the services of the University, and any indication of University affiliation should be accompanied by a statement that it is for identification purposes only.

B. Responsibilities of a Faculty Member as a Professional Individual. A faculty member is expected to instruct his assigned courses in a manner consistent with the scheduled time, the course content, and the course credit as approved by the faculty. Within these constraints, he is entitled to freedom in the classroom in developing and discussing, according to his area of competence, the subjects which he is assigned. If the faculty member is unable to meet his class, he has the obligation to offer alternate instruction to meet the course requirements. If he is unable or unwilling to do so, his department or college must assume this responsibility.

During those times when events of national or local importance tend to dominate the attention of members of the university community, the teacher must be especially mindful of his responsibility, freedom, and power. He must avoid using his position as instructor to coerce students into adopting or feigning positions similar to his, or otherwise to infringe upon the rights of any student to hold views opposed to his. Such an act destroys the freedom of his students to pursue the very sort of unbiased inquiry that he should at all times promote.

Experimentation and innovation in teaching functions are professional responsibilities and should be consistent with professional conduct and subject to the knowledge and concurrence of the appropriate academic bodies.

Since University policy calls for the comparison of a student's performance with that of other students in the University for the several purposes that grades serve, every faculty member has the responsibility to provide the University with an evaluation of the work of each student in his classes. Evaluation of academic achievement is a difficult task; a member of the faculty should establish appropriate academic criteria and determine the extent to which his students have met those criteria.

This assessment must be on an individual student basis. The indiscriminate assignment of a grade or the rigid *a priori* determination of a percentage of a class that shall receive a specific grade are equally inimical to academic responsibility and the rights of the individual. Students should have protection through orderly procedures against prejudiced or capricious evaluations.

Each faculty member has the right to criticize and seek alteration of regulations and policies by appropriate means. Among means deemed inappropriate are committing or inciting: acts of physical violence against or coercion of individuals; acts which interfere with academic freedom, freedom of speech, or freedom of movement; and acts of destruction of property.

C. The Maintenance of Academic Rights and Faculty Responsibilities. With respect to matters of academic freedom and faculty responsibility, fundamental principles for university governance and for evaluation of faculty performance are rooted in the historic tradition of higher education in our society, in the position papers of the many professional societies, and in the Statutes of this Institution. It is abundantly clear that all members of the academic community share the responsibility to maintain an atmosphere in which violations of academic and personal rights are unlikely to occur, and to develop processes by which these rights are fully assured. In particular, those faculty who hold administrative positions must constantly be alert to the needs of the academic community; must give full and fair hearing to expressions of grievances; and must respond promptly to such expressions. In making decisions, administrative officers are expected to consult with those affected by the decisions and with appropriate academic advisory bodies. Alleged abuse of the proper role of the faculty with regard to academic freedom and faculty responsibility should be identified and adjudicated by appropriate faculty bodies already in existence in the University community in accordance with established principles and procedures of due process. The University Statutes indicate that these evaluations are initially made by departmental administrators with the counsel of faculty bodies; subsequent evaluation is made by academic deans, campus and university level administrators, and the Board of Trustees with adequate counsel of faculty bodies. At the campus level, the Faculty Advisory Committee and the Senate Committee on Academic Freedom and Tenure are charged with a responsibility both in the judicial and review process.

The Board of Trustees, which has ultimate legal authority over the University has the right to expect that the University faculty and administration will fairly judge those of its members who are alleged to have abused these rights and responsibilities. In turn, it follows that sound and established policy indicates that the Board of Trustees should not exercise original jurisdiction or overrule the judgment of academic bodies in these matters of internal administration.

Appendix 2:
Oregon State Board of Higher Education — Statement Relating to Faculty Conduct, 1970

Society has for long recognized the necessity for protecting colleges and universities against undue outside interference in order that an environment of freedom, which is indispensable to their effective service to society, might be assured.

In recent times it has become apparent that they must be protected also from coercion from within. It is this need that prompts the board to adopt the new provisions of the *Administrative Code*. . . . These include specific prohibitions of some overt conduct inimical to the maintenance of public order. They also contain more general language directed at failure to meet professional standards of conduct.

The board recognizes the difficulty of defining such conduct and the desirability of preciseness to ensure due process. It urges the institutions and their faculties:

1 To develop and adopt in faculty codes any definitions particularly appropriate to the individual institutions.

2 To develop and suggest to the board any more precise or supplemental definitions which should be incorporated in the *Administrative Code.*

3 To develop procedures for advisory interpretive rulings by responsible members of the profession as applied to factual situations posed by members of the academic community.

The changes in the *Administrative Code* are being made by the board in the interest of protecting the integrity of its institutions and the freedoms of the faculty, staff, and students of its institutions, the great majority of whom have not participated nor would participate in or condone the conduct proscribed in these additions to the *Administrative Code.*

The following statement is not intended to preclude any of the institutional and faculty development urged above. Rather, it is a starting point reflecting current board concern and thinking with respect to the difficult and continuing process of defining professional obligations.

FACULTY
ROLES

The faculty member is at one and the same time:

- A citizen
- A member of a learned profession
- An employee of the institution and of the state
- An officer of the institution

To each of these roles there attach certain opportunities, certain responsibilities and obligations.

1 As a *citizen of the broader community,* the faculty member is the beneficiary of all of the rights and the bearer of all of the obligations that citizenship offers or imposes upon any other citizen, including the right to express himself freely and openly.

As a matter of policy the board of higher education does not attempt to control the personal opinion of any faculty member, nor the public expression of that opinion.

But the board does share with the American Association of University Professors the view that the faculty member's special position in the community as a man of learning and an educational officer does impose upon him special responsibilities when he speaks or writes as a citizen. For the public may judge his profession or his institution by his utterances or his actions. It is imperative, therefore:

- That he strive to be accurate at all times, to exercise appropriate restraint, and to show respect for the opinions of others.
- That he strive to make clear that he is not a spokesman for the institution or for the state system of higher education.

As the board would not have individual faculty members presume to present their views publicly as being institutional views when they act in their role as citizens, so the board would not wish any of its institutions to speak out with a corporate voice on public issues — except in those extremities in which the institution's own health or independence, or the freedom of its scholars is at stake. Our colleges and universities are centers of learning, not agencies of direct political action. A center of learning is, by definition, a place of divergent views, independence of thought, diversity of voices.

This is not to suggest that our institutions can be or ought to be remote from the great issues of our day. An education insulated from these would be sterile. But there is a significant difference between individual members of the academic community — or groups bound together by common beliefs and loyalties — setting out to cure social ills by direct political and social action, and the institution, as a corporate body, speaking with one voice for the diversity of views and judgments that are to be found within the faculty and student body on controversial public issues.

The urgency of society's problems and the interest that youth have in seeking their solution offers institutions a unique impetus for devising more creative and productive ways of providing students and faculty the means of studying the issues of our time. Within the context of a center of learning, with due regard for the requirements of scholarship and intellectual rigor, ideas may be formulated, criticized, tested, and applied. Thus armed, let individuals, or groups of like-minded individuals in our academic communities, move to the correction of society's ills, while society rests secure in the knowledge that whatever the ideas proposed or applied in the attempted amelioration of its problems, they will be subject to the careful scrutiny, honest criticism, and candid judgment that only a free and independent academic community can offer.

It is in this vein that the board has said, and now reiterates, that the facilities, equipment, supplies, and other resources of its institutions must not be diverted to partisan political use. This affirmation is not intended to interfere with the traditional use of campus facilities as public forums nor with the political rights of faculty members and students. Nor it is intended to modify relationships with any of the duly recognized student organizations on campus, including the Young Republicans and Young Democrats, and any other political groups characteristically functioning on the campuses. What it seeks to avoid is the colleges and universities becoming agents of direct political action contrary to the views expressed in the paragraphs above.

2 As a *member of a learned profession* that depends upon freedom of opinion, freedom of inquiry, and freedom of expression for its health, vitality, and integrity, the faculty member has a special responsibility to support and defend these freedoms against incursions from within the academic community with the same vigor with which he defends them against outside incursions which would limit or abridge their free exercise.

Such defense requires continuing adherence to the high standards of scholarly commitment that have generally characterized our institutions, and a vigorous rejection of those attitudes which, though rarely encountered in state system institutions, have elsewhere jeopardized academic freedom and public confidence—such attitudes as:

- The attitude that violence, physical threats, destruction of property or other coercive activities are appropriate forms of behavior within an academic community.

- The attitude that scholarly requirements can be abandoned, transforming classrooms from centers of learning to centers of propaganda.

- The attitude that "academic freedom" means an absence of restraint and an absence of accountability to the institution and to society which has established and supports the institution.

3 As an *employee of the institution,* the faculty member has a contractual obligation to perform the services he was employed to provide.

If without authority of his department, school, or institution, the faculty member deliberately withholds the services he was employed to provide, he is breaching his contract and jeopardizing the institution's ability to meet its contract with its students— entered into when the students were admitted and their tuition accepted. In such circumstances, the institutions must take appropriate action to protect themselves and the rights of the students with whom they have contracted. Willfull withholding of services is grounds for withholding pay for the period involved and may be considered as evidence of cause for termination of employment as determined by due process, as set forth in the *Administrative Code.*

This is not to question the right of the faculty—and students, too—to criticize and seek revision of institutional policies, rules, or regulations, or to give free and vigorous expression to their views on public affairs, or to engage in protests carried on in a manner consistent with the maintenance of institutional integrity and the protection of the rights of all members of the academic community, including those whose views may not be congruent with those of the protesters. It is, rather, to suggest that faculty members have professional responsibilities that must be fulfilled if they are to honor their contracts; that the board does not, and the institutions must not, condone the confusion of the faculty member's concern (as a citizen) with public affairs with his obligation to teaching and learning, which forms the basis of his employment agreement with the board and of his obligation to his students.

Nor is there justification for certain other kinds of actions less obvious than deliberate withholding of services, but which undermine the integrity of the institutional programs. Although not often encountered in state system institutions, such practices are to be condemned when they are, and should be dealt with by appropriate action. Illustrative of such practices are the following:

- The devaluation of the institution's credits by grading practices that have no foundation in institutional standards or in an honest professional evaluation of the student's true merit.

- The abandonment to students of the full instructional responsibility for courses for which the faculty member has been given primary responsibility.

  Objection to this action is not to raise question concerning the use of qualified graduate assistants who are under departmental assignment to instruct, nor is it intended to preclude supervised practice teaching by qualified students under controlled conditions concurred in by the department or school in which the faculty member is employed. What it is intended to speak to is the unjustifiable lending of a faculty member's name to a course which is subsequently taught by a student.

- The abandonment, in substantial measure, of the subject matter of the course and the substitution therefor of subject matter unrelated to the discipline in which the course lies.

  Objection to the foregoing practice is not intended to preclude those special circumstances in which the institution, school, or department may, for good and sufficient reasons, authorize faculty to use class time for special functions for a limited period. Nor it is intended to inhibit the ingenuity of the faculty member in relating the content of his course to current problems. The objection is, rather, to those circumstances in which a faculty member, without the knowledge and concurrence of his department, school, or institution, makes the unilateral decision to "reconstitute" his course by abandoning the content of the discipline in favor of some unrelated content considered by him to be more "relevant" to the times.

The habitual or persistent introduction into a course of controversial matter that has no relation to the course content.

Although it is imperative that the teacher have freedom in the classroom in discussing his subject, if he persistently and habitually introduces into his teaching controversial matter which is irrelevant to his subject, the integrity of the course is sacrificed.

When controversial matter appropriate to the subject matter of the course is dealt with, the instructor has the obligation, in the words of AAUP's founding fathers,

". . . to set forth justly without suppression or innuendo, the divergent opinions of other investigators . . . [to] cause his students to become familiar with the best published expressions of the great historic types of doctrine upon the questions at issue; and he should, above all, remember that his business is not to provide his students with ready-made conclusions, but to train them to think for themselves, and to provide them access to those materials which they need if they are to think intelligently."

As an *officer of the institution* by which he is employed, the faculty member shares in the exercise of authority through which the institution is managed and gets its work done. The board of higher education has delegated to the institutional executives responsibility for the operation of their institutions. But in so doing, the board recognizes that the academic community is of a nature, and its constituency of a character that makes it wise for the executive to share with faculty members the exercise of this grant of authority from the board.

Thus it is that the faculty has important responsibilities in the realm of faculty status (appointments, reappointments, decision not to reappoint, promotions, granting of indefinite tenure, and dismissal). And they participate actively in the deliberations relating to such crucial areas as curriculum, subject matter, methods of instruction, research, and those aspects of student life which relate to the educational process.

This shared responsibility is matched by the faculty's shared obligation to the institution itself—to colleagues and to students—and to society which created and maintains the institutions—an obligation to ensure that the institutions remain open, both literally and figuratively. They must not be closed by action of faculty or students. And their tradition of free and open inquiry, discourse, and opinion must remain unchallenged. The board of higher education has committed itself to these aims and urges that faculties give voice to their obligation to share in this avowal of resolve to protect our institutions against the challenges to their continued effective operation to which this statement and the accompanying amendments to the *Administrative Code* speak.

Appendix R: Stanford Chapter of the American Association of University Professors — Report on Faculty Self-Discipline, January 1971

It may be helpful in considering what follows to summarize the essential features of our recommendations. We have provided for:

1   A set of standards for faculty members (see I);

2   A discriminating series of graduated sanctions (see II);

3   A randomly selected panel from which a randomly selected tribunal is to be chosen (see V.A. and VI.A.);

4   A Faculty Screening Agent, chosen by the Chairman of the Senate, to provide a faculty voice in screening complaints (see V.B.);

5   A Prosecutor, chosen by the President, to gather evidence and to present the case (see V.C.);

6   A choice of hearing methods (see V.D.); and

7   A set of procedures to govern the hearings (see VI.D.).

I. STANDARDS The first question that faces anyone who considers this problem is how general or specific must the "substantive law" be. It is clear that too generalized a standard (*e.g.,* whoever does anything wrong shall be punished) simply won't work because it furnishes no warning to the people to whom it is addressed and because it exerts no control over the discretion of those who must apply it. The Tenure Statement (see Appendix E), the Fundamental Standard (see Appendix F), the AAUP Statement on Professional Ethics of 1966 (see Appendix G) all suffer in some degree from these defects.

At the same time, we think that a detailed statement of rules, like that apparently suggested by President Hitch for the University of California (see Appendix H), is objectionable because it affords no flexibility in application, inevitably contains lacunae, and strikes us as being inconsistent with the spirit that ought to obtain in an academic community. Detailed rules may have some place; but we think that a statement of standards that can be applied through a combination of adjudication and legislation must be the starting point.

Accordingly, we propose a set of standards that should enable faculty members (as defined in Part III hereof) to understand what their institutional responsibilities are. By "institutional," we mean those responsibilities that arise out of the individual's place (see Part IV hereof) in this academic community. These standards, as will be noticed, incorporate the spirit of certain provisions of the Tenure Statement. As will also be noticed, we regard those provisions as necessary but insufficient. The standards are as follows (the words "faculty member" are used as shorthand for the people defined in Part III hereof):

[N.B. Throughout this document, bold face type is used to indicate our legislative recommendations. Non-bold face language is intended to be either a preamble to or a commentary on the bold face language.]

It is to be hoped that every person will assist in maintaining the standards set out below.

1. No faculty member shall knowingly violate, or attempt to violate, any provision or the University's Regulations that have been duly promulgated and approved by the Faculty Senate.

2. No faculty member shall engage, or attempt to engage, in professional misconduct in the performance of his academic duties within the University.

3. No faculty member shall intentionally neglect the academic duties which he has undertaken to perform within the University.

4. No faculty member shall prevent, or directly exhort or incite anyone (including, without limitation, students) to prevent, or attempt to prevent anyone from performing his duties within the University.

Paragraph 1 is intended to make it possible for the President and the Senate to define what Regulations of the University should be binding on the faculty. At the present time, with the sole exception of the Disruption Policy, there is no way for any faculty member to know what the University's Regulations are. The word "academic" modifying "duties" in Paragraphs 2 and 3 is used to restrict faculty duties for the purpose of agreeing to standards for faculty self-discipline. We prefer to leave to case-by-case determination the question of what academic duties are. We prefer a common-sense construction which we are quite certain the tribunal (see Part V hereof) will give to these words. In Paragraph 4, we omitted the word "academic" because there are numerous situations in which we think that a "person" (a) ought not to "exhort or incite" anyone (b) to prevent anyone (c) from "performing his duties within the University." For example, a faculty member (a), we think, should not directly incite students (b) to attack police (c) who have been summoned to do their duty on the campus. This is an extreme example, to be sure, but we think that the standard should be the same whether or not a faculty member physically prevents a fellow faculty member from teaching his class, or "directly incites" students to keep a faculty member from teaching his class. By "directly exhort or incite" we mean saying "go do *x*." Of course, we intend that "directly exhort or incite" should be interpreted by the tribunal (see Parts V and VI hereof) strictly so as to permit the broadest possible freedom of speech. Yet, there are occasions when the use of words may justify penalties. We cite the familiar example of yelling "fire" in a crowded theater. We expect this provision to be used extremely sparingly.

5. **No faculty member shall refuse to appear when summoned in connection with any proceeding under this Statement, except that one who appears may, in answer to any question, invoke**
   a. **his privilege not to incriminate himself; or**
   b. **his privilege not to divulge a confidential communication from a student or a colleague made with the understanding that it would be kept confidential;**
   c. **his privilege not to testify against his spouse.**

While we think that it should be a violation of these Standards for a faculty member to refuse to appear when he is summoned, we recognize that his refusal to testify must be privileged in certain circumstances. The three examples that we have given exhaust, in our opinion, the justifiable categories of privilege. We rule out all but the most cursory inquiry by the tribunal into whether the refusal is justified. We think that the claim of privilege, once made in response to a specific question, normally should not be pursued any further.

It will be noticed that, while the substance of certain provisions of the Tenure Statement have been included, this Statement is not intended as a complete substitute for the Tenure Statement. We have used the words "professional misconduct" because we think that the Tenure Statement might be interpreted to cover more of the individual's personal life than we think it wise to include in a Statement of Standards for Faculty Self-Discipline. We prefer to leave it to the Senate to consider whether any attempt to change the Tenure Statement, which was adopted before the Senate came into existence, should be made. We have not included any paraphrase of the Tenure Statement's "incompetence" provision, because we do not think that the question of "incompetence" has any legitimate place here. In so saying, we do not mean to express any opinion as to whether the Tenure Statement should be amended in any way.

II. SANCTIONS As the recent AAUP Statement on Freedom and Responsibility dated Oct. 31, 1970 stated:

". . . systematic attention should be given to questions relating to sanctions other than dismissal, such as warnings and reprimands, in order to provide a more versatile body of academic sanctions."

We recommend that sanctions should be classified in the following manner:

1. Moderate Sanctions. Moderate sanctions should include in ascending order of severity:
   a. a warning;
   b. a censure by the President of the University;
   c. a monetary fine deducted from the offender's pay.

2. Severe Sanctions. Severe sanctions should include in ascending order of severity:
   a. Suspension from duty without pay for a specified period;
   b. Reduction in pay;
   c. Dismissal from the University. (This sanction is intended to be used only in extreme or flagrant cases of violations of the standards.)

In Part VI. D. 10 and 11, we have tried to make clear the significance of the proposed distinction between Moderate and Severe Sanctions.

III. APPLICA-
BILITY

These Standards and Sanctions are intended to apply to every member of the Academic Council.

While there may be much to say for including such people as instructors, lecturers and the like, we concluded that until and unless they are included in the Academic Council, separate procedures are necessary; until such persons have a voice in the Council and in the selection of the Faculty Senate, the procedures we have recommended are inappropriate. As to teaching and research assistants who are also students, there is definitely a problem as to how their responsibilities may be maintained. We learned during our investigations of some instances of neglect of duty or unprofessional conduct by members of this group. We concluded that it was impractical and inappropriate to include them here. We recommend as strongly as we can that the problem of disciplining members of the teaching staff who do not belong to the Academic Council be studied by an appropriate body.

IV. THE
QUESTION OF
CONTRAC-
TUAL STATUS

From the very beginning of our deliberations, we pondered a good deal about the extent to which the people affected by our study have any contractual status. We suggest that the Senate, the President, and the Board of Trustees should all consider this question and should study the implications that it raises, particularly with regard to clarification of each person's academic duties within the institution.

V. THE
PANEL AND
PRELIMINARY
PROCEEDINGS

We begin this section with the assertion that we regard the Advisory Board as an unsatisfactory tribunal for hearing disciplinary cases. We say this, not because the Advisory Board has heard no cases nor in spite of that fact. We believe that the Advisory Board, composed as it is of full professors, and having the very important function of reviewing all appointments and promotions before the President transmits them to the Board of Trustees is not the appropriate instrumentality to pass on disciplinary cases. This is especially true if our recommendations as to sanctions are carried out. If the process that we have in mind is to be used, two kinds of considerations militate against using the Advisory Board to carry it out. One is efficiency. The Advisory Board is already heavily burdened with the functions of passing on appointments and promotions and rendering advice to the President. The other consideration is fairness. How, for example, can we expect a non-tenured Assistant Professor to be satisfied that he has received justice from a panel of full professors, elected by the faculty from its most eminent members? We believe that the tribunal should be drawn from a panel of Academic Council members. The legislative recommendations that follow are interspersed with our commentary, in which we try to give our reasons for each specific legislative recommendation.

A. Selecting the Panel.

1. **The Panel should be chosen annually by the Academic Secretary by random selection and should include not less than one member for every 20 members of the Academic Council.** We favor random selection because we believe (a) that it is fair, (b) that it avoids the dangers of self-selection by volunteers, (c) that it avoids the dangers of having a panel wholly composed of extremists of any type.

2. **Every member chosen for the Panel should serve unless it is impossible for him to do so.** If a faculty member is on leave or ill, the Academic Secretary should replace him by someone else chosen at random. We think that it should be easier to get a commitment to serve on the panel, which may never entail serving on a tribunal, than to get a commitment to serve on the tribunal when a case arises. For this reason, we prefer the two-step process outlined herein.

3. **In selecting the panel, the Academic Secretary should be required to follow a ratio of tenured to nontenured members that reflects the ratio that obtains in the Academic Council.** Our reasons for imposing this requirement should be obvious. We rejected rank distinctions because we believe them to be for this purpose irrelevant. The sole relevant distinction, in our judgment, is whether or not the faculty member has tenure until retirement.

B. The Faculty Screening Agent.

1. **The Chairman of the Senate shall each year appoint a member of the Academic Council whose duty it shall be to screen a complaint against a faculty member and to determine whether or not the complaint shall be forwarded to the officer described in Part V. C. hereof.** We believe that anyone—be he a fellow-faculty

member, a student, a member of the Administration, an alumnus, or a "stranger"—should be entitled to file a complaint against a faculty member. We refer herein to "complainant" as the person who files a complaint and to "respondent" as the faculty member against whom the complaint is filed. No doubt, some procedures are required to see to it that all complaints are received, recorded, and acknowledged. We have not considered those issues. By interposing this faculty member between the complainant and the respondent it is our intention to provide for a faculty scrutiny of the charges and to prevent ill-founded prosecutions. As hereinafter provided, the Faculty Screening Agent, who should be a faculty member who is cognizant of faculty mores and attitudes, can decide on the basis of the complaint, and whatever informal inquiries he may choose to make, whether the complaint stands any chance of resulting in sanctions being applied.

2. **If the Faculty Screening Agent decides to forward the complaint, he shall state to the officer described in Part V. C. hereof what the maximum sanction is that that officer may seek.** We thereby seek to make an additional protection available to the faculty member. We think that whoever receives the complaint, whether it is the President's Office, a Dean, a Department Chairman, or the Chairman of the Senate, should be required to forward it to the Faculty Screening Officer rather than to the Officer, hereafter described, who presents the case. We believe that if that Officer shall inadvertently first receive a complaint he should immediately transmit it to the Faculty Screening Agent. There should also be some provision made for the Chairman of the Senate to appoint an alternative Screening Agent at the beginning of the academic year to handle cases as to which the principal Screening Agent may be disqualified for any reason. We think, nonetheless, that there should be one principal Faculty Screening Agent. We considered the idea of entrusting the screening function to a committee; we unanimously concluded that the difficulties quite outweighed whatever advantages might accrue from such a diffusion of responsibility.

3. **The Faculty Screening Agent shall never be subject to being called to testify in any case that he has screened.** We want to give the Faculty Screening Officer the maximum opportunity to conduct as free-wheeling an investigation as he may desire to conduct. He should, for example, be free to consult whichever of the faculty member's colleagues he wishes to. We visualize his role

as being to consider whether the complaint constitutes a *prima facie* case against the faculty member. In most cases, we think that he can, and thus should, accomplish his function simply from scrutiny of the complaint.

C. Investigation and Presentation of the Case.

1. The President shall designate a member of his staff whose duty it shall be to investigate the case and to present the evidence. Once a case has been cleared by the Faculty Screening Agent, we think that an administrative officer should have the duty of investigating the case, of gathering evidence and of presenting the evidence. We refer to this officer hereafter as the "Prosecutor."

2. After investigation, the Prosecutor may determine that a *prima facie* case does not exist. If that is his decision, he may choose not to prosecute the case. Thus, we provide *two* opportunities for the complaint to be dropped.

3. If the prosecutor decides to drop the case, he shall so inform the Faculty Screening Officer, who shall thereupon cause the complainant to be notified. We do not make any explicit provision for who shall notify the complainant. But we believe that he should be notified if either the Faculty Screening Officer or the Prosecutor decides that the case should proceed no further. In any event, we think that all existing informal methods of settling disputes should remain open and should be used.

D. Choice of Hearing Methods.

1. The Prosecuting Officer, after consultation with the respondent, shall decide as between (a) a hearing before the cognizant Dean followed if demanded either by complainant or respondent by a *de novo* proceeding before the tribunal hereinafter specified or (b) a hearing before the tribunal. The reason why we think that these two options are appropriate can be summarized as follows: It will often occur that the alleged violation is administrative in nature. For example, it may consist of a violation that involves neglect of duty. In such cases, the cognizant Dean may be presently authorized to order the sanction. If, for example, the violation is alleged to be an unauthorized absence from work, the President has the power to order that the violator's pay be docked. That power may obviously be delegated to the cognizant Dean (see Appendix I). Often, the alleged violator will prefer that the complaint be heard administratively. We give the Prosecutor this option because we think that the Administration will ordinarily initiate disciplinary action. However, we believe that, whoever

initiates disciplinary action, the possibility of review by the faculty should always be kept open. Some of us would prefer to see option (a) be the avenue for faculty discipline. Others believe that option (b), which represents the traditional avenue, should be the avenue. Yet we have all concluded that both avenues should be kept open, subject to the restrictions and rights specified hereafter.

It should be noted that when complainant demands review by the tribunal under option (a), on the ground that the penalty imposed by the Dean is insufficient, the prosecutor has discretion not to press the case further, but to allow the Dean's decision to stand.

E. Interim Decisions Under Option (a).

In cases in which option (a) is used, the decision should be automatically stayed for an appropriate period after the respondent is notified of the tentative decision, and, if he elects to seek a review, through the period consumed by the subsequent proceedings. The only exception to this principle that we would advocate is in a case where the President thinks that immediate harm to the community or the respondent would occur were the respondent not immediately suspended from duty. Any such emergency suspension should always be with pay. As we have already implied, any hearing before the tribunal that complainant or respondent demands under option (a) shall have the effect of wiping out the interim decision and the interim decision shall never be referred to in the proceeding before the tribunal.

VI. PROCEED-INGS BEFORE THE TRIBUNAL

A. Selection of the Tribunal.

1. The Academic Secretary shall choose a tribunal of five members from the panel by random selection. Just as the panel is chosen by random selection, we believe that the tribunal to hear any given case should be selected by the same method.

2. If the Faculty Screening Agent determines that the Prosecutor may seek the sanction of Dismissal, then unless the Prosecutor states that he will not do so;

a. The respondent, if he so chooses, shall be entitled to a tribunal made up of at least three members who have the same contractual status, *i.e.,* permanent tenure or nonpermanent tenure, as he does; or

b. The respondent, if he so elects, shall be entitled to a tribunal made up exclusively of persons with permanent tenure. This provision represents the one exception we decided to make to the principle that the tribunal should be composed completely of faculty members chosen at random from the Panel. In cases in which the sanction of Dismissal is sought, we decided that the respondent should be entitled to one of the two options as to tribunal membership set out in the text. A further provision regarding this matter is found in VI. D. 9.

3. **No panel member may be called on to hear more than one case.** Since we think it vital to insure that faculty members serve on tribunals, we deemed this provision to be as much as we could legitimately recommend by way of incentive. We argued a good deal about this point, but we felt it inappropriate to *require* any faculty member to serve either on the panel or on a tribunal.

4. **The Chairman of the Senate or his designee shall select a non-voting Chairman of the Tribunal from the Faculty of the School of Law or from such other faculty members who have similar experience.** It is the Chairman's function to conduct the hearing and to rule on points that any party may raise, subject to having his rulings overruled.

B. **Written Pleadings.**

1. **The complaint shall be served on the respondent by the prosecutor.**

2. **The respondent shall be accorded a reasonable time to submit a written answer and to prepare his defense.**

3. **The tribunal may decide by majority vote that no issues of fact exist and that the case can be determined without taking evidence.**

C. **Challenges to the Tribunal.**

1. **The prosecutor and the respondent shall each be allowed one preemptory challenge.**

2. **Any challenge for cause shall be upheld only on a vote of at least three members of the tribunal.** We vacillated between this provision and the alternatives of allowing the Chairman to break a 2–2 tie and allowing him to determine the decision on the challenge. The challenged member, of course, does not vote on the challenge.

D. **Procedures Before the Tribunal.**

These procedural principles shall apply whether the case is heard by a Dean or by the tribunal under option (a) or option (b). We list these principles without explanation because we believe that they are recognized universally as being necessary.

1. **The respondent shall be presumed to be innocent.**

2. In order to find a violation, the tribunal must be satisfied that the respondent has violated the Standards in the respect or respects charged.

3. The respondent shall be entitled to be represented by anyone of his choice. (At the end of this section, we discuss the question of legal aid to the respondent.) He shall have the rights of cross-examination and confrontation.

4. Technical legal rules of evidence need not be followed.

5. The Chairman shall rule on all questions of admissibility. If either party objects to any such ruling, a majority vote of the Tribunal shall be necessary to overrule the decision of the Chairman.

6. A stenographic record or tape or other verbatim record shall be made and shall be available to both parties.

7. Oral argument may be made by both sides after the hearing, and written briefs may be submitted.

8. Respondent shall have the choice of a public or a private hearing.

9. (a) Except as prescribed in subparagraph (b) hereof, a decision of the tribunal shall require the concurrence of at least three members.

(b) The tribunal shall not impose the sanction of Dismissal without the concurrence of at least four members.

10. If the tribunal imposes Moderate Sanctions, it shall notify the President of that fact. If the President concurs, appropriate action to carry the decision out shall be taken.

11. If the tribunal imposes Severe Sanctions, it shall notify the President of that fact. Unless the President thinks that the respondent is not guilty of the violation or reduces the sanction to a Moderate Sanction, he shall transmit the decision to the Board of Trustees. Unless the Board of Trustees at its first meeting after it has received the decision shall not accept the decision, the President shall carry it out.

12. The decision shall be transmitted to both complainant and respondent.

13. If a hearing is disrupted, the Chairman may declare the hearing closed and exclude all persons; provided, that respondent may name up to 20 faculty members who shall be admitted to the hearing. Should any of these faculty members disrupt the hearing, they may be excluded. Should respondent disrupt the hearings, he may be excluded and the tribunal shall proceed without him.

14. Any faculty member who disrupts a hearing shall be subject to charges under this Statement.

15. In cases in which the tribunal finds that the prosecution has been frivolous or without substantial merit, it may recommend that the University reimburse respondent for all or part of his expenses of defense.

[N.B. We think that a respondent may need to have part or all of the expenses of his defense reimbursed as the case progresses, quite without reference to its outcome. We have tried to find out whether the national AAUP will help him. The answer seems to be quite equivocal. We suggest that, if the need develops, the local chapter of the AAUP should try to set up a defense fund for disciplinary cases under this Statement.]

VII. COUNTER-CLAIMS BY A RESPONDENT

If a respondent to an action under this Statement believes that the University has violated any of his rights, he may assert that by way of counterclaim in his written response in the proceeding against him. The tribunal shall consider any such counterclaim and, if it decides by a vote of three members that the counterclaim is meritorious, may take the counterclaim into consideration in deciding the original case. The tribunal may, it if finds the counterclaim to be meritorious, either (a) dismiss the original proceeding or (b) mitigate the sanction that it would otherwise have recommended. Any such excuse or mitigation shall be explicitly stated in the tribunal's decision.

CONCLUSION

The views of a few members of the Commission diverge on some of the recommendations. All members join in the essential recommendations . . . reserving the right to state their separate views at an appropriate time.

We submit our Report, hoping that the results of our study will be useful to the members of the AAUP chapter, to the Senate of the Academic Council, to the President and to the Board of Trustees of Stanford University.

Appendix S: American Association of State Colleges and Universities — Basic Rights and Responsibilities for College and University Presidents, 1970

The history of American higher education strongly supports the contention that no college or university has made important progress except under the leadership of an outstanding president. At the present time, unfortunately, colleges and universities are experiencing increasing difficulty in attracting and holding able persons as chief adminstrative officers. And individuals remaining in such positions stand virtually unanimous in the opinion that their role has become much more difficult and demanding.

It is the purpose of this document, therefore, to identify certain basic principles that must be accepted if colleges and universities are to function in an orderly, purposeful way and to lay down those conditions necessary to insure the presence of effective leadership on the campus.

Basic principles

1 Before anything else, a college or university (particularly a public one) exists to serve the general society which created it and which supports it; such an institution does not belong to a particular group of persons within that society or within that institution.

2 A college or university serves many constituencies—faculty, staff, students, alumni, and parents of students being the closest ones. All of these constituencies have a stake in the institution and its

development, and all should be provided with an opportunity to be informed and heard.

Legally defined, a college or university does not consist of any one or combination of these constituencies. In the eyes of the law, a college or university is its governing board, most commonly known as the board of trustees.

The major functions of a public college or university are teaching/ learning, scholarship/research, and appropriate public service, as determined ultimately by the board of trustees. These functions cannot be illegally interfered with or eliminated except at the risk of destroying the institution.

The role of the college president

I. Executive officer: The president serves as chief executive officer of the college or university. In this capacity, he reports and recommends directly to the board of trustees. Although the president listens to the voices of all constituent groups, it must be recognized that he functions primarily as the administrative arm of the board and that all legal governing authority resides with the board.

II. Authority: The selection of the president is the board of trustees' most important decision. Having once made that selection, the board must insure that the president is vested with all the authority necessary to carry out the duties and responsibilities for which he is held accountable. The board (and, if the institution is part of a multi-college system, its central staff) must operate in a manner which does not erode the authority of the president but which enhances the autonomy of the institution.

III. Responsibilities: As chief executive officer, the president is responsible for recommending broad policies for consideration by the board and implementing these policies once they have been approved by the board. Major areas of presidential responsibility include:

The direction of current and long-range planning related to institutional goals, academic programs and teaching approaches, research, public service, enrollment projections, and physical plant development.

The development and maintenance of appropriate administrative organization and policy-making structure for the most efficient and effective utilization of institutional resources.

The development and maintenance of a personnel system concerned with the recruitment, selection, assignment, supervision, evaluation, and promotion and tenure of all personnel employed by the institution.

The preparation and presentation of the financial budget and the allocation and supervision of all appropriated and other funds that finance any activities under the jurisdiction of the college.

The development and maintenance of the facilities and equipment necessary for the support of the college's functions.

IV. Relationship with governing board: As chief executive officer of the institution, the president deserves to have a clear understanding with his governing board concerning the following working relationships:

The board of trustees should invite the president to attend all meetings of the board (the only exception being when the board meets in executive session to act on the president's salary and other personal matters). The board should not meet with any representatives of the college's various constituencies without the presence of the president.

The board of trustees should ask the president for his recommendations on all matters before the board that may affect the college. No changes affecting an institution in any regard should be made by the board (or a coordinating board, commission for higher education, central staff, or other state agencies) without appropriate prior consultation with and recommendations from the president of that institution.

The board of trustees should hold the president free of any personal liability in the execution of his duties and responsibilities so long as he is acting as the board's chief executive officer. This should include protection against claims from damage suits and physical and psychological harassment.

The board of trustees should recognize that it, and not the president, holds final responsibility for the health, safety, and welfare of the institution and its personnel, particularly students. The president's main responsibility is that of providing students with reasonable opportunities to obtain an education, in accordance with the laws of the surrounding community, the policies of the board, and the resources of the institution.

Carnegie Commission on Higher Education

Sponsored Research Reports

ALTERNATIVE METHODS OF FEDERAL
FUNDING FOR HIGHER EDUCATION
Ron Wolk

INVENTORY OF CURRENT RESEARCH ON
HIGHER EDUCATION 1968
Dale M. Heckman and Warren Bryan Martin

The following reprints and technical reports are available from the Carnegie Commission on Higher Education, 1947 Center Street, Berkeley, California 94704.

INSTITUTIONS IN TRANSITION, *by* Harold Hodgkinson *(out of print); expanded version to be published by McGraw-Hill in 1971.*

. . . AND WHAT PROFESSORS THINK: ABOUT STUDENT PROTEST AND MANNERS, MORALS, POLITICS, AND CHAOS ON THE CAMPUS, *by* Seymour Martin Lipset *and* Everett Carll Ladd, Jr., *reprinted from* PSYCHOLOGY TODAY, November 1970.

DEMAND AND SUPPLY IN U.S. HIGHER EDUCATION: A PROGRESS REPORT, *by* Roy Radner *and* Leonard S. Miller, *reprinted from* AMERICAN ECONOMIC REVIEW, May 1970.

THE UNHOLY ALLIANCE AGAINST THE CAMPUS, *by* Kenneth Keniston *and* Michael Lerner, *reprinted from* NEW YORK TIMES MAGAZINE, November 8, 1970 .

PRECARIOUS PROFESSORS: NEW PATTERNS OF REPRESENTATION, *by* Joseph W. Garbarino, *reprinted from* INDUSTRIAL RELATIONS, *vol. 10, no. 1, February 1971.*

RESOURCES FOR HIGHER EDUCATION: AN ECONOMIST'S VIEW, *by* Theodore W. Schultz, *re-printed from* JOURNAL OF POLITICAL ECONOMY, *vol. 76, no. 3, University of Chicago, May/ June 1968. (Out of print.)**

INDUSTRIAL RELATIONS AND UNIVERSITY RELATIONS, *by* Clark Kerr, *reprinted from* PRO-CEEDINGS OF THE 21ST ANNUAL WINTER MEETING OF THE INDUSTRIAL RELATIONS RE-SEARCH ASSOCIATION, *pp. 15–25. (Out of print.)**

NEW CHALLENGES TO THE COLLEGE AND UNIVERSITY, *by* Clark Kerr, *reprinted from Kermit* Gordon *(ed.),* AGENDA FOR THE NATION, *The Brookings Institution, Washington, D.C., 1968. (Out of print.)**

PRESIDENTIAL DISCONTENT, *by* Clark Kerr, *reprinted from David C. Nichols (ed.),* PER-SPECTIVES ON CAMPUS TENSIONS: PAPERS PREPARED FOR THE SPECIAL COMMITTEE ON CAMPUS TENSIONS, *American Council on Education, Washington, D.C., September 1970. (Out of print.)**

STUDENT PROTEST—AN INSTITUTIONAL AND NATIONAL PROFILE, *by* Harold Hodgkinson, *reprinted from* THE RECORD, *vol. 71, no. 4, May 1970. (Out of print.)**

WHAT'S BUGGING THE STUDENTS?, *by* Kenneth Keniston, *reprinted from* EDUCATIONAL RECORD, *American Council on Education, Washington, D.C., Spring 1970. (Out of print.)**

THE POLITICS OF ACADEMIA, *by Seymour Martin Lipset, reprinted from David C. Nichols (ed.)*, PERSPECTIVES ON CAMPUS TENSIONS: PAPERS PREPARED FOR THE SPECIAL COMMITTEE ON CAMPUS TENSIONS, *American Council on Education, Washington, D.C., September 1970. (Out of print.)**

*The Commission's stock of this reprint has been exhausted.

DATE DUE